Focus on GRAMMAR 5

FOURTH EDITION

Jay Maurer

ALWAYS LEARNING

PEARSON

FOCUS ON GRAMMAR 5: An Integrated Skills Approach, Fourth Edition
Teacher's Resource Pack

Pearson Education, 10 Bank Street, White Plains, NY 10606

Staff credits: The people who made up the *Focus on Grammar Teacher's Resource Pack* team, representing editorial, production, design, and manufacturing, are Iris Candelaria, Dave Dickey, Christine Edmonds, Nancy Flaggman, Ann France, Shelley Gazes, Lester Holmes, Stacey Hunter, Pamela Kohn, Theodore Lane, Christopher Leonowicz, Jennifer McAliney, Lise Minovitz, Jennifer Raspiller, Mary Perrotta Rich, Debbie Sistino, Ken Volcjak, Marian Wassner, and Adina Zoltan.

Contributing writers (Level 5): Carol Chapelle, Nan Clarke, Evelyn Fella, Leslie Grant, Bethany Gray, Joan Jamieson, Xiangying Jiang, Hsin-Min Liu, Ruth Luman, Kathleen Smith, Gabriele Steiner, BJ Wells, and Kevin Zimmerman.

Cover image: Shutterstock.com
Text composition: ElectraGraphics, Inc.
Text font: New Aster

ISBN 10: 0-13-216997-5
ISBN 13: 978-0-13-216997-4

Printed in the United States of America

1 2 3 4 5 6 7 8 9 10—V001—16 15 14 13 12 11

CONTENTS

ABOUT THE TEACHER'S RESOURCE PACK

This Teacher's Resource Pack offers a multitude of ideas for working with the material for the new edition of *Focus on Grammar 5: An Integrated Skills Approach*. The Teacher's Resource Pack includes:

- a **Teacher's Manual** (including General Teaching Notes, Unit Teaching Notes, Student Book Audioscript, and Student Book Answer Key)
- a **Teacher's Resource Disc** (including interactive PowerPoint® grammar presentations, placement test, reproducible Unit and Part assessments, and test-generating software)

THE TEACHER'S MANUAL

The Teacher's Manual includes the following sections:

- **General Teaching Notes** (pages 1–13) provide general suggestions for teaching and assessing the activities in the Student Book. A Strategies for Teaching Grammar section offers a quick reference for some of the most common and useful grammar teaching techniques. A Frequently Asked Questions section answers some of the most common issues that teachers encounter.
- **Unit Teaching Notes** (pages 14–133) provide step-by-step instructions on how to teach each unit and supplementary "Out of the Box Activities." They also include suggestions on when to use activities and tests from **www.myfocusongrammarlab.com**, assignments from the workbook, and materials from the Teacher's Resource Disc.
- The **Student Book Audioscript** (pages 134–145) includes scripts for the Listening and Pronunciation exercises in the Student Book.
- The **Student Book Answer Key** (pages 146–179) includes answers for the exercises in the Student Book.

THE TEACHER'S RESOURCE DISC

The Teacher's Resource Disc includes additional teaching resources and a complete assessment program:

Teaching Resources

- **PowerPoint® Presentations** of all Grammar Charts for each unit in the Student Book offer an alternative teaching tool for introducing the grammar presentation in the classroom. For select units, animated theme-based grammar presentations provide interactive follow-up practice activities for the contextualized instruction of grammar.
- **Internet Activities** for each unit in the Student Book provide opportunities for students to expand on the content and interact with each other creatively and fluently.

Assessments

- **Placement Test** in PDF format can be printed and used to place students into the appropriate level. Along with this 40-minute test is an audioscript and an answer key in PDF format, and audio as an MP3 file.
- **Part and Unit Tests** in PDF format can be printed and used in class. These include Part Pre-Tests, Part Post-Tests, and Unit Achievement Tests. Also included are assessment audioscripts and answer keys in PDF format, and audio as MP3 files.
- **Test-Generating Software** provides thousands of questions from which teachers can customize class-appropriate tests.

GENERAL TEACHING NOTES

These notes are designed to guide you in teaching and assessing the recurring sections of the Student Book. Experimenting with the various options will enliven your classroom and appeal to students' different learning styles.

In the following section and in the Unit Teaching Notes, the icon (⏱) indicates an optional step you may wish to include if time permits.

PART OVERVIEW

The **Part Overview** previews the grammar and themes covered in each unit.

(⏱) Part Pre-Tests

Before beginning each part, you may want to have students complete a diagnostic test. There are two options.

1. You can use the Part Pre-Tests to help you determine how well students know the material they are about to study in the next part of the Student Book. Since the material is usually new, students often score low on these tests. Each test takes about 50 minutes and includes about 60 items. The test begins with a listening exercise, includes several contextualized grammar exercises, and ends with an editing exercise. The tests are offered in two formats:
   - automatically graded tests at **www.myfocusongrammarlab.com**
   - reproducible tests on the Teacher's Resource Disc in this manual
2. You can use the Test-Generating Software on the Teacher's Resource Disc to create customized Part Diagnostic Tests of any length. The test items focus on grammar.

UNIT OVERVIEW

The **Grammar Overview** portion of the Unit Overview (offered in this Teacher's Manual) highlights the most important grammar points of each unit. It also points out common grammar trouble spots for students. You may also find it helpful to review the Grammar Charts and Grammar Notes in the Student Book before teaching each unit. The **Unit Overview** previews the unit theme.

Step 1: Grammar in Context

Each unit opens with a reading selection designed to raise students' interest and expose them to the target grammar in a realistic, natural context. The selections include newspaper and magazine excerpts, reviews, short stories, opinion columns, biographies, transcripts from radio and television programs, and other formats that students may encounter in their day-to-day lives. All of the texts are recorded and available on the audio program or at **www.myfocusongrammarlab.com.**

Before You Read (5 minutes)

This prereading activity creates interest, elicits students' knowledge about the topic, and encourages students to make predictions about the reading.

Suggested Procedure

1. Have the class look at the illustrations.
2. Ask students to respond to the questions. Ask these questions in a conversational way, instead of reading them from the book.

Option A

- Have the class read the questions in pairs or small groups and discuss their answers.
- Call on pairs to share their ideas with the class.

Option B

- Ask students to prepare questions they have about the topic in pairs.
- Call on pairs to share their questions and write them on the board.

Read (15–20 minutes)

Depending on the needs of your class, have students complete the reading in class or at home. Encourage students to read with a purpose, and to read the passage once or twice without stopping to look up new words.

Suggested Procedure

1. Write the comprehension questions from the Unit Teaching Notes on the board.
2. Play the audio and have students follow along in their books. Have them underline any new words.
3. Have students read the passage again silently, looking for answers to the questions.
4. ⏱ Have students discuss their answers with a partner or in small groups.
5. ⏱ Put students in pairs or small groups to discuss the reading. Invite them to respond to the reading in a way that is meaningful to them: What was most interesting? What did they learn? Refer to the discussion topics in the Unit Teaching Notes to help generate ideas for discussion.

Option A (At Home / In Class)

1. Write the comprehension questions on the board for students to copy or prepare them as a handout for students to take home.
2. Have students read the passage and answer the questions at home.
3. ⏱ Have students write a few additional questions about the reading.
4. Have students discuss their answers in pairs or small groups.
5. ⏱ Have students take turns asking and answering the questions they prepared at home.
6. Follow Steps 3 through 5 in the Suggested Procedure for Read above.

Option B (In Class)

- Have students work in pairs. Divide the reading in half and have each student in the pair read one half.
- Have students summarize the information in their half of the reading for their partner.
- Follow Steps 3–5 in the previous notes for Suggested Procedure for Read.

After You Read (10–20 minutes)

Depending on the needs of your class, have students complete the exercises in class or at home. Following the Student Book practice, you may want your students to go to **www.myfocusongrammarlab.com** for automatically graded Vocabulary or Reading homework. The Vocabulary homework provides additional practice with the words in the Student Book; the Reading homework is on related topics.

A. Vocabulary (5 minutes)

These questions help students develop vocabulary skills by focusing on the meaning of targeted words in the opening text. The words are recycled throughout the unit.

Suggested Procedure

1. Have students find and circle the target words in the opening text.
2. Elicit or explain the meanings of any new words.
3. Have students complete the exercise individually or in pairs.
4. Call on volunteers to read their answers aloud.
5. ⏱ Direct students to record new words in a notebook or on vocabulary cards. Have them write the word, part of speech, meaning, and a sample sentence.

B. Comprehension (5 minutes)

These post-reading questions help students focus on the meaning of the opening text. In some cases, they may also focus on the target grammar without explicitly presenting the grammar point.

Suggested Procedure

1. Have students answer the questions individually.
2. Have students compare answers in pairs.
3. Call on volunteers to read their answers aloud.

Step 2: Grammar Presentation

There are many ways to teach the material in the Grammar Presentation. As a general rule, the more varied and lively the classroom activities, the more engaged students will be—and the more learning will occur. Approaching grammar from different angles and trying out different classroom management options can help increase student motivation. The Strategies for Teaching Grammar on page 10 provide some guidelines to keep in mind when presenting a new grammar point. In addition to these strategies and the procedures outlined on the following pages, you can find specific suggestions for presenting the unit's grammar in the Unit Teaching Notes.

Grammar Charts (5–10 minutes)

The Grammar Charts provide a clear reference of all the forms of the target grammar. Students also become familiar with grammatical terminology. The charts also enable you to pre-teach some of the Grammar Notes that follow. You may want to use the charts in the PowerPoint® presentations on the Teacher's Resource Disc to help direct all of your students' attention to the same focus point. Select presentations also include colorful graphics, animations, and interactive practice activities that reinforce the grammar point.

Suggested Procedure

1. Using the examples from the charts and/or the PowerPoint® presentations, draw students' attention to important features in the models by asking them questions or by pointing out the key features.
2. Confirm students' understanding by engaging them in some recognition activities. Try one or two activities from Strategies 3, 4, 5, or 6 (page 10).
3. Get students to manipulate the new structures through substitution or transformation drills. See Strategy 7 (page 10) for an example of a transformation drill.
4. Encourage students to make sentences that are personally meaningful using the new grammar.

Option A

- Have students study the Grammar Charts at home.
- In class, follow Step 1 in the suggested procedure above.
- Move directly to the Grammar Notes section. Carry out Steps 2, 3, and 4 in the suggested procedure above using the notes together with the charts.

Option B

- Assign individual students responsibility for presenting a topic to the class by combining the information in the charts and the relevant notes. You may want to give them large pieces of paper and markers to prepare posters.
- ⏱ Meet with students individually. Allow them to practice their presentations. Provide any coaching needed.
- Call on students to present their topics to the class. Encourage questions from the class.
- Choose appropriate practice activities from Strategies 4–8 (page 10) or move directly to the Grammar Notes section.

Grammar Notes (20–30 minutes)

These notes provide helpful information about meaning, use, and form of the grammatical structures that students have encountered in the opening text and Grammar Charts. They include the following features to help students understand and use the forms.

- Where appropriate, timelines illustrate the meaning of verb forms and their relationship to one another.
- *Be Careful!* notes alert students to common errors among English language learners.
- Additional *Notes* provide guidelines for using and understanding different levels of formality and correctness.
- References to related structures are provided below the notes.

Suggested Procedure

1. Have students read each note at home and/or in class.
2. For each note, write examples on the board and elicit or point out the key features of the form (see Strategy 1, page 10).
3. If possible, demonstrate the meaning of the grammatical form(s) by performing actions (see Strategy 6, page 10).
4. Model the examples and have students repeat after you so that they become comfortable with the appropriate stress, intonation, and rhythm.
5. Engage students with the grammar point by choosing appropriate activities, for example:
   - Elicit examples of the target structure.
   - Confirm students' understanding by having them categorize examples or perform actions that illustrate the structure (see Strategies 5 and 6, page 10).
   - Provide controlled practice with quick substitution or transformation drills (see Strategy 7, page 10).
   - Encourage students to make personally meaningful sentences using the new grammatical forms.
   - Use the Focused Practice exercises in the Student Book.
6. You may want to repeat Steps 2 through 5 for each Grammar Note.

Option

- Photocopy one set of Grammar Notes for each group of three or four students in your class. Cut them up so that the notes and their corresponding examples are not attached.
- Divide the class into groups of three or four students and give a set of cut-up notes to each group.

- Give students their task:
  1. Match the examples with the correct notes.
  2. Attach the notes and corresponding examples to a sheet of newsprint (a large piece of paper).
  3. Have students create more examples for each note.
- Circulate to ensure that students are on the right track and provide help as needed.
- Have students post their results around the room and invite groups to look at each other's work.
- Regroup as a class to answer questions.

Identify the Grammar (5–10 minutes)

This optional activity helps students identify the target grammatical structures embedded in the context of the opening text. This helps students learn the form, meaning, and usage of the target grammar point and helps you make a smooth transition from the Grammar Presentation to Discover the Grammar in Focused Practice.

Step 3: Focused Practice

The exercises in this section provide practice for the structures in the Grammar Presentation. You may want to have students complete the corresponding exercise immediately after you have presented the relevant Grammar Note. Another option is for students to complete one or more of the exercises at home.

If you decide to have students complete the exercises in class, you can keep them motivated by varying the order of the exercises and/or the way you conduct them. Following are various ways of conducting the exercises.

Following the Student Book practice, you may want students to go to **www.myfocusongrammarlab.com** for automatically graded grammar homework or to the workbook for traditional grammar exercises. You may want to assign these to be completed in class or as homework.

Discover the Grammar (5–10 minutes)

This opening activity gets students to identify the target grammar structures in a realistic context. It also sometimes checks their understanding of meaning. This recognition activity raises awareness of the structures as it builds confidence.

Suggested Procedure
1. Go over the example with the class.

2. Have students complete the exercise individually or in pairs.
3. Elicit the correct answers from the class.

Controlled Practice Exercises (5–10 minutes each)

Following the Discover the Grammar activity are exercises that provide practice in a controlled but still contextualized environment. The exercises proceed from simpler to more complex and include a variety of exercise types such as fill in the blanks, matching, and multiple-choice. Students are exposed to many different written formats, including letters, electronic bulletin boards, résumés, charts, and graphs. Many exercises are art-based, providing a rich context for meaningful practice.

Options
- Have students complete the exercises in pairs.
- If the exercise is in the form of a conversation, have students practice the completed exercise in pairs and role-play it for the class.
- When going over answers with students, have them explain why each answer is correct.
- Whenever possible, relate exercises to students' lives. For example, if an exercise includes a timeline, elicit from students some important events that have happened in their own lives.

Editing (10 minutes)

All units have an editing exercise to build students' awareness of incorrect usage of the target grammar structures. Students identify and correct errors in a contextualized passage such as a student's composition, a journal entry, or an online message-board posting. The direction line indicates the number of errors in the passage.

Suggested Procedure
1. Have students read the passage quickly to understand its context and meaning.
2. Tell students to read the passage line by line, circling incorrect structures and writing in the corrections.
3. Have students take turns reading the passage line by line, saying the structures correctly. Alternatively, read the passage aloud to the class and have students interrupt you with their corrections.
4. There are also usually examples of the correct usage of the structures in each editing exercise. After students have identified the errors, point out the correct usages and ask why they are not errors.

Step 4: Communication Practice

These in-class exercises give students the opportunity to use the target structure in communicative activities. These activities help develop listening and speaking fluency and critical thinking skills, as well as provide opportunities for students to "own" the structures. As with the Focused Practice exercises, you may wish to vary the order of these activities to keep student motivation high.

Since there are many different exercise types in the Communication Practice section, specific ideas and guidelines are provided in the Unit Teaching Notes. Following are general suggestions for the main types of exercises. (Note: See the FAQs on pages 11–13 for more information about setting up pair work and group work.)

Following the relevant Student Book practice, you may want your students to go to **www.myfocusongrammarlab.com** for automatically graded Listening, Pronunciation, Speaking, or Writing exercises and activities. The Pronunciation homework provides additional practice with the pronunciation feature from the Student Book; the Listening, Speaking, and Writing homework exercises and activities are on related topics.

Listening (10 minutes)

The first or second exercise in each Communication Practice section deals with listening comprehension. Students hear a variety of listening formats, including conversations, television scripts, weather forecasts, and interviews. After listening, students complete a task that focuses on the form or meaning of the target grammar structure. The recordings for the listening exercises are on the audio program and at **www.myfocusongrammarlab.com**, so students can complete the exercises outside of class.

Suggested Procedure

Before Listening
1. Explain the situation or context of the listening passage. Provide any necessary cultural information and pre-teach any vocabulary students may need to know. Since some of these words and phrases may appear in the listening, not in the exercise itself, refer to the audioscript at the back of this manual as necessary.
2. Ask students to read the exercise questions first so that they know what to listen for.

First Listening Task
1. Play the audio. Have students listen with their pencils down.
2. Play the audio again. Have students listen and complete the task.
3. You may want to let students listen as many times as necessary to complete the task.

Second Listening Task
1. See Steps 2 and 3 from the first listening task for general instructions.
2. Have students compare their answers in pairs or small groups.

After Listening
1. Elicit answers for the exercise items and write them on the board. Answer any questions the students may have.
2. ⏱ Students listen a final time and review the passage.

Option A
- Rather than play the audio, read the audioscript aloud.
- Speak with a lot of expression and at a natural pace. Change positions and tone of voice to indicate who the speaker is.
- Draw stick figures on the board and label them with the characters' names. Then point to the appropriate character as you change roles.

Option B
- Make photocopies of the audioscript and hand it out to students.
- Play the audio recording and have students read along with it in chorus. Explain that this exercise will help them to hear and practice the rhythms, stresses, and clusters of English sounds.

Option C
Have students listen and complete the exercise at home or in a language lab.

Pronunciation (10 minutes)

The first or second exercise in each Communication Practice section deals with pronunciation. The pronunciation exercise generally focuses on the grammar presented in the unit or a difficult sound that appears in the opening text. It also prepares students for the speaking activities that follow. The recordings for the pronunciation exercises are on the audio program and at **www.myfocusongrammarlab.com**, so students can practice the exercises outside of class.

Suggested Procedure

First Task

1. Go over the instructions and point out the Pronunciation Note.
2. Play the audio.

Second Task

1. Play the audio. Have students close their eyes and notice the pronunciation feature.
2. ⏱ Play the audio again. Have students listen again and follow along in their books.

Third Task

1. Play the audio again.
2. Have students repeat in pairs or small groups. Circulate and monitor their pronunciation.
3. ⏱ Call on volunteers to practice in front of the class.

Information Gaps (10–20 minutes)

Information Gaps are designed to encourage communication among students. In these activities, each student has a different set of information. Students have to talk to their partners to complete tasks such as solving a puzzle or completing a text.

Advantages of Information Gaps

- Information Gaps are motivating and fun.
- There is a real need for communication in order to combine the information to solve a problem and complete the task.
- Information sharing allows students to extend and personalize what they have learned in the unit.

Suggested Procedure

1. Explain how the Student A and Student B pages relate to each other (how they are different or similar).
2. Refer students to the examples and to any language provided.
3. Divide the class into pairs (Student A and Student B). Have them position themselves so that they cannot see the contents of each other's books.
4. Tell the Student Bs what page to turn to. Circulate to check that they are looking at the correct page.
5. Have students read their separate instructions. Check comprehension of the task by asking each group, "What are you going to do?"
6. Remind students not to show each other the contents of their pages.

7. As students are working, circulate to answer individual questions and to help students with the activity.

Games (10–20 minutes)

Games are designed to encourage communication among students. In these activities, students compete in pairs or small groups to complete a task such as guessing something or winning points.

Advantages of Games

- They can create a fun and stress-free environment.
- They involve friendly competition and keep students engaged.
- They can improve students' ability to speak in a communicative way.

Suggested Procedure

1. Go over the instructions to make sure students understand the task.
2. Have students model the example or provide one of your own.
3. Have students carry out the instructions. Circulate and help as needed.
4. ⏱ Go over answers as a class or ask who won.
5. ⏱ Note any incorrect uses of grammar. Write the sentences on the board and have students correct them.

Discussions (10–20 minutes)

In these classroom speaking activities, students express their ideas about a variety of topics. These activities include Picture Discussion, Group Discussion, Pair Discussion, Story Discussion, and Personal Inventory.

Advantages of Discussions

- They help students move from speaking accuracy to speaking fluency.
- They help students develop critical thinking skills as they explore the pros and cons of a given topic.
- They help students build confidence in their ability to express opinions on a variety of topics.

Suggested Procedure

1. Go over the instructions so that students understand the task.
2. Elicit or present useful language and write it on the board.
3. Have two or three students model the example discussion.
4. Divide the class into the suggested groupings and give them a fixed time limit for completing the task.

5. Circulate while the students discuss the topic. Help with language or monitor their grammar as needed.
6. Ask volunteers for each group to summarize the discussion or conclusions.
7. ⏱ Write any sentences with incorrect grammar you noticed on the board. Have the students correct them as a class.

Writing (15–25 minutes)

These activities give students the opportunity to develop their writing skills and provide additional practice using the target grammatical structures. There is a variety of realistic formats, including paragraphs, narrative essays, opinion essays, descriptive writing, and academic essays. The themes are related to material covered in the unit so that students already have some preparation for the writing task.

Suggested Procedure

Prewriting (in class)
1. Go over the instructions with the class.
2. Brainstorm ideas for the assignment with the class and write them on the board.
3. Encourage students to include grammar and vocabulary from the unit in their assignment.

Writing and Editing (at home)
1. Have students compose a draft of the writing assignment at home.
2. Have students use the Editing Checklist to correct their work.

Wrap-Up (in class)
1. Have students submit the draft to you or share it with a partner in class.
2. Give students a score on the draft. You can comment on the following features:
   - Content: Has the student responded appropriately to the task? Are the main points well supported?
   - Organization: Is the flow of ideas logical and effective?
   - Accuracy: Are there any major errors in the grammar points taught in the unit?
3. ⏱ Depending on your class's needs, you may want to have students complete a second draft at home. When you check these drafts, point out any further areas needing correction, concentrating especially on errors in the target grammar point or grammar points from a previous unit.

Option A

Have students share their final drafts in class. For example:
- Post students' work on the class bulletin board.
- Publish their work on a website or in a class magazine.
- Have students exchange papers with a partner.
- Have students read their papers aloud in small groups or to the class.

Option B

Have students put the final drafts of their written work in a folder, or portfolio, which you can review at the end of the course. This will allow your students and you to see the progress they have made.

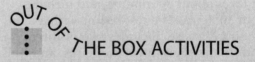

OUT OF THE BOX ACTIVITIES

One or more activities for further practice (in the Teacher's Manual only) can be found at the end of every unit in the Unit Teaching Notes. These exercises offer additional communicative practice with the target structure of the unit. Many can be done in class with no before-class preparation. The activities often involve a combination of skills, such as grammar and speaking or grammar and writing.

Unit Review

The last section of each unit of the Student Book is a review feature that can be used as a self-test. These exercises test the form and use of the grammar content presented and practiced in that unit. They give students a chance to check their knowledge and to review any problematic areas before moving on to the next part. An answer key is provided at the back of the Student Book.

Suggested Procedure
1. Have students complete the exercises at home and check their answers in the Answer Key.
2. During the next class, go over any remaining questions students may have.

Option

- Have students complete the exercises in class. Give them a time limit of 10 minutes and circulate as they work.
- Have students use the Answer Key to check and correct their answers in pairs or you can go over the answers as a class.

⏱ Unit Achievement Tests

After the Unit Review, you may want to have students complete an achievement test. There are two assessment options.

1. You can use the provided **Unit Achievement Tests** to help you assess students' knowledge of the specific grammatical topics presented in the unit. If students have mastered the material presented in the unit, they should answer most of the questions correctly. Each test takes about 30 minutes and includes about 30 items. The test begins with a listening exercise, includes two or three contextualized grammar exercises, and ends with an editing exercise. The tests are offered in two formats:
   - automatically graded tests at **www.myfocusongrammarlab.com**
   - reproducible tests on the Teacher's Resource Disc in this manual
2. You can use the **Test-Generating Software** on the Teacher's Resource Disc to create customized unit achievement tests of any length. The test items focus on grammar.

⏱ Part Post-Tests

At the end of each part, you may want to have students complete an achievement test. There are three assessment options.

1. You can have students go to **www.myfocusongrammarlab.com** for an automatically graded review. Students can complete the review on a computer in class, at home, or in a language lab. Each review takes about 25 minutes and includes about 30 items. The test focuses on grammar.

2. You can have students take the **Part Post-Tests** to help you determine how well they have mastered the material they have studied in that part of the Student Book. If students have mastered the material presented in the part, they should answer most of the questions correctly. Each test takes 50 minutes and includes about 60 items. The tests begin with a listening exercise, include several contextualized grammar exercises, and end with an editing exercise. The tests are offered in two formats:
   - automatically graded tests at **www.myfocusongrammarlab.com**
   - reproducible tests on the Teacher's Resource Disc in this manual
3. You can also use the **Test-Generating Software** on the Teacher's Resource Disc to create customized Part Achievement Tests of any length. The test items focus on grammar.

From Grammar to Writing

The From Grammar to Writing section at the end of each part of the Student Book integrates grammar presented in the units. It also goes beyond the grammar in the unit and gives additional information about writing in English. This information may include cohesion (e.g., parallel structure, subject-verb agreement), coherence (e.g., avoiding sentence fragments), and structure (e.g., topic sentences, transitions). Following these exercises, students practice prewriting strategies. These strategies may include the use of graphic organizers, such as charts, notes, and outlines. Finally, students apply the teaching point in a writing task. Text types include both formal and informal writing, such as academic essays, opinion essays, personal narratives, and humorous stories. The section concludes with peer review and editing.

Depending on your class's needs, you may want to have students go to an additional From Grammar to Writing exercise at **www.myfocusongrammarlab.com**.

Suggested Procedure

Prewriting

1. Have students complete the controlled practice exercises individually. Then have them exchange books and compare answers.
2. Go over the answers as a class and answer any questions.
3. Explain the prewriting task. Where appropriate, provide a model for students on the board or on an overhead.
4. Have students complete the prewriting task in pairs or small groups. Circulate and answer any questions.

Composing and Correcting

1. Go over the instructions to make sure students understand the task.

2. Have students complete the writing assignment at home.
3. In class, complete the peer review portion of the task. Circulate while students are working together to make sure they are on task and to provide appropriate feedback. (See Suggested Procedure for Writing on page 7 for examples.)
4. ⏱ Have students revise their writing and turn in the second draft to you.

Option

- Have students complete the controlled practice exercise(s) at home.
- In class, have students compare answers in pairs.
- Follow the suggested procedure for Steps 3 and 4 in the prewriting phase.

STRATEGIES FOR TEACHING GRAMMAR

1. Develop awareness
Ask questions that help students become aware of the form of the structure. For example, for modals to express degrees of certainty (Student Book page 72), read the affirmative statement "It may be true; we may solve it soon," and ask, "How do you form affirmative statements with *may* and other modals?" *(modal verb + base form of verb)* Ask students what *base form* means. *(the simple form without an ending)* Then ask, "Does the modal change when the pronoun changes?" *(No.)* Compare information in the Grammar Charts. For example, for conditionals (Student Book pages 381–384) there are Grammar Charts for present real conditionals and for present unreal conditionals. Ask: "In the present real conditional, what form does the verb take in the *if* clause?" *(simple present or present progressive)* Ask: "In the present unreal conditional, is the verb form in the *if* clause the same or different?" *(different; verbs are in simple past form)*

2. Present meaning
Show the meaning of a grammatical form through a classroom demonstration. For example, to illustrate the use of present perfect progressive, you could show a picture of a person carrying grocery bags full of food. *(He/She has been shopping.)*

3. Identify examples
Ask students to go back to the Grammar in Context section and label examples in the reading passage with the grammatical terms in the Grammar Charts.

4. Generate examples
Find examples from the reading or elsewhere that could fit into the Grammar Charts. An interesting way to do this is to photocopy and enlarge the Grammar Chart. White out the targeted structures and draw a blank line for each missing word. Make copies and distribute them to students in pairs or small groups. Have students fill in the blanks, using examples from the reading. Then generate more examples. Books can be open or closed, depending on the level of challenge desired.

5. Show understanding by categorizing
Check comprehension of a grammatical principle by asking students to label multiple examples appropriately. For example, students can label verbs "present" or "future," or they can label examples "correct" or "incorrect."

6. Show understanding by performing actions
Ask students to show their understanding of the meaning of a grammatical form by following instructions or devising a demonstration. Ask students, for example, to think of and perform a set of actions that they could describe using the present progressive.

7. Manipulate forms
Have students manipulate the examples in the Grammar Charts to practice the form. Drills such as substitution or transformation help students to build fluency. For example, in Unit 1 (Student Book page 4) you might put one present-time form on the board *(She lives downtown)* and then elicit other forms by saying, "present progressive" *(She's living downtown)*, "present perfect" *(She has lived downtown)*, "present perfect progressive" *(She has been living downtown)*, and so on to get students to produce the other forms rapidly.

8. Personalize
Ask students to provide personal examples. For example, on page 199 of the Student Book, students see the example "I remember the café where we met." Ask students if they remember a place where they met someone important in their lives or something significant happened.

9. Repeat, reinforce
Students need to be exposed to new grammar many times in order to internalize it completely. You can first present a new structure on the board, then point it out in the book, then have students use it in an informal oral exercise, then do a written exercise in pairs, and finally review the same structure in homework. Varying the content and focus of these activities will keep students interested, and the grammar will be reinforced almost automatically.

FREQUENTLY ASKED QUESTIONS (FAQs)

1. When should I have students work in pairs or groups rather than individually or as a whole class?

Varying your classroom organization to suit particular activity types will result in more effective and more interesting classes. Many students are not accustomed to working in pairs or groups, so it is important to use these groupings only when they are most beneficial.

- **Whole-class teaching** maximizes teacher control and is especially good for:
  — presenting information, giving explanations, and providing instructions
  — showing material in texts and pictures or on audio or video recordings
  — teacher-led drills (such as substitution or transformation) or dictations
  — reviewing answers or sharing ideas after students have completed an activity
  — enabling the whole class to benefit from teacher feedback to individuals
- **Students working individually** allows quiet, concentrated attention and is most effective for:
  — processing information or completing a task at the students' own pace
  — performing writing tasks

For objective exercises such as fill-in-the-blank, matching, multiple-choice, and editing, vary your class organization to keep student motivation high. Students can sometimes complete these exercises individually, and sometimes they can work with a partner.

- **Students working in pairs** maximizes student speaking time, breaks up the routine and "teacher talk," and is ideal for:
  — information-gap activities
  — role plays
  — writing and/or reading dialogues
  — predicting the content of reading and listening texts
  — comparing notes on what students listen to or see
  — checking answers
  — peer assessment

Pair work can also be very effective for completing objective exercises such as fill-in-the-blank, matching, multiple-choice, and editing.

- **Students working in groups** creates ideal conditions for students to learn from each other and works well for:
  — generating ideas
  — pooling knowledge
  — writing group stories
  — preparing presentations
  — discussing an issue and reaching a group decision

2. How should I set up pair work and group work?

Here are a few different techniques:

- **Streaming.** Grouping students according to ability or participation has certain advantages.
  — **ability:** Grouping weaker and stronger students together allows more able students to help their less fluent classmates.
  — **participation:** If you see that some students participate less than others, you could make a pair or group of weak participators. By the same token, you can also put especially talkative students together.
- **Chance.** Grouping students by chance has many benefits, especially if it results in students working with varied partners. You can group students by chance according to:
  — **where they sit:** Students sitting next to or near one another work in pairs or groups. This is the easiest option, but if students always sit in the same place, you will want to find other ways of grouping them.
  — **the "wheels" system:** Half the class stands in a circle facing outward, and the other half stands in an outer circle facing inward. The outer circle revolves in a clockwise direction, and the inner circle revolves in a counterclockwise direction. When you tell them to stop, students work with the person facing them. This is an effective way to have students engage in meaningful repetition, such as asking the same question of many different partners.
  — **assigned letters:** Assign each student a letter from A to E. Then ask all the As to form a group, all the Bs to form a group, and so on.

— **birthdays:** Students stand in a line in the order of their birthdays (with January at one end and December at the other). The first five students form one group; the second five students another group; and so on.

— **native language:** If possible, put students in groups or pairs with others who don't share a native language. This helps create an "English-only" classroom.

3. How can I make activities more successful?

Before the activity:

• **Motivate students and explain the purpose.** Make it clear that something enjoyable or interesting is going to happen. Explain the rationale for the activity. Make sure that students understand that the purpose of the activity is to help them practice what they have learned and encourage them to participate.

• **Provide clear directions.** Explain what students should do in every step of the activity. Have students paraphrase or demonstrate the task to be sure they understand it.

• **Demonstrate.** Show the class what is supposed to happen in an activity. This might involve asking a student to demonstrate the activity with you or having two students role-play at the front of the room.

• **Provide a time frame.** It is helpful for students to know how much time they have and exactly when they should stop. Approximate times are given for all the activities in this Teacher's Manual.

For open-ended activities, such as the writing exercises, you will also want to:

• **Stimulate thinking.** When there are choices for students to make, it is often helpful to set up small-group and/or whole-class brainstorming sessions to define the focus and/or content of their task.

• **Prepare language.** Review grammar and vocabulary that students may need to complete the task. This can be done as a follow-up to a brainstorming activity where you elicit ideas and write key language on the board.

During the activity:

• **Observe students.** Walk around the room watching and listening to pairs or groups.

• **Provide assistance as needed.** See FAQ 5 for suggestions on giving feedback and correcting errors.

After the activity:

• **Elicit student responses.** For some activities, you may ask for volunteers or call on students to share some of their ideas with the class. For other types of activities, a few pairs or groups can be asked to role-play their discussions to demonstrate the language they have been using.

• **Provide feedback.** In many cases, this is most conveniently done in a whole-class setting. It may be preferable, however, for you to meet with individuals, pairs, or groups. While the principal focus in a grammar class is language use, it is also important to acknowledge the value of students' ideas. See FAQ 5 below for suggestions on feedback and error correction.

4. What can I do to encourage students to use more English in the classroom?

It is perfectly natural for students to feel the need to use their first language in an English class. There are a number of actions that teachers can take to promote the use of English.

• **Set clear guidelines.** Some teachers in monolingual classes find that activities such as providing vocabulary definitions, presenting a grammar point, checking comprehension, giving instructions, and discussing classroom methodology are best done in the students' native language.

• **Use persuasion.** Walking among the students during speaking activities and saying things such as "Please speak English!" or "Try to use English as much as possible" helps to ensure that students will speak English most of the time.

5. What's the best approach to giving feedback and correcting errors?

Here are two considerations:

• **Be selective in offering correction.** Students can't focus on everything at once, so concentrate first on errors relating to the target grammar point and grammar points from units previously studied, as well as any errors that interfere with communication. Whether you respond to other errors depends on your judgment of students' readiness to take in the information. If you see a teachable moment, seize it. Rather than correct every error individual students make in the course of activities, it is generally preferable to note commonly occurring mistakes and give a short presentation for the whole class at the end of the activity.

- **Recasting.** If a student makes an error, for example, "I *didn't came* to class yesterday because I was sick," you can recast it as, "You *didn't come* to class yesterday because you were sick?" The student ideally notices the difference and restates the original sentence: "Right. I didn't come to class yesterday because I was sick." This process can be effective because the student has the opportunity to self-correct an error that is still in short-term memory. As a variation, you can restate but stop, with rising intonation, right before the potential error: "You didn't . . . ?"

6. What can I do to accommodate different learning styles?

Focus on Grammar recognizes different styles of learning and provides a variety of activities to accommodate these different styles. Some learners prefer an analytical, or rule-learning (deductive), approach. Others, especially younger learners, respond best to an inductive approach, or exposure to the language in meaningful contexts. Indeed, the same students may adopt different styles as they learn, or they may use different styles at different times.

As teachers, we want to help the students in our classes who prefer to follow rules become more able to take risks and plunge into communicative activities. We also want to encourage the risk-takers to focus on accuracy. *Focus on Grammar* provides the variety to ensure that students achieve their goal: to learn to use the language confidently and appropriately.

UNIT TEACHING NOTES

PRESENT, PAST, AND FUTURE

UNIT	GRAMMAR FOCUS	THEME
1	Present Time	The Digital World
2	Past Time	Marriage
3	Future Time	Travel

Go to **www.myfocusongrammarlab.com** for the Part and Unit Tests.

Note: PowerPoint® grammar presentations, test-generating software, and reproducible Part and Unit Tests are on the *Teacher's Resource Disc.*

UNIT 1 OVERVIEW

Grammar: PRESENT TIME

Unit 1 focuses on the meanings and uses of four aspects of the present time frame and the contrasts among them: the simple present, present progressive, present perfect, and present perfect progressive.

- Use the simple present to show actions, events, or states that are true in general or happen habitually. Also use the simple present to narrate events that happen in sequence.

- Use the present progressive to show actions or events in progress at the moment but not yet complete.

- Use the present perfect and the present perfect progressive to connect the past with the present and show actions and states that began in the past and continue until now.

- Use the present perfect to describe completed actions with a connection to the present.

This unit also reviews the distinction between action and non-action verbs and explains their use in the present progressive. Some non-action verbs that are commonly used in the present progressive are highlighted.

- Action verbs, also called active verbs, describe actions. Adverbs are usually used with action verbs. Non-action or stative verbs describe states such as appearance, emotion, mental state, perception, possession, and desire. Non-action verbs are most often used in the simple rather than the progressive form. When used to describe states, non-action verbs are usually accompanied by adjectives.

- There are some non-action verbs that can express either states or actions. This use usually gives the verb a different meaning. Both adjectives and adverbs can be used with these verbs, depending on their meaning.

Theme: THE DIGITAL WORLD

Unit 1 focuses on language that is used to discuss various elements of modern technology and their application to personal communication.

Step 1: Grammar in Context (pages 2–4)

See the general suggestions for Grammar in Context on page 1.

Before You Read

- Have students discuss the questions in small groups.
- Call on students to share the group's ideas with the class.

Read

- Write these questions on the board:
  1. Does the author think digital communication and modern technology have a positive or negative effect on our lives? *(Overall he thinks the influence is positive, with some negative effects.)*
  2. Who are the people that the author uses as examples to support his point of view? *(his daughter, son, wife, and himself)*
  3. What is the primary form of communication that each person uses? *(daughter Allison—social networking sites; son Nick—texting; wife Elena—email; author—blogging)*
- Establish a purpose for reading. Call on students to read the questions. Remind students to think about these questions as they read and listen to the text.

- Have students read the text, or play the audio and have students follow along in their books. Have students discuss the questions in pairs or groups of three. Call on pairs or groups to share answers with the class.

After You Read

A. Vocabulary
- Have students complete the vocabulary exercise on page 3 individually. Then have them compare answers in pairs.
- Circulate as students compare answers. Call on pairs to read their answers aloud.

B. Comprehension
- Have students complete the exercise on pages 3–4 individually. Then have them compare answers in pairs.
- Call on pairs to share their answers with the class. Have each student point out the place in the text where he or she found the answer to the question.

Go to **www.myfocusongrammarlab.com** for an additional reading, and for reading and vocabulary practice.

Step 2: Grammar Presentation (pages 4–6)

See the general suggestions for Grammar Presentation on page 2.

Grammar Charts
- Have students look over the first two charts. Write these questions on the board and then have students work in groups to discuss them. Then discuss the answers as a class.
  — How many time periods (e.g., past, present, or future) are represented in these two charts? *(only one—the present)*
  — According to the charts, how many different ways are there to talk about this time period? What are they? *(four—simple present, present progressive, present perfect, and present perfect progressive)*
  — Which two ways do we use to talk about this time period in general or right now? *(simple present and present progressive)*
  — Which two ways do we use to talk about a time in the past until now? *(present perfect and present perfect progressive)*
  — What form does each of these have? *(simple present—base form of verb + -s or -es for third-person singular; present progressive—be + base form of verb + -ing; present perfect—have + past participle; present perfect progressive—have been + base form of verb + -ing)*

- Have students look at the next chart, "Action and Non-Action Verbs." Have students name the action verbs and non-action verbs in the chart. Write them on the board in two separate lists. (Action verbs: *drive, take*; Non-action: *know, want*) Ask: "How are these verbs different?" *(Action verbs describe actions, but non-action verbs describe states such as appearance, possession, and mental states.)* Elicit additional examples of each type of verb. Write them on the board. Ask: "Which kind of verb can be used in progressive forms?" *(action verbs)*
- Have students read the next chart, "Some Non-Action Verbs." Explain that some verbs have an action meaning and a non-action meaning. Have students read the example sentences aloud. Call on students to explain how the meaning changes in each pair of sentences.
- Have students read the last two charts. Explain that you can use adverbs with action verbs but not with non-action verbs. Similarly, adjectives usually go after certain non-action verbs (e.g., *look, taste, feel*) rather than with action verbs.

Grammar Notes

Note 1
- Divide the class in half. Have one half read the first part of Note 1 and the example sentences in small groups. Have the other half look at the second part of Note 1 and the example sentences.
- Have groups in the first half of the class look through the opening reading for other examples of the use of the simple present to show actions, states, or events that are true in general or happen habitually. Have groups in the other half find examples of the simple present that show narration of events in a sequence.
- Circulate as students are working and provide help as needed. Call on students from each group to say which use they were looking for and some of the examples they found.

Note 2
- Have a student read the note aloud.
- Set up a competitive activity. Establish a time limit (1 to 3 minutes) and have students work in groups or pairs to reread the opening text and find examples of the present progressive used to show actions in progress at the moment. The group that finds the most correct examples wins.

Note 3

- Using either procedure described in Note 1 or Note 2, have students look for examples of the present perfect or present perfect progressive.
- Call on groups to read aloud the examples they found. Ask them why each example is in the present perfect or present perfect progressive, and whether the tense could be changed without changing the meaning.

Note 4

- Have students read the note and the examples. Make sure they understand the difference in meaning between the last two example sentences.
- Put students in pairs and have them write similar example sentences in simple and progressive form. (Example: *I speak three languages: Spanish, English, and French. Right now I'm speaking English.*) Call on pairs to share their sentences.

Note 5

- Have students look over the first two parts of the note. Make sure they don't look at the section that talks about non-actions verbs that can be used to express action. Then write these six headings on the board: *Appearance, Emotions, Mental States, Perceptions, Possession,* and *Want*. Elicit non-action verbs for each category and write them on the board. (Examples: appearance—*seem*; emotions—*love*; mental states—*know*; perceptions—*hear*; possession—*own*; want—*need*)
- Point out that one of the most common non-action verbs is *be*. For example: *He is a nice fellow.* Ask students: "Do you think *be* could also be used to express an action?" If students answer *yes*, have students give an example sentence. For example: *Today he's not being nice.* In this example, *be* is similar to *behaving* so it can be used in the present progressive.
- Have students look at the next section of Note 5, where they will see the examples using *be* that you have just given. Have each group look over the list of verbs again. If they think the verbs can be used in the present progressive, have them try to come up with a synonym for the verb. For example: *She has a new house.* (owns or possesses) and *She's having a baby* (giving birth to).

Note 6

- In pairs, have students choose two or three verbs from each category in Note 5 that can be both non-action or action verbs.

- Have groups write sentences with each of these verbs, adding adjectives or adverbs as appropriate. For example: *She looked great!* (adjective) *She looked quickly at the letter.* (adverb)
- Call on students from each pair to share their sentences with the class.

🕐 **Identify the Grammar:** Have students identify the grammar in the opening reading on pages 2–3. For example:

Most of us hardly **go** anywhere today without a cell phone or iPhone, an iPod, or a laptop—or so it **seems**.

We**'re trying** to stay in 24/7 communication with each other.

MySpace **has been** around since 2003 and Facebook since 2005.

Right now Nick **is texting** friends—he's **been doing** that for the last half hour—and **shows** no signs of stopping.

Go to **www.myfocusongrammarlab.com** for grammar charts and notes.

Step 3: Focused Practice (pages 6–9)

See the general suggestions for Focused Practice on page 4.

Exercise 1: Discover the Grammar

A

- Go over the example with the class. Make sure everyone understands why the example answer is correct.
- Have students complete the exercise individually. Then have them compare answers in small groups. Go over the correct answers as a class.

B

- Go over the example with the class. Have students complete the exercise individually. Then have them compare answers in groups.
- Go over the answers as a class. Have students identify the non-action verbs that could be used as action verbs and give an example sentence for each one. (Example: Item 7—*feels: The doctor is feeling his leg carefully, but she doesn't think it's broken.*)

Exercise 2: Simple Present / Present Progressive

- Have students complete the exercise individually. Then go over the answers as a class.
- As students provide correct answers, have them explain why the answer is correct. For example: *I telecommute* is correct because it is describing a habit.

Exercise 3: Present Perfect / Present Perfect Progressive

- Read the instructions aloud. Make sure students understand that if both the present perfect and present perfect progressive forms are possible, they should use the present perfect progressive form.
- Have students complete the exercise individually. Then have them compare answers in pairs. Have pairs explain to each other why the present perfect progressive is or is not appropriate in each case.
- Go over the answers as a class. Call on students to explain why the present perfect progressive is or is not appropriate. Elicit the cases in which the present perfect progressive is inappropriate because the verb is non-action (stative).

Exercise 4: Action / Non-Action Verbs; Adverbs / Adjectives

- Have students complete the exercise individually. Then have them check answers in small groups.
- Have each group think of a synonym for the verbs in the sentences that clarifies why they are non-action or action. For example, *Your new iPhone appears similar to mine* (Item 1).

Exercise 5: Editing

- Have students complete the exercise and check answers in pairs. Then call on students to explain each error and correction.

Go to **www.myfocusongrammarlab.com** for additional grammar practice.

Step 4: Communication Practice (pages 10–13)

See the general suggestions for Communication Practice on page 5.

Exercise 6: Listening

A

- Establish a purpose for listening. Read the instructions and have students read the topics. Elicit key words, phrases, or questions students might hear for each topic. Write them on the board.
- Play the audio and have students complete the exercise. Go over the answers as a class.
- (!) Play the audio again. Have students compare what they hear with the words you wrote on the board.

B

- Establish a purpose for listening. Have students read the questions. Remind students to think about these questions as they listen.

- Play the audio. Allow students time to write their answers. Have students work in small groups to compare answers. Then go over the answers as a class.
- (!) Provide students with a copy of the audioscript. In pairs, have them identify the examples of simple present, present progressive, present perfect, and present perfect progressive and explain why each one was used.

Exercise 7: Pronunciation

A

- Have students read and listen to the Pronunciation Note. Have them repeat the key words *English* and *sing* several times as you say them.
- (!) Deliberately mispronounce *sing* to point out the incorrect pronunciation. Then pronounce several words with the /ng/ sound correctly and incorrectly. Have students raise their hands when they hear an incorrect pronunciation.

B

- Go over the example with the class. Play the audio and have students complete the exercise.
- Have students check their answers in pairs. Replay the audio as needed.

C

- Have students take turns saying the sentences for Part C. Have each pair practice the sentences twice, so that each person has the chance to say all of the sentences.
- Circulate as pairs practice saying the sentences. Make corrections as needed.

Exercise 8: Group Discussion

A

- Have students read the devices in the chart and the column headings. Allow students a few minutes to complete the chart with information about themselves, including comments.

B

- Model the example conversation with a student. Point out that the example conversation is based on the answers in the chart.
- Have students discuss their answers in small groups. Circulate, helping as needed.

C

- Call on a student from each group to summarize the group's answers for the class.

- **Note:** As a variation, have students exchange charts and report to the class about their partners' use of electronic devices.

Exercise 9: Class Discussion

A

- Explain that students will read some information about texting while driving and then discuss the issue. Ask: "Let's have a quick show of hands. Who thinks texting while driving should be banned?" Count the votes and write them on the board.
- Have students read the text to see if the information affects their opinion. Call on a few students to read each paragraph of the text (or give students a few minutes to read the text silently). Answer any questions about the vocabulary, grammar, or cultural content in the text.
- ⏲ Have students practice reading the text aloud to each other in pairs. Remind them to focus on the correct pronunciation of the /ng/ sound. Point out that the /ng/ sound in *dangerous* is different from the sound in *English*. In *dangerous*, the *g* sounds more like a /j/ sound (as in *jury*).

B

- Go over the questions as a class. Have students complete the class discussion.
- ⏲ Note common grammar errors students make during the discussion. Then write the errors on the board and have the class correct them.

Exercise 10: Writing

A

- If needed, review the definition and structure of a paragraph. *(A paragraph is a group of sentences that discuss one topic. The **topic sentence** expresses the main idea of the paragraph, and the remaining sentences provide details about the main idea.)*
- Have students look at the example and identify the topic sentence. Point out that the writer makes a statement that is true for him in the topic sentence. The rest of the sentences support his main idea by giving reasons why the statement is true.
- Have students write topic sentences for each of their paragraphs. Have them compare topic sentences in pairs. Call on a few students to share their topic sentences. Correct the sentences as needed. Then have students write their paragraphs, either in class or as homework.

B

- Have students work in pairs to correct each other's work using the Editing Checklist. Have each student revise and rewrite as needed.
- ⏲ Have students post their papers in the classroom so the class can read them. You can also publish them together in a booklet or on a class website.

OUT OF THE BOX ACTIVITIES

Reading, Writing, Listening, and Speaking

- Have students choose a topic from the unit:
  — staying connected through technology
  — the advantages or disadvantages of a particular electronic device or communication medium, such as texting or email
  — identity theft
- Have students who chose the same topic work in groups. Then have each student find and read an article about the topic. Have them bring to class enough copies of the article for the group. The groups then read and discuss the articles.
- Have each student write two or three paragraphs about the chosen topic. They can use any of the text in the unit as a model for their writing. The opening reading on pages 2–3, the text in Exercise 2 on page 7, the corrected text in Exercise 5 on page 9, and the text in Exercise 9 on page 13 all provide good models for students to use. Remind them to focus on the use of present time verbs in their writing and encourage them to incorporate all four of the target structures in their writing. Remind them to be mindful of the form and use of non-action verbs.

Reading, Listening, and Speaking

- Bring in (or have students bring in) short articles from newspapers, magazines, or websites about the various topics included in this unit. Have enough articles for every two or three students. Have students work in pairs or groups to identify examples of this unit's target structures.

- Have pairs or groups work together to prepare a short oral presentation to the class about the article. Remind them that they can use notes for their presentations, but they should not read word for word or copy sentences directly from the article. Remind them to use target structures from this unit in their presentations. Circulate as students are working and help as needed.
- Have each pair or group present to the class. If you have a very large class, you may want pairs or groups to give their oral presentations to each other.

Go to **www.myfocusongrammarlab.com** for additional listening, pronunciation, speaking, and writing practice.

Note:
- See the *Focus on Grammar Workbook* for additional in-class or homework grammar practice.

Unit 1 Review (page 14)

Have students complete the Review and check their answers on Student Book page UR-1. Review or assign additional material as needed.

Go to **www.myfocusongrammarlab.com** for the Unit Achievement Test.

UNIT 2 OVERVIEW

Grammar: PAST TIME

Unit 2 focuses on the meanings and uses of a variety of past forms and how these forms can work alone and together to convey a range of meanings regarding past time: the simple past, the past progressive, the present perfect, *used to / would* + base form, past perfect, past perfect progressive, and the "future in the past."

- The simple past expresses an action, event, or state completed at a general or specific time in the past. The simple past is the definite past.
- The past progressive expresses an action that was in progress or not completed at a time in the past.
- The present perfect expresses an action, event, or state completed at an indefinite time in the past. The present perfect is the indefinite past. Remember that the present perfect also connects the past and the present.
- *Used to* and *would* + base form express a habitual action, event, or state that was true in the past but is no longer true.
- The past perfect shows an action, event, or state that happened before a certain time in the past. Use the past perfect with the simple past to show which of two past actions, events, or states happened first.
- The past perfect progressive expresses an action that was in progress before another past event.
- Use *was / were going to / would* + base form to describe an action, event, or state that was planned or expected before now. This is sometimes called the "future in the past."

Theme: MARRIAGE

Unit 2 focuses on language that is used to talk about an arranged marriage in the United States.

Step 1: Grammar in Context (pages 15–17)

See the general suggestions for Grammar in Context on page 1.

Before You Read
- Have students work in groups to discuss the questions.
- Call on students to share their groups' answers with the class.

Read

- Write these questions on the board:
  1. How many Americans have arranged marriages? *(not very many)*
  2. Why did Weinlick choose the date of his wedding before he found a bride? *(He got tired of being asked when he was going to tie the knot.)*
  3. Whose idea was the selection process for a bride? *(It was the idea of his friend Steve Fletcher.)*
  4. Where did Runze and Weinlick get married? *(at the Mall of America in Minneapolis)*
- Establish a purpose for reading. Call on students to read the questions to the class. Remind students to think about the questions as they read and listen to the text.
- Have students read the text. Discuss the answers to the questions as a class.

After You Read

A. Vocabulary

- Have students cover the definitions in the right-hand column. Have them read the sentences in the left-hand column and try to guess the meanings of the boldfaced expressions. Then have students discuss what they mean in pairs and write a brief definition for each one.
- Have students complete the exercise individually and go over the answers as a class. Have students compare the definition they wrote with the correct answers.
- (!) Point out that when people guess at meaning by reading the words and sentences around a word or phrase they don't know, they are using *context* to get meaning. Developing this reading skill will help students understand unknown words and expressions more easily and increase their overall reading comprehension.

B. Comprehension

- Have students complete the exercise individually and then compare answers in pairs or groups of three, sharing their corrected false sentences with each other.
- Call on students to share their corrected sentences with the class.

Go to **www.myfocusongrammarlab.com** for an additional reading, and for reading and vocabulary practice.

Step 2: Grammar Presentation (pages 17–19)

See the general suggestions for Grammar Presentation on page 2.

Grammar Charts

- Have students read the first three grammar charts. Ask students:
  — Which structures are used to express a definite time in the past? *(the simple past and past progressive)*
  — What time frame is the present perfect used to express? *(indefinite time in the past)*
  — What two structures are used to talk about habitual or repeated past time? *(used to or would + base form)*
- Have students work in pairs to identify other examples of these structures in the opening reading and go over them as a class.
- Have students read the last two grammar charts. Write the two example sentences on the board and underline the target structures:
  He <u>had met</u> her before the wedding.
  He <u>had been planning</u> the wedding for months.
- Point to the first sentence and ask: "Is the wedding in the past, present, or future?" *(the past)* "Which was first: he met her, or they had the wedding?" *(he met her)*
- Point to the second sentence and ask: "Did the wedding happen yet?" *(yes)* "Was he planning before or after the wedding?" *(before)*
- Have students work in pairs to identify other examples of these structures in the opening text. Go over them as a class.

Grammar Notes

Note 1

- Point out the examples of general and specific time and elicit more examples of each.
- If needed, refer students to Appendix 1 on page A-1 for a list of irregular verbs.

Note 2

- Write this example from Note 2 on the board: Runze <u>was studying</u> . . . when she <u>decided to get married</u>. Have students label the verb forms.
- Remind students that the restrictions regarding non-action verbs in the progressive discussed in Unit 1 apply to the past progressive as well as the present progressive. If needed, refer students to Appendices 2 and 3 for more information.

- ⏱ Have students share stories about what they (or people they know) were doing when they decided to get married. Then erase the verbs and elicit other examples.

Note 3

- To clarify the contrast in meaning between the simple past and the present perfect, have students work in pairs to write five to eight *Have you ever . . . ?* questions. Have two pairs work together to ask and answer their questions. When the answer is *yes*, the question *When?* can be asked, prompting a response in the simple past with a specific time stated or implied. Call on students to share their questions and answers with the class.
- ⏱ Remind the class that the present perfect shows a connection between the past and the present. Point out the example sentence in the note. You can also point out that *Did you eat dinner yet?*, while not considered "correct," is commonly used these days. In combination with the words *yet, already*, and *just*, the simple past is becoming increasingly more common as a substitute for the present perfect in informal speech.

Note 4

- To clarify the difference in usage between *used to* and *would* write on the board: I used to____. I would ____.
- Have students use the words on the board to make sentences with these cues: *have a guitar, be a good student, live in the city.* Ask students: "Why do these phrases all require *used to*?" *(The verbs express past possession, state, or location.)* Ask students: "Can *used to* be used with active verbs as well?" *(Yes.)*
- On the board write: Luis used to play the guitar. Then ask: "Does he still play the guitar?" *(No.)* Then write: Tania <u>would</u> practice the piano for hours when she was young. Ask: "Does she still practice the piano?" *(Maybe; we don't know.)* Point out that in order to use *would*, we generally include a time reference such as *when she was young* above, whereas *used to* can stand alone.

Note 5

- Illustrate the use of the past perfect by listing your actions on a particular day in chronological order. For example: *At 6:30, I got up. I took a shower, and I had breakfast. I also walked the dog and read the newspaper. Then I left for work at 8:15.*

Show students how the usage changes when you use *by* or *by the time*. Explain that this is a point in the past, so all actions before it will use the past perfect. For example: *By 8:30 A.M., I had gotten up, taken a shower, eaten breakfast, walked the dog, read the newspaper, and left for work.* OR: *By the time I left for work, I had gotten up, taken a shower, eaten breakfast, walked the dog, and read the newspaper.*

- ⏱ Have students make a similar list of actions on a particular day. Then have them discuss the events in small groups. Encourage them to use the past perfect. Circulate as students talk and give help as needed.

Note 6

- Have students read the note and the example sentence aloud. Ask students: "When did she start working: before she got married or when she got married?" *(before)*
- ⏱ Have students use the past perfect to describe amazing things about their childhood in groups. The events can be true or imaginary. Be sure they include a specific time reference. For example: *By the time I was four, I had been playing the piano professionally for three years. By the time I was twelve, I had been making movies for six years.*

Note 7

- The term "future in the past" may be a bit difficult for students to understand. Explain that it simply refers to states and actions planned or expected in the past. Remind students that *be going to* is used to show future intention.
- Model some sentences using the target structures in Note 7. For example: When I was in high school, I knew I was going to be a teacher. I also knew I wouldn't begin my career in the United States. I knew that after college I would probably live in a foreign country for a while.
- ⏱ Have students write several sentences about "future in the past" plans or goals. Then have them share their sentences in pairs.

⏱ **Identify the Grammar:** Have students identify the grammar in the opening reading on pages 15–16. For example:
How many Americans **have** ever **considered** asking friends or relatives to select their spouse for them?
Yet this is exactly what David Weinlick **did**.
He **had** long **been pondering** marriage and **had known** for quite some time that he **was going to get** married in June of 1998.

When the wedding **would take place** and who **would be invited** he already **knew**. He just **didn't know** whom he **would be marrying**.

Go to **www.myfocusongrammarlab.com** for grammar charts and notes.

Step 3: Focused Practice (pages 19–24)

See the general suggestions for Focused Practice on page 4.

Exercise 1: Discover the Grammar

A

- Go over the example with the class. Have a student explain why the action or state on the left occurred before the one on the right. (*Because the past perfect* —Weinlick had known—*refers to an event in the past, and the "future in the past"* —was going to get married—*refers to a future event that was expected in the past.*)
- Have students complete Part A. Review the answers as a class. Have students explain why each event is before or after the other.
- ⏱ Have students look again at the opening reading. In pairs, have them write three to five more sentences about the people and events. Call on students to write their sentences on the board. Then have the class identify the earlier and later occurring states/events.

B

- Have students complete the exercise individually and check answers in pairs.
- Call on students from each pair to share their answers.

Exercise 2: Simple Past / Present Perfect

- Have students complete the exercise individually and work in pairs to check answers.
- Go over the answers with the class. Call on students from each pair to provide correct answers.
- ⏱ Have students read the text aloud to each other in pairs.

Exercise 3: *Used To / Would*

- Read the instructions and go over the example with the class. Make sure students understand that they should use *would* in their answers whenever possible.
- Have students complete the exercise individually. Go over the answers as a class. Call on students to provide the correct answers and to explain why each choice is correct.

- ⏱ Have students practice the conversation in pairs, changing roles after the first practice.

Exercise 4: Simple Past / Past Perfect

- Go over the example with the class. Ask if there are any other ways to combine the sentences. (*Yes: Jim Garcia and Jennifer O'Leary had known each other for three years when they graduated from high school.*)
- Have students complete the exercise individually. Call on students to write their sentences on the board and read them aloud to the class. Make sure that students use a comma if the dependent clause comes first.
- ⏱ For further practice, after students read each sentence aloud, have another student say the sentence with the statements in reverse order. For example:
  S1: When they graduated from high school, Jim Garcia and Jennifer O'Leary had known each other for three years.
  S2: Jim Garcia and Jennifer O'Leary had known each other for three years when they graduated from high school.

Exercise 5: Weinlick / Runze Updated

- Have students read the questions. Then have them read the article for the answers. Allow students time to write their answers.
- Have students work in pairs to check their answers. Have students in each pair take turns asking and answering the questions.

Exercise 6: Editing

- Go over the example with the class. Then have students complete the exercise individually.
- To check answers, have several students write their corrected sentences on the board. Have these students tell the class why each error is a mistake and how their correction resolves the problem.

Go to **www.myfocusongrammarlab.com** for additional grammar practice.

Step 4: Communication Practice (pages 24–30)

See the general suggestions for Communication Practice on page 5.

Exercise 7: Listening

A

- Establish a purpose for listening. Have students read the question. Remind them to think about the question as they listen.
- Play the audio. Ask the class the question and go over the answer. Replay the audio if needed.

B

- Have students read the questions. Remind them to think about the questions as they listen. Play the audio again.
- Call on students to read and answer the questions.
- You may want to play the audio again to clarify any discrepancies in students' answers.

Exercise 8: Pronunciation

A

- Have students read and listen to the Pronunciation Note.
- If more practice is needed, say the example sentences aloud and have students repeat.

B

- Read the instructions. Play the audio, pausing as needed so students can repeat the sentences.
- Play the audio again and have students underline the auxiliary verb in each sentence. Go over the examples and have students name the auxiliary verb that has been contracted. For example, for Item 1, the verb is *has*.

C

- Read the instructions. Play the audio, pausing as needed so students can repeat the sentences.
- Allow students time to underline the auxiliary verbs. Go over the answers as a class.

D

- Have students complete this exercise in pairs. Have them take turns saying the sentences, randomly choosing either the contracted or full forms. The listener should write what he or she hears. Then have pairs check what they wrote with each other.

Exercise 9: Information Gap

A

- Divide students into pairs, Student A and Student B. Have the Student Bs turn to page 30. Explain that they are looking at the same story, but each person is missing information that their partner has. They should ask and answer questions to find the information.
- Have a pair read the example conversation aloud. Make sure everyone understands that the information Student A asks for is in Student B's text, and vice versa.
- Have students complete the activity in pairs. Circulate and help as needed.

B

- Have students compare their stories in pairs and confirm that the information they wrote matches.
- Have students read and discuss the questions in pairs. Circulate and help as needed. Call on a few students to share their answers with the class.
- ⏱ Have pairs write three to five questions about the story. Encourage them to use as many target structures from the unit as possible. Them have pairs exchange questions and answer them

Exercise 10: Picture Discussion

- Read the instructions aloud. Have students look at the picture and read the questions.
- Have students discuss the picture in pairs. As students are sharing ideas with the class, make notes about the discussion on the board or have a student take notes.
- ⏱ Have students write a paragraph about the picture on page 28. Encourage them to use the target structures from this unit in their paragraphs. Then have them share their paragraphs in pairs. You may also want to post them on the walls or a bulletin board in your classroom.

Exercise 11: Group Discussion

- Have groups complete the exercise. Then have two groups work together. Each student tells the larger group about the significant life change of another student in his or her first group. Then call on students to share information with the class.

Exercise 12: Writing

A

- Have students read the example. Then have them find examples of the target structures from the unit, including the present perfect and the use of "future in the past."
- Read the writing instructions. For each topic mentioned (a marriage, a job, college plans, a move), have students suggest how the situation could turn out differently than expected. For example: *Before I moved to a new city, I didn't think I would miss my family very much, but I did.*
- Have students compare ideas in pairs. Then have students write their paragraphs, either in class or as homework.

B

- Have students work in pairs to correct each other's work using the Editing Checklist. Have each student revise and rewrite as needed.

- ⏲ Have students post their papers in the classroom so the class can read them. You can also publish them together in a booklet or on a class website.

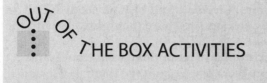

OUT OF THE BOX ACTIVITIES

Listening and Speaking

- Bring in pictures of married people in your family and describe their courtship and/or marriage to the class.
- Have students think of couples they know well (e.g., their parents, their grandparents, themselves) and prepare some notes describing their courtship and marriage. Have them bring in a photo of the couple if possible.
- Have students share their stories in small groups. Encourage them to use a variety of past-time forms. Tell them that *would* + base form should be especially useful here. Have each group select one story to tell the whole class.

Listening and Writing

- Choose a movie that deals with the topic of marriage—for example, *My Best Friend's Wedding, Green Card,* or *Leap Year.* Have students watch the movie—or parts of it— and then write a summary of what they've seen, using the past forms studied in this unit.
- **Note:** For variation, you can bring in photocopies of a magazine or newspaper article about a famous couple whose marriage is in trouble. This kind of article often looks back on the couple's story, which can also be discussed using the past forms.

Writing and Speaking

- Construct a timeline of significant events or a significant time period in your life. Write it on the board or prepare it as a handout.

- Using the timeline, talk about the various events using the target structures in this unit. For example:
  By the time I was six, I had lived in three different countries and spoke two languages. My father worked for the government, and my parents had been living in Germany for two years when I was born. Before I was born, my parents used to travel a lot around Europe. They had been to France, Spain, and Portugal, and thought they would go to Belgium next. Then I arrived. They never got to Belgium! When I was a year old . . .
- Have students construct a similar timeline of significant events or a significant time period in their lives. Have them work in pairs to practice talking about the events or time period using the target structures in this unit. Then have two pairs work together and tell each other about the events or time period.

Go to **www.myfocusongrammarlab.com** for additional listening, pronunciation, speaking, and writing practice.

Note:
- See the *Focus on Grammar Workbook* for additional in-class or homework grammar practice.

Unit 2 Review (page 31)

Have students complete the Review and check their answers on Student Book page UR-1. Review or assign additional material as needed.

Go to **www.myfocusongrammarlab.com** for the Unit Achievement Test.

Grammar: FUTURE TIME

Unit 3 focuses on the meanings and uses of a variety of tenses and aspects that are used to express future time. There are four aspects of the future time frame: simple future, future progressive, future perfect, and future perfect progressive. In addition, the simple present and present progressive may also be used to express the future.

- Use the simple future —*will* or *be going to* + the base form of a verb— to express what you think will happen in the future. To express a future action decided on in the moment, use *will*, not *be going to*. We most often use *be going to* to talk about a planned or already developing future situation.

- Use the future progressive to talk about an action that will be in progress at a certain time in the future. You can use *will be* or *going to be* + the base form of a verb + *-ing* to form the future progressive.

- You can also use the simple present to talk about a future action, state, or event that is part of a schedule. You can use the present progressive to talk about a future action or event that has already been arranged.

- To talk about two separate actions in the future, use *will* or *be going to* in the independent clause and the simple present in the dependent clause.

- Use the future perfect or the future perfect progressive to talk about an action, state, or event that will happen or will be happening before a certain time in the future.

Theme: TRAVEL

Unit 3 focuses on language that is used to discuss future plans and suggestions for travel.

Step 1: Grammar in Context (pages 32–34)

See the general suggestions for Grammar in Context on page 1.

Before You Read

- Have students look at the pictures included in the article. Ask them what problem the people have and elicit the term *jet lag*.
- Have students work in pairs or small groups to discuss the questions.
- Call on students from each pair or group to share ideas with the class.

Read

- Write these questions on the board:
  1. Why is the author of the article a good source for travel tips? *(because she is the* Times *travel editor)*
  2. What are the five travel topics that the author gives tips about in this article? *(jet lag, tours, accommodations, money / valuables, and language / culture)*
  3. What is the primary purpose of this article? *(to offer tips to people who are planning a trip in the future)*
- Establish a purpose for reading. Have students read the questions. Remind students to think about these questions as they read and listen to the text.
- Have students read the text, or play the audio and have students follow along in their books. Then have students work in pairs to discuss the questions. Call on students to share answers with the class.
- **Note:** You may want to point out that the answers to the first and third questions require students to make inferences—an important reading comprehension skill. When we make inferences, we use what we already know along with information in a text to draw a conclusion about something that is not stated explicitly. In the first question, the text tells us that the author is a travel editor for the *Times*. Based on prior knowledge of what a travel editor does, we infer that the author would be a good source of information about travel tips.

After You Read

A. Vocabulary

- Have students scan the reading for each of the boldfaced words and underline them. Have them read the sentence in which they find the word, make a guess about what each word means, and write it in their notebooks.
- Have students complete the exercise individually. Call on students to read their answers aloud. As students share their answers, have them recall their guesses about the meanings of the words. Were their guesses accurate?
- ⏱ Point out that guessing meaning by reading the sentences around the word is using context to understand meaning. This reading skill will help students better understand unfamiliar texts with unknown words.

B. Comprehension

- Have students complete the exercise individually. Then have them compare answers in pairs.
- Call on students to share their answers with the class. Have them point out the place in the text where they found the answers.
- ⏱ Have the class discuss how their travel experiences relate to the tips given in the article.

Go to **www.myfocusongrammarlab.com** for an additional reading, and for reading and vocabulary practice.

Step 2: Grammar Presentation (pages 35–36)

See the general suggestions for Grammar Presentation on page 2.

Grammar Charts

- Write these questions on the board:
  — How many different forms can we use to express the future? *(six)*
  — What are they? *(simple future, future progressive, simple present, present progressive, future perfect, and future perfect progressive)*
  — Which two of these forms can be used to express a different time frame? What time frame can they express? *(The simple present and present progressive can be used to express the present time frame.)*
- Have students look over the grammar charts. Then have them work in pairs to discuss the questions.
- Go over the answers as a class.

Grammar Notes

Note 1

- Divide the class into three groups. Have one group read the first part of Note 1 and the example sentences. Have the second group look at the second part of Note 1 and the example sentences. Have the last group look at the third section of Note 1.
- Have each of the groups look through the opening reading for other examples of the use of *will* or *be going to*. Circulate as students are working and provide help as needed.
- Have students from each of the groups work together. Have them share information about the use of *will* and *be going to* that their original groups focused on and the examples they found in the opening reading.

Note 2

- Have a student read Note 2 aloud.
- Write the last example sentence on the board: Next week at this time we'll be climbing Kilimanjaro.
  Change the information in the sentence so it's true for you. (Example: *Next week at this time I'll be having lunch with my friend.*) Call on a few students to say similar sentences about themselves.

Note 3

- Have students read Note 3 aloud. Point out that simple present can refer to a future event that is part of a schedule or timetable. Brainstorm some examples of things that fall under this category. (Examples: *flights, buses, trains, classes, meetings, appointments, etc.*)
- Have students look at the example sentences. For example, ask: "What events are part of a schedule?" *(a departure, a plane's arrival)*
- ⏱ Have students list things they are scheduled to do in the next week. Then have them describe these events in pairs using the simple present. (Example: *I have biology class tomorrow at three o'clock.*)

Note 4

- Go over Note 4 as a class. Have students identify examples in the opening reading that show use of the present progressive to talk about a future action or event that has already been arranged.
- Point out that this use of present progressive is similar to the use of the simple present explained in Note 3.

Note 5

- On the board, illustrate that when two future actions are described in two clauses, one independent and one dependent, the one in the dependent clause shows the earlier of the two actions and is expressed in the simple present.

     1   2

  We will get to Italy. Then we will rent a car.
  When we get to Italy, we will rent / are going to rent a car.
- Write these sentences on the board:
  As soon as <u>class is over</u>, I'm going to <u>go shopping</u>.
  When I <u>get home</u>, I'll <u>make a list</u>.
  I'm going to <u>watch a movie</u> after <u>I finish dinner</u>.
- First have students identify the sequence of actions by writing *1* over the first and *2* over the second one. Then have them generate more examples, replacing the underlined words with their own ideas.

Note 6

- To make the concept of the future perfect more clear, it may help to start with a simple example. Ask students what time today's class started, what time it is now, and what time the class ends. Then write:

  We started class at [start time]. It is now [current time]. Class will end at [ending time].

  So far we have been in class for _____ minutes.

  By [ending time], we <u>will have been</u> in class for _____ minutes.

- Elicit the correct number of minutes for each sentence and write them in the blanks. Then have students read the completed sentences aloud. Point out that class is not over, but the last sentence describes what things will be like when class ends.

- Have students read the explanation and examples in Note 6. For each example sentence, ask: "When is the speaker saying this?" *(before their trip ends, before the end of the summer, before they finish their trip).* "What is the sentence describing?" *(what things will be like when the trip or the summer ends)*

🕐 **Identify the Grammar:** Have students identify the grammar in the opening reading on pages 32–33. For example:

  So you**'re visiting** some new countries this year?

  You already have your tickets, and you **leave** in exactly four weeks.

  A month from now you**'ll be relaxing** in the sunshine or **visiting** famous landmarks.

  By the time you **arrive**, you**'ll have been flying** for eight to ten hours and **won't be able to keep** your eyes open.

Go to **www.myfocusongrammarlab.com** for grammar charts and notes.

Step 3: Focused Practice (pages 37–40)

See the general suggestions for Focused Practice on page 4.

Exercise 1: Discover the Grammar

A

- Read the instructions. Quickly review the different future forms covered in this unit and write them on the board. (*Simple future with* will / be going to, *future progressive with* will / be going to, *simple present, present progressive, future perfect, future perfect progressive*.) Write these terms on the board.

- Have students complete the exercise individually and compare answers in pairs. Go over the answers as a class.

B

- Have students complete the exercise. Then have them compare answers in small groups.
- Go over the answers as a class.

Exercise 2: Present Progressive Future

- Read the instructions. Make sure students understand to use the present progressive whenever it is possible. Go over the example answer with the class and make sure students understand why the present progressive is *not* possible in this sentence.
- Have students complete the exercise. Go over the answers as a class.

Exercise 3: Two Actions in the Future

- Have students complete the exercise individually. Then have them compare answers in pairs.
- 🕐 In pairs, have students identify the sequence of the actions by writing *1* over the first action and *2* over the second one. Call on students to share their answers with the class.

Exercise 4: Personal Inventory (Future)

- Have students complete the exercise individually. Then have them compare answers in pairs.
- 🕐 Have two pairs work together. Each person in the pair tells the other pair three things his or her partner just shared. For example:

  S1: Thong thinks he'll be an engineer. In five years he'll be living in Vietnam. As soon as he leaves class today, he's going to work.

Exercise 5: Editing

- Have students complete the exercise and work in pairs to check their answers.
- Call on students to explain each error and correction.

Go to **www.myfocusongrammarlab.com** for additional grammar practice.

Step 4: Communication Practice (pages 41–43)

See the general suggestions for Communication Practice on page 5.

Exercise 6: Listening

A

- Establish a purpose for listening. Read the instructions and the question. Remind students to think about the question as they listen.

- Play the audio. Go over the answer as a class.

B

- Establish a purpose for listening. Have students read the sentences. Remind students to think about whether these statements are true or false as they listen.
- Play the audio. Have students work in small groups to compare their answers. Then go over the answers as a class.
- 🕐 Have students correct the false statements in pairs. Go over the answers as a class.

Exercise 7: Pronunciation

A

- Have students read and listen to the Pronunciation Note.
- If more practice is needed, say the example sentences aloud and have students repeat.

B

- Read the instructions. Play the audio for the first item and pause the audio to go over the example answer.
- Play the rest of the audio and have students complete the exercise. Have students compare answers in pairs.
- Play the audio again. Pause after each item to check the correct answer as a class.

C

- Play the audio, pausing as needed so students can repeat the sentences.

Exercise 8: Pair Discussion

A

- Have students read the items in the *Event* column in the chart. For each item, ask for a show of hands: "Who thinks this will happen in the next 25 years?"
- Elicit other events that might or might not happen in the next 25 years. Write them on the board. (Examples: *wars end, flying cars become popular, global warming gets worse*)
- Have students check their predictions in the chart and write another item in the last row.

B

- Read the example conversation with a student. Then have students share their predictions in pairs.
- Circulate and help as needed. Encourage students to give reasons for their predictions and ask follow-up questions.

C

- Call on pairs to share their answers with the class or, for large classes, with a group.

- **Note:** For variation, you may want students to exchange charts and report to the class about their predictions and how they compare or contrast with their partner's predictions.

Exercise 9: Group Discussion

A

- Ask students: "How many countries do you think there are in the world?" Write their guesses on the board. Then ask: "How many countries have you been to?"
- Have students read the paragraph and compare their answers to the information in the paragraph.

B

- Go over the questions as a class. Have students quickly reread the text in Part A with these questions in mind.
- Model the example conversation with a student. Point out that Speaker B asks a follow-up question to keep the conversation going. Have the students discuss the questions in groups. Circulate and encourage them to ask follow-up questions.

C

- Call on groups to share their ideas with the class.
- **Note:** If you have a large class, you may want two or three groups to share their ideas with each other rather than the whole class.

Exercise 10: Writing

A

- Have students read the two suggested writing topics and the example. Ask: "Which topic is the example about?" *(the second one)* Have students look at the example and identify the topic sentence. Point out that, in this example, the writer makes a statement about his dream vacation in the topic sentence and then other sentences support his main idea by giving details about that vacation.
- If students choose to write about the first topic, the topic sentence will state an opinion and the other sentences will provide reasons and examples that support the opinion. Students who would like to respond to the first question will be well prepared from the ideas generated from the preceding small group discussion.
- For those writing about their dream vacation, write these questions on the board to generate ideas and elicit vocabulary:
  — What are some places you have always wanted to go?

— Imagine you're going to visit this place. What will you do while you are there?

— What time of year will you go? For how long?

— Will you go alone or with someone? Who?

• Have students write their paragraphs, either in class or as homework.

B

• Have students work in pairs to correct each other's work using the Editing Checklist. Have each student revise and rewrite as needed.

• ⏱ Have students post their papers in the classroom so the class can read them. You can also publish their writing in a booklet or on a class website.

OUT OF THE BOX ACTIVITIES

Listening, Reading, and Speaking

• To provide practice for students to make the distinction between using *will* for unplanned actions and *be going to* to express a planned or developing situation, play "Let's Have a Party!" Explain that you're planning a party, and start by offering to do something to organize it. For example: *I'll bring some fruit and cheese.* Then ask a student: "What will you bring?" That student says what he or she will bring and asks another student: "What will you bring?" Emphasize that the use of *will* here represents each person spontaneously expressing what he or she will bring. As students say what they'll bring, write the items on the board, along with each student's name or initials.

• Have students recall what each person is bringing. Stress that since the action is now preplanned, the future with *be going to* should be used. Point out that the present progressive would also be appropriate. Model the first statement and then have students ask and answer questions about what they're going to bring. For example:

T: Tomiko is going to bring napkins. Raoul, what is Olga going to bring?

S1: Olga is bringing paper plates. Felipe, what's Song Hee going to bring?

S2: Song Hee is going to bring the music. Chen, what's Sui going to bring?

Writing. Reading, Speaking, and Listening

• Have each student write four to five tips about travel in his or her own country, using the opening reading as a model. Encourage students to use target structures from the unit.

• Post the tips around the classroom. Then have students walk around the class and read them.

• Have students discuss the tips in pairs.

Go to **www.myfocusongrammarlab.com** for additional listening, pronunciation, speaking, and writing practice.

Note:

• See the *Focus on Grammar Workbook* for additional in-class or homework grammar practice.

Unit 3 Review (page 44)

Have students complete the Review and check their answers on Student Book page UR-1. Review or assign additional material as needed.

Go to **www.myfocusongrammarlab.com** for the Unit Achievement Test.

From Grammar to Writing (pages 45–49)

See the general suggestions for From Grammar to Writing on page 9.

Go to **www.myfocusongrammarlab.com** for an additional From Grammar to Writing Assignment, Part Review, and Part Post-Test.

MODALS AND OTHER AUXILIARIES

UNIT	GRAMMAR FOCUS	THEME
4	Modals to Express Degrees of Necessity	Cultural Differences
5	Modals to Express Degrees of Certainty	Puzzles

Go to **www.myfocusongrammarlab.com** for the Part and Unit Tests.

Note: PowerPoint® grammar presentations, test-generating software, and reproducible Part and Unit Tests are on the *Teacher's Resource Disc.*

Grammar: MODALS TO EXPRESS DEGREES OF NECESSITY

Unit 4 focuses on the meanings and uses of modals that are used to express varying degrees of necessity.

- Modals are auxiliary verbs and have only one form for first, second, and third person.
- Use simple modals (modal + base form of verb) to show degrees of necessity in the present and future.
- Use perfect modals (modal + *have* + past participle of verb) to show degrees of necessity in the past.
- Modals show speakers' attitudes: obligations, advice, expectations, and suggestions.
- Some expressions have meanings that are similar to modals. *Have to* and *have got to* are similar to *must. Be supposed to* is similar to *should. Be allowed to* is similar to *may.*
- Use *must, have to,* and *have got to* to show strong necessity. Use *must* in more formal language to express a strong obligation that cannot be avoided. Use *have to* in all forms and situations, formal or informal. Use *have got to* in conversation and informal writing. Use *don't have to* to express the negative of *have got to.* Use *will have to* to express future necessity. Use *had to* + base form of the verb to express past necessity.
- Use *must not* to talk about something that is prohibited. Use *didn't have to* + base form of the verb to talk about something that was not necessary in the past. Although *must* and *have to* are similar in meaning, *must not* and *don't have to* have very different meanings.

- Use *should* or *ought to* to offer advice. They usually mean that something is a good idea or the right thing to do. *Should* not rather than *ought to* is used in questions and negatives. Use *should have* or *ought to have* to express advice about the past. *Should have* and *ought to have* suggest that something did not happen, while *shouldn't have* and *ought not to have* suggest that it did. We can also use *shall* in questions that ask for advice.
- *Had better* is stronger than *should* and *ought to.* Use *had better (not)* to give a warning that something negative will happen if advice isn't followed.
- Use *be supposed to* to show an expectation. You can use *be to* + base form in formal English to express a strong expectation.
- Use *could* or *might* to make suggestions about the present or future that are not too strong. Use *could have* or *might have* to talk about a missed opportunity in the past.

Theme: CULTURAL DIFFERENCES

Unit 4 focuses on language that is used to discuss suggested, required, or prohibited customs in other cultures

Step 1: Grammar in Context (pages 50–52)

See the general suggestions for Grammar in Context on page 1.

Before You Read
- Have students work in small groups to discuss the questions.
- Call on a few students to share their answers with the class.
- ⏱ Ask students what they know about the origins of specific customs in their cultures.

Read
- Write these questions on the board:
  1. What were some of the social (cultural) errors that the author and his wife made during their visit to Masayuki and Yukiko's home? *(They didn't leave their shoes pointing toward the door. They brought a gift that was both inappropriate and unwrapped. Helen took more food than she was able to finish. Helen offered to help in the kitchen. They accepted an additional drink instead of politely refusing.)*
  2. What did the author do as a result of feeling uncomfortable about aspects of the evening with his Japanese friends? *(He asked his friend Junichi about it because he had lived in the United States and Japan.)*

3. The author says that Masayuki and Yukiko never gave any indication that anything was wrong during the evening. What might this say about Japanese culture? *(Japanese people are very polite and will not show that they are upset about something.)*

- Establish a purpose for reading. Have students read the questions. Remind students to think about these questions as they read and listen to the text.
- Have students read the text or play the audio and have students follow along in their books. Have students discuss the questions in pairs or groups of three. Call on students to share answers with the class.

After You Read

A. Vocabulary
- Have students complete the exercise individually.
- Have students compare answers in pairs. Circulate as students compare answers, helping as needed. Call on students to read their answers aloud.
- ⏱ You may want to have students find the vocabulary words in the opening text and read the sentences where they appear.

B. Comprehension
- Have students complete the exercise individually. Then have them compare answers in pairs.
- Call on students to share their answers with the class. Have each student point out the place in the text where he or she found the answer for the question.

Go to **www.myfocusongrammarlab.com** for an additional reading, and for reading and vocabulary practice.

Step 2: Grammar Presentation (pages 53–56)

See the general suggestions for Grammar Presentation on page 2.

Grammar Charts
- Since this unit will be partly review and consolidation, focus on those modals or uses of modals that are likely to be new to your class.
- Have students work in four groups. Assign each group a section of the grammar chart: obligation (necessity), advice, expectation, and suggestion / no obligation (no necessity). Have each group write out the negative forms and affirmative forms of each of the modals in the chart, as well as an example of the modal from the opening reading.

- Have students form new groups of four. In each group there should be a student who has a completed chart for a different meaning / use, so that students have access to all four meanings and uses: obligation (necessity), advice, expectation, and suggestion / no obligation (no necessity). Have each student in the group share with the others the information from his or her completed chart. Call on students from each group to share information with the class.
- Review subject-verb agreement with the class. Ask:
  — Does the modal *should* change when the subject changes? (*No. For example, both* you *and* he *are followed by* should.)
  — Which of the other modals are like this? (*must, ought to, could, might, can*)
  — For which modals does this rule not apply? (*have to, have got to,* and *be supposed to*)
- Make sure students notice the verb forms following the modals and elicit from them that the base form is used after simple modals and the past participle is used after perfect modals.

Grammar Notes

Note 1
- Do a listening exercise in which students discriminate between the simple and perfect forms of *should, could,* and *might*. Write on the board (or have students write in two columns on a sheet of paper):

Present	Past
should	*should have*

- Have students listen and point to the one they hear (or have them respond on paper, placing a check under the appropriate column) as you say a series of sentences at normal speed. (Examples: *We should invite him. We should have invited him. We should have called her. I could write them. I could have written them.*)
- Remind students that the formation of the perfect modal requires the past participle, which is often irregular. Elicit a few examples (e.g., *should have* [write] *written* and *might have* [come] *come*).

Note 2
- Have students read the modal-like expressions and the example sentences. Have them practice saying each variation of the

sentence. For example, for the first example sentence:
You must finish everything on your plate.
You have to finish everything on your plate.
You have got to finish everything on your plate.
- Explain that the meaning of these three sentences is basically the same, but there are small differences that will be discussed in the notes below.

Note 3
- Have a student read Note 3 aloud.
- Ask: "Which expression is most often used to express strong necessity?" *(have to)* "Which expression is used in conversation and informal writing?" *(have got to)*
- Point out that *must* is very rarely used in speech to express necessity but is more commonly seen in signs. (Example: *Employees must wash hands before returning to work.*)

Note 4
- Have students read the note. Draw special attention to the *Be Careful!* explanation.
- Write sentences on the board using the modals and have students identify the meaning by using the equivalent expressions. For example:

You must leave now.	= It is necessary that you . . .
You have to leave now.	
You must not leave now.	= It is necessary that you not . . .
You don't have to leave now.	= It is not necessary that you . . .
You didn't have to leave then.	= It was not necessary that you . . .

Note 5
- Point out that *should* is more commonly used than *ought to*, particularly in past forms.
- Explain that *shall* used to be used as a form of *will*. North Americans still occasionally use *shall* for the future, but when they do, they are being very formal or trying to sound funny or different.

Note 6
- Point out the forms of *had better* and that it is sometimes used in the past: *You'd better not have scratched my car.* (You're in trouble if you did.) The question form is also worth mentioning: *Hadn't we better get going soon?*

- Explain to students that they need to be careful in using *had better*. It is a strong expression and can seem rude or impolite if not used correctly. It is usually used by people who have authority over others or with people they know very well.

Note 7
- Point out the difference between *have to* and *supposed to*. For example: *You have to have a license to drive.* (It's a requirement.) *You're supposed to obey the speed limit.* (This is the expectation and the law, but many people don't obey it.)
- Explain to students that *be to* + base form is a very strong expression and can seem rude or impolite in both speech and writing. It is usually used to express strong rules or by people in a position of authority over others.

Note 8
- Tell students that these polite forms will be very useful to them. You could also point out that *could have* and *might have* referring to past opportunity are close in meaning.

⏱ **Identify the Grammar:** Have students identify the grammar in the opening reading on pages 50–51. For example:
Recently my wife and I had a cross-cultural experience that taught us about some things we **should have done** differently.
Now we know what we **should** and **shouldn't have done**.
We knew you're **supposed to take** them **off** in a Japanese home.
It's OK to bring it in a plastic bag, but the gift **has to be wrapped**.
". . . you **could have taken** some flowers."
"You mean you**'ve got to eat** everything that's offered?" I asked.
"You **don't have to**. But if you take something, you **must finish** it."

Go to **www.myfocusongrammarlab.com** for grammar charts and notes.

Step 3: Focused Practice (pages 56–61)

See the general suggestions for Focused Practice on page 4.

Exercise 1: Discover the Grammar
- Have students complete the exercise. Then have them compare answers in small groups.
- Call on students from various groups to share their answers with the class. Clarify any discrepancies in answers among groups.

- ⏱ Have students look at the "wrong" answer choices for the items and write an appropriate restatement of these sentences using modals. For example, for Item 1, the wrong answer choice was *It doesn't matter whether or not you wear your shoes in a Japanese home.* Students should restate this using modals: *You don't have to take off your shoes in a Japanese home.*

Exercise 2: Modals

- Have students quickly read the dialogue for main ideas. Ask: "What is the conversation about?" *(tipping customs in Japan and in another country, probably the United States)*
- Have students read the expressions with modals in the box. You may want to review which expressions describe obligation, necessity, advice, and so on. You may also want to review which expressions are about the past or the present.
- Have students complete the exercise individually. Then have them compare answers in pairs. Have students work in pairs to practice the conversation twice, changing roles after the first practice.

Exercise 3: *Must / Have To / Should / Be Supposed To*

A

- Read the instructions. Write the following questions on the board:
  1. Which two cultures are compared in the text? *(Bali in Indonesia and the United States.)*
  2. What are two differences in the way babies are treated? *(In Bali, it is not good to let babies cry or put them on the floor.)*
- Have students read the text to find the answers to the questions. Go over the answers as a class.

B

- Have students read the sentences in pairs and quickly try to complete the blanks based on what they remember about the text. Then have students read the text again and complete the exercise individually. Have them compare answers in pairs.
- Go over the answers as a class. Have students explain why their answers are correct.

Exercise 4: *Should Have / Could Have*

- You may want to have students quickly reread the opening text on pages 50–51 to remind themselves of the topic and ideas in the article.

- Have students complete the exercise individually. Then have them work in groups to compare answers.
- Have students from various groups share their sentences with the class.

Exercise 5: Editing

- Have students complete the exercise and work in pairs to check their answers. Then call on students to explain each error and correction.

Go to **www.myfocusongrammarlab.com** for additional practice.

Step 4: Communication Practice (pages 62–67)

See the general suggestions for Communication Practice on page 5.

Exercise 6: Listening

A

- Establish a purpose for listening. Read the instructions and the question. Remind students to think about the question as they listen.
- Play the audio. Go over the answer as a class.

B

- Establish a purpose for listening. Have students read the questions. Remind students to think about the questions as they listen.
- Play the audio. Have students work in small groups to compare their answers. Then go over the answers as a class.
- ⏱ You may also want to provide students with a copy of the audioscript and have them work in pairs to practice reading the conversation. Call on a pair to role-play the conversation for the class.

Exercise 7: Pronunciation

A

- Have students read and listen to the Pronunciation Note.
- If more practice is needed, read the examples aloud and have students repeat.

B

- Read the instructions. Play the audio, pausing as needed so students can repeat the sentences.
- If students have difficulty, you may want to replay the audio so they can listen and repeat again.

C

- Have students complete this exercise in pairs. Have them take turns saying the sentences, randomly choosing either the full form or the reduced form. The listener responds by saying the other form of the sentence.

- Circulate as pairs practice saying the sentences. Make corrections as needed.

Exercise 8: Information Gap

- Divide students into pairs, with one person Student A and the other Student B. Have the Student Bs turn to page 67. Explain that they are looking at the same story, but each person is missing information that their partner has. They should ask and answer questions to find the information.
- Have a pair read the example conversation aloud. Make sure everyone understands that the information Student A asks for is in Student B's text, and vice versa.
- Have students complete the activity in pairs. Circulate and help as needed. Have students compare their completed stories when finished. Go over the answers as a class.
- 🕐 You may want to have students read through their versions of the story and underline unfamiliar vocabulary. Write these items on the board and ask students what they think the words mean. Discuss the definitions. Some of these might be:

be on a tight budget	to have very little extra money to spend
astonished	very surprised about something, especially because it is unusual or unexpected
grateful	feeling that you want to thank someone because of something kind that they have done
miserable	extremely unhappy
broadening	if an experience is broadening, it makes it easier for you to accept other people's beliefs or ways of doing things

Exercise 9: Discussion

A

- Have students read the list of behaviors in the chart. Answer any questions about vocabulary.
- Have students check the word that best describes their opinion about each behavior.

B

- Model the example conversation with a student.

- Divide the class into small groups. If possible, include students from different cultures in each group. Have them compare answers. Circulate, helping as needed. Encourage students to give reasons and examples for their opinions.
- Call on each group to share their answers with the class. You may also want to spend some time talking about other customs or behaviors that are obligatory or prohibited in different cultures.

Exercise 10: Writing

A

- Have students read the instructions. Brainstorm some examples of situations people often feel they should have handled differently. (Examples: *attending a gathering in another culture, tipping while on vacation*)
- Have students look at the example and identify the topic sentence. Point out that the writer begins by briefly describing the situation in the topic sentence. The other sentences support his description by giving specific details about the situation.
- Have students write their paragraphs, either in class or as homework.

B

- Have students work in pairs to correct each other's work using the Editing Checklist. Have each student revise and rewrite as needed.
- 🕐 If time permits, you may want to have students post their papers in the classroom so the class can read them. You could also publish them together in a booklet or on a class website.

OUT OF THE BOX ACTIVITIES

Listening, Speaking, Reading, and Writing,

- Point out to students that any behavior can be misinterpreted across cultures. Even positive actions such as expressing appreciation can lead to misunderstanding. For example, in some countries, if you say "Thank you" a lot as Americans typically do, you can be seen as cold, distant, or superior. Instead, you say nice things about the person who did the kindness rather than thanking the person for the kindness.

- Have students work in small groups. Give each group a scenario. For example:
  — A classmate invites you to dinner.
  — A friend gives you a book for your birthday.
  — Someone offers to show you the sights of the city.
  — Your teacher shows you how to do something.
- Have groups discuss how people in these situations show appreciation in their cultures. Then have them write short dialogues and role-play them for the class.

Reading, Writing, Listening, and Speaking

- Do a search on the Internet (or have pairs or groups of students do the search) on cross-cultural etiquette and / or cultural awareness. Print out (part of) a test that reflects cultural awareness.
- Have students take the test to find out how much they know about other cultures. Have students work in small groups to comment on the test and discuss what people must / should / are supposed to / are not allowed to do in other cultures. Encourage students to use the test as the basis for a discussion of related experiences they might have had.
- As students share their experiences, have them encourage their classmates to give their opinion by saying what they think the person should / ought to have done or could / might have done in the situations described.

Go to **www.myfocusongrammarlab.com** for additional listening, pronunciation, speaking, and writing practice.

Note:
- See the *Focus on Grammar Workbook* for additional in-class or homework grammar practice.

Unit 4 Review (page 68)

Have students complete the Review and check their answers on Student Book page UR-1. Review or assign additional material as needed.

Go to **www.myfocusongrammarlab.com** for the Unit Achievement Test.

Grammar: MODALS TO EXPRESS DEGREES OF CERTAINTY

Unit 5 focuses on the meanings and uses of modals and modal-like expressions that express varying degrees of certainty.

- When we use modals and modal-like expressions to express certainty, we speculate based on logic and facts. These structures can be used with both simple and progressive forms.
- Use *must, have to,* and *have got to* + base form to express near certainty about the present. Use *can't, couldn't,* and *must not* + base form to express negative speculation. *Must not* is slightly less certain and is generally not used in the contracted form. For questions, use *could* or *couldn't.*
- Use *may, might,* and *could* + base form to express less certain speculation about the present. For negative speculation, use *may not* or *might not* + base form. *May not* is never contracted, and the contracted form of *might not* is rare. For questions, use *could* or *might.*
- Use *must have* and *had to have* + past participle to express near certainty about the past. For negative speculation about the past, use *can't* or *couldn't have* + past participle to express impossibility. Use *must not have* + past participle when you are less certain. For questions, use *can have* or *could have.*
- When you are speculating about the past and are less certain (about 50 percent), use *may have, might have,* or *could have* + past participle. Remember that *could have* + past participle has two meanings: possibility or missed opportunity. For negative speculation about the past, use *may not have* or *might not have* + past participle. For questions, use *might have* or *could have* + past participle.
- For speculation about the future, use *should* or *ought to* + base form to express near certainty. Use *may, might,* or *could* + base form to express less certainty about the future. For negative speculation about the future, use *may* or *might* + *not / never* + base form.

Theme: PUZZLES

Unit 5 focuses on language that is used to talk about mysterious events, myths, and legends of the past.

Step 1: Grammar in Context (pages 69–71)

See the general suggestions for Grammar in Context on page 1.

Before You Read
• Have students work in pairs to discuss the questions.
• Call on students to share their answers with the class.

Read
• You may want to point out unfamiliar vocabulary. Write the words on the board and ask students what they think the words mean. Discuss the meanings as a class. For example:

fragment	a small piece that has broken off or that comes from something larger
pottery	objects made out of baked clay
candidate	a person, group, or idea that is a good choice for something
hemisphere	one of the halves of the earth

• Write these questions on the board (or prepare them as a handout):
1. According to the reading, who are the best-known candidates for the title of "discoverers" of the New World? *(the Vikings)*
2. What evidence is offered that the Vikings found the New World? *(Viking records and artifacts)*
3. What evidence is offered that the Irish reached North America? *(a written account, religious artifacts, and stone carvings found in Virginia)*
4. Who were the real discoverers of America? *(the Native Americans who migrated across the Bering Strait more than 10,000 years ago)*
5. In what sense did Columbus "discover" America? *(he started two-way communication between the Old and New Worlds)*

• Establish a purpose for reading. Call on students to read the questions to the class. Remind students to think about the questions as they read and listen to the text. Have students read the text. Discuss the answers to the questions as a class.

After You Read
A. Vocabulary
• Have students cover the definitions in the right-hand column. Have them read the sentences in the left-hand column and try to guess the meanings of the boldfaced expressions. Then have students work in pairs to discuss what they mean and write a brief definition for each one.
• Have students complete the exercise and go over the answers as a class. Have students compare the definition they wrote with the correct answers.
• ⏱ You may want to point out to students that when they guess at meaning by reading the words and sentences around a word or phrase they don't know, they are using *context* to get meaning. Developing this reading skill will help them understand unknown words and expressions more easily and increase their overall reading comprehension.

B. Comprehension
• Have students complete the exercise individually and then compare answers in pairs or groups of three, sharing their corrected false sentences with each other.
• Call on students to share their corrected sentences with the class.

Go to **www.myfocusongrammarlab.com** for an additional reading, and for reading and vocabulary practice.

Step 2: Grammar Presentation (pages 72–74)

See the general suggestions for Grammar Presentation on page 2.

Grammar Charts
• Students will most likely be familiar with the forms and sentence patterns of modals, so in general their attention will be more on meaning than on form in this unit. However, one aspect of form and meaning regarding these modals that is quite challenging is that some modals are used only in affirmative statements. In addition, for some modals, the negative form does not mean the opposite of the affirmative form. Students will need to learn which modals to use to form negatives and questions that convey the desired meaning.

- Have students study the charts and look for examples where the affirmative and negative form are both used and have the expected, opposite meanings. (Answers: *must / must not, may / may not* for present and future, *might / might not* for present and future, *must have / must not have, may have / may not have, might have / might not have*)
- Have them look for examples where the negative form of the modal does *not* have the opposite meaning. (Answers: *has (got) to, can't, couldn't, could* for present and future, *had to have, can't have, couldn't have, could have*) Write these modals on the board.
- For each modal on the board, elicit the modal with the opposite meaning. Draw lines on the board to connect pairs of modals with opposite meanings.
  has (got to)—can't / couldn't / must not
  could (present)—may not / might not
  had to have—can't have / couldn't have / must not have
  could have—may not have / might not have
  could (future)—may not / might not

Grammar Notes

Note 1
- Your students will probably already have some ideas about using modals to show certainty. Draw a line on the board and label it *0% certain* on one end and *100% certain* on the other. Have students tell you where to place the modals *should, must, may, might,* and *could* on this scale.
- Leave the diagram on the board for reference as you discuss the rest of the Grammar Notes.

Note 2
- Have students read the note. Ask students: "Where do *have to* and *have got to* go in the diagram on the board?" (*with* must, *close to 100%*)
- Ask students: "How are *have to, have got to,* and *must* different?" If they generalize what they have already learned about *must,* they may think that *must* is formal and more restricted in speech than *have to* or *have got to*. Point out that, on the contrary, when *must* is used for probability, it is quite common in informal speech. In fact, it is probably the most usual way to express that something is almost certainly true. On the other hand, *have got to* is decidedly informal and is therefore somewhat less useful than the other two.

- Ask students how they would express the opposite of *It must be true.* They will probably say, *It must not be true.* Ask if they can think of other ways. (*It can't be true.*) Ask which of these shows stronger certainty. (*It can't be true.*)

Note 3
- Have students read the explanation and the example sentences.
- You may want to point out that to express possibility, *may* and *might* are used more frequently than *could* in affirmative statements. However, in questions, *could* is more commonly used than *might*. *May* cannot be used at all.
- Ask students: "Which of these modals can be used with *not?*" (*may* and *might*) "Can *may* or *might* be contracted?" *(no)*

Note 4
- Have students read Note 4. Read the example sentences aloud and have students repeat.
- Point out that *must have* + past participle and *had to have* + past participle are similar in meaning, but *had to have* shows a greater certainty. For example:
  John must have gone home. (I'm almost certain that he did.)
  John had to have gone home. (It's almost impossible that he didn't.)

Note 5
- Students will need some practice with these past modals. Go over Note 5, model the examples, and have students repeat.
- Provide examples of the two meanings of *could have* + past participle:
  Mary could have left early. (It's possible that she left early.)
  Mary could have left early. (She didn't leave early, but it was possible to do so.)

Note 6
- Review the "certainty scale" with students. Have them place *should* and *ought to* on it.
- Point out that the negative form of *should* and *ought to* are not used to speculate about the future. Instead, students can use nonmodal expressions like *probably won't*.

Note 7
- Have students read the note. Read the example sentences aloud and have students repeat.

- To contrast *should* and *ought to* with *may*, *might*, and *could*, have students work in pairs to decide which modals they would use in the following sentences:
  1. It's four o'clock. Their train _____ be here in a few minutes. (*should, ought to*)
  2. A: What are you going to wear to the party?
     B: I don't know. I _____ wear my blue suit. (*may, might*)
  3. A: When will we see you again?
     B: I _____ be back on the East Coast next spring. There's a conference I'm planning to go to in April. (*should*)

🕐 **Identify the Grammar:** Have students identify the grammar in the opening reading on pages 69–70. For example:

However, Columbus **may not have been** the first non-Native American to visit the Western Hemisphere.

So many other potential discoverers have been nominated that the question **might** almost **be rephrased** as "Who *didn't* discover America?"

Scholars originally thought Vinland **must have been** Newfoundland, but today it is believed Vinland **couldn't have been** that island since it is too far north for grapes to grow.

Could the climate **have been** warmer in Erickson's day?

Go to **www.myfocusongrammarlab.com** for grammar charts and notes.

Step 3: Focused Practice (pages 74–79)

See the general suggestions for Focused Practice on page 4.

Exercise 1: Discover the Grammar
- Have students complete the exercise. Go over the answers as a class.
- 🕐 To provide additional practice, you may want to have students look again at the opening reading and work in pairs to write three to five more sentences similar to the ones in the exercise that are based on the reading. Have pairs exchange papers. At the bottom or on the back of the paper, have students make a scale with *certain* at one end and *impossible* at the opposite end. Then have pairs work together to place the sentences in the correct spot along the scale.

Exercise 2: Affirmative Modals
- You may want to call students' attention to these two words, which may be unfamiliar. Ask students what they think they mean and discuss the definitions.

cohorts	colleagues or associates
retirement home	a building where older people live that provides various services such as food, social activities, and medical care

- Have students complete the exercise individually. Have them compare answers in pairs. Call on students from each pair to provide correct answers.
- Have students work in groups of three to practice reading the conversation, changing roles after each practice.

Exercise 3: Affirmative / Interrogative Modals
- You may want to point out vocabulary that may be unfamiliar. Ask students what they mean and discuss the definitions.

dwelling	a house, apartment, etc. where people live
flourishing	growing or developing well
devastate	to damage something very badly or to destroy something completely

- Have students complete the exercise individually. Go over the exercise as a class.
- 🕐 Have students work in pairs to practice reading the text to each other.

Exercise 4: Personal Inventory (Future)
- Have the students read the instructions and the examples. Brainstorm some accomplishments to write about. (Examples: *have children, win a prize, buy a home, become famous*)
- Have students complete the exercise individually. Then have them share their personal inventories in pairs. Call on students to tell the class one or two things about their partners they thought were the most interesting.

Exercise 5: Editing
- Go over the example with the class. Make sure everyone understands why the example is a mistake and how the correction resolves the problem.
- Have students complete the exercise individually. Then have a few students write their corrected sentences on the board. Have students explain their corrections to the class.

- (!) Have students work in pairs to read the corrected text aloud to each other.

Go to **www.myfocusongrammarlab.com** for additional grammar practice.

Step 4: Communication Practice (pages 80–83)

See the general suggestions for Communication Practice on page 5.

Exercise 6: Listening

A

- Establish a purpose for listening. Have students read the question in Part A, then play the audio. Remind them to think about the question as they listen.
- Play the audio and allow students time to answer the question. Go over the answer as a class.

B

- Have students read the statements. Remind them to think about the statements as they listen. Play the audio, pausing after each statement so students can circle their answers.
- Go over the answers as a class. You may want to play the audio again to clarify any discrepancies in students' answers.
- (!) You may want to ask students how the listening tasks in each part are different. (*In Part A, they are listening to get the gist, or the main idea. In Part B, they are listening for details.*) Point out that these two purposes for listening require different skills that both need to be developed.

Exercise 7: Pronunciation

A

- Have students read and listen to the Pronunciation Note.
- If students have difficulty with this, say the full and reduced pronunciations of *to* and *have*. Have students repeat.

B

- Go over the example with the class. Play the audio and have students complete the exercise.
- Have students work in pairs to check their answers. Replay the audio as needed.

C

- Have students practice the conversations in pairs. Have each pair practice the conversations twice, so that each person has the chance to say all of the sentences.
- Circulate and make corrections as needed.

Exercise 8: Pair Discussion

A

- Read the instructions aloud. Explain that students will read four paragraphs that are puzzles or riddles. Then they will try to solve the puzzle in pairs.
- Call on different students to read each puzzle aloud. Answer any questions about vocabulary.
- Go over the example answer. Have students explain why this is one solution to the puzzle. (*If the bank had a security camera, there would be evidence that the thief cashed the woman's check.*) Brainstorm other possible answers using the target language. (Example: *The thief must have given the woman his name so she could write the check, so that made it easy to catch him.*)
- Have students work in pairs to discuss the puzzles. Circulate and help as needed.

B

- Call on students from each pair to share their ideas with the class.

Exercise 9: Group Discussion

A

- Have students quickly reread the information about Atlantis on pages 77–78. Have them look for explanations, interpretations, or opinions about the existence of Atlantis in the text.
- Elicit the explanations, interpretations, and opinions from the text. Write them on the board. Examples:
  — Atlantis is a myth and never existed.
  — The present-day Basques might be descendants of Atlantis.
  — Reports of a disaster on the island of Thira may have influenced the Atlantis legend.
- Have students compare ideas in groups. Circulate and help as needed.

B

- Call on students from each pair to share their ideas with the class.
- As students are sharing ideas in their groups, have a student make notes about the discussion on the board. Leave the notes on the board for the next exercise.

Exercise 10: Writing

A

- Read the instructions, the topic list, and the examples. You may want to offer students the option of writing about the mystery they discussed in the previous activity.

- Have students write their paragraphs, either in class or as homework.

B
- Have students use the Editing Checklist to revise and rewrite as needed. As an alternative, have them work in pairs to correct each other's work.
- ⏱ If time permits, you may want to have students post their papers in the classroom so the class can read them. You could also publish them together in a booklet or on a class website.

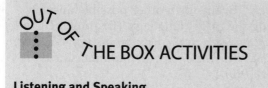

OUT OF THE BOX ACTIVITIES

Listening and Speaking
- **Note:** As a rule, the lives of important figures are surrounded by myths and legends. When George Washington was a little boy and used his new hatchet to cut down a cherry tree, his angry father confronted him with the evidence. Little George, realizing he had done wrong and understanding that he would be severely punished, said, "I cannot tell a lie. I did it with my hatchet." Many American school children have heard and believe this story. Yet it is totally false.
- Have students discuss similar legends in small groups. Have them say whether they think each is true and explain why it is important, even if it is not true.
- Have each group share one of the legends they discussed with the class.

Listening, Speaking, and Reading
- Bring in several newspaper articles with headlines that lend themselves to discussion and speculation. Cut out the headlines to separate them from the articles.
- Have students work in small groups. Give each group a headline, and have students make speculations about what could be happening, what could have happened, and what could happen next. Encourage the use of a variety of modals to express degrees of certainty.

- Give students the articles that match their headlines so they can confirm their guesses. Follow up by having students write the headline on the board and report to the class about their guesses and what actually happened.

Writing, Reading, Speaking, and Listening
- Have students bring in a photo that was taken at an event with family or friends.
- Have pairs exchange photos. Tell students the task is to look at the photo and speculate about the event it represents. Their speculations should include the past, present, and future.
- Have students write about the photo using various modals of certainty to express their speculations. Have students read what their partners wrote about their photos and then tell each other true details of the event.

Go to **www.myfocusongrammarlab.com** for additional listening, pronunciation, speaking, and writing practice.

Note:
- See the *Focus on Grammar Workbook* for additional in-class or homework grammar practice.

Unit 5 Review (page 84)
Have students complete the Review and check their answers on Student Book page UR-1. Review or assign additional material as needed.

Go to **www.myfocusongrammarlab.com** for the Unit Achievement Test.

From Grammar to Writing (pages 85–87)
See the general suggestions for From Grammar to Writing on page 9.

Go to **www.myfocusongrammarlab.com** for an additional From Grammar to Writing Assignment, Part Review, and Part Post-Test.

NOUNS

UNIT	GRAMMAR FOCUS	THEME
6	Count and Non-Count Nouns	Health
7	Definite and Indefinite Articles	Environmental Concerns
8	Quantifiers	Money
9	Modification of Nouns	Expectations

Go to **www.myfocusongrammarlab.com** for the Part and Unit Tests.

Note: PowerPoint® grammar presentations, test-generating software, and reproducible Part and Unit Tests are on the *Teacher's Resource Disc.*

Grammar: COUNT AND NON-COUNT NOUNS

Unit 6 focuses on the meanings and uses of count and non-count nouns.

- Nouns name persons, places, and things. There are two types of nouns: common and proper. Proper nouns name particular persons, places, or things that are usually unique. In writing they are capitalized. Common nouns refer to persons, places, or things in general and are not the names of particular individuals, places, or things.

- The two types of common nouns are count and non-count. Count nouns refer to things that you can count separately. They can be singular or plural. Non-count nouns refer to things that you cannot count separately. They usually have no plural form. We normally use a singular verb with a non-count noun and a singular pronoun to refer to it.

- There are several categories of non-count nouns: abstractions, diseases, food and drink, natural phenomena, particles, and other things.

- Many nouns have both count and non-count meanings. Examples: *experience, fish, history, space, talk.*

- We can make certain non-count nouns countable by adding a phrase that describes their form, limit, or the container in which they are found. We use these phrases to be more specific or emphatic.

- Many non-count nouns are given a countable meaning by using the plural form to mean kind, type, or variety. For example, *Many tasty cheeses are produced in France.*

- Some non-count nouns end in *-s*, such as *news* or *physics*. Some count nouns have irregular plural forms.

- *People* and *police* are plural count nouns and need a plural verb.

Theme: HEALTH

Unit 6 focuses on language that is used to discuss factors that relate to health and wellness.

Step 1: Grammar in Context (pages 90–92)

See the general suggestions for Grammar in Context on page 1.

Before You Read

- Have students discuss the questions in small groups or as a class.
- 🕐 Have students share information about health issues in their cultures.

Read

- Write these questions on the board:
  1. What does Dr. Brand say about fast food? *(It's OK in moderation. It's full of salt, sugar, cholesterol, and calories.)*
  2. What are some ways to avoid the dangers of being in the sun? *(wear sunblock and a hat with a brim)*
  3. What does Dr. Brand tell Martina about her husband? *(He's overweight and needs to start exercising and losing weight.)*
- Establish a purpose for reading. Call on students to read each of the questions. Remind students to think about these questions as they read and listen to the text.
- Have students read the text, or play the audio and have students follow along in their books. Have students discuss the questions in pairs or groups of three. Then call on students to share answers with the class.

After You Read

A. Vocabulary

- Have students complete the exercise individually. Then have them compare answers in pairs. Have pairs work together to take turns asking each other for the definitions of the vocabulary words in the box. For example:

  S1: What is BMI?

  S2: It's a numerical measurement of body fatness.

B. Comprehension

- Have students complete the exercise individually. Then have them compare answers in pairs.
- Call on students to share their answers with the class. Have each student point out the place in the text where he or she found the answer for the question.

Go to **www.myfocusongrammarlab.com** for an additional reading, and for reading and vocabulary practice.

Step 2: Grammar Presentation (pages 93–96)

See the general suggestions for Grammar Presentation on page 2.

Grammar Charts

- Write these questions on the board (or prepare them as a handout):
  — What are the two types of nouns found in the first section of the chart? *(common and proper)*
  — What types of words precede count nouns? *(articles or numbers)* What are some examples of these types of words? *(a, an, the, one, two)*
  — What are some examples of non-count nouns? *(rice, nutrition)*
  — What are some examples of nouns that can have both count and non-count meanings? *(hair, chicken, time, coffee, cheese, light)*
  — What are some examples of phrases that are used to make non-count nouns countable? *(a piece of, a game of, a spoonful of, a loaf of, a pound of, a package of)*
- Have students work in pairs or groups to answer the questions using the grammar charts. For the last three questions, have students provide additional examples of their own. Call on students to share their answers with the class.

Grammar Notes

Note 1

- Point out that some nouns that are considered proper and capitalized in English are not capitalized in some other languages. For example, in Spanish and French, days of the week, months of the year, names of languages, nationalities, and religions are not capitalized. On the other hand, some languages capitalize words that are not considered proper nouns in English. For example, in German, the first letter of all nouns is capitalized.

Note 2

- Have students read the explanation and example sentences. Point out the boldfaced nouns in each sentence. For each noun, ask students: "Can you count this separately?"
- ⏱ Write additional common nouns on the board (for example, *information, idea, problem, time*). Ask if they are count or non-count.

Note 3

- Give students a few minutes to read the categories and examples. Explain any unfamiliar vocabulary items.
- Have students work in small groups and assign each group two or three categories. Have them add five more non-count nouns to each category. If needed, refer students to Appendix 5 on page A-4 for a list of non-count nouns.
- Call on students to share their categories and examples with the class.

Note 4

- Ask a question with a non-count noun that can also have a countable meaning (for example, "Do you drink coffee?"). Then ask: "What is a common way of asking for three orders of coffee?" *(three coffees)*
- Point out that in countable use, a given noun can usually be singular or plural.
- Elicit examples of non-count nouns that can also have a countable meaning. (Examples: *television, radio, chance, business, philosophy, film, theater*) Have students try to make sentences that express the count and non-count meanings of these nouns.

Note 5

- Students will probably need practice with the use of non-count nouns in a count sense. First, model the phrases in the right column. Then have students repeat them after you.

- Have students work in pairs or groups to think of other words they can make countable by preceding them with these phrases:
  a piece of *(fruit, fish, cake, information, advice)*
  a grain of *(sand, salt, truth)*
  a cup of *(coffee, tea, milk, sugar, flour)*
  a pound of *(meat, cheese, rice)*
- Have groups continue to work together to think of other common phrases that are used to make non-count nouns countable and provide examples of the nouns with which they are used. Then call on students to share their ideas with the class.

Note 6
- Have students read the note and the example sentences.
- Point out that, as Note 6 explains, there are many non-count nouns that are used in a countable sense to mean a kind or type. Have students brainstorm a list of others and write them on the board. (*Food, soup,* and *fruit* are just a few.)

Note 7
- Elicit examples of other nouns ending in -*s* that are usually singular (for example: *linguistics, economics*).
- Give students example sentences using *criterion, phenomenon,* and *nucleus* in both the singular and plural.
- If needed, refer students to Appendix 4 on page A-3 for a list of irregular noun plurals.

⏱ **Identify the Grammar:** Have students identify the grammar in the opening reading on pages 90–91. For example:
  Welcome to Ask the **Expert**.
  I'm Miranda Olson. My **guest** today is Dr. Mel Brand, and we're going to devote today's entire **program** to your **questions** about **health**.
  So let's get right to it. . . . Tell us your **name** and where you're from.
  We hear a lot of negative **stuff** about fast **food**, but my **husband** and **kids** love **hamburgers** and **fries** and **sodas**.

Go to **www.myfocusongrammarlab.com** for grammar charts and notes.

Step 3: Focused Practice (pages 96–100)

See the general suggestions for Focused Practice on page 4.

Exercise 1: Discover the Grammar
- Have students complete the exercise and compare their answers in small groups.

- Call on students from various groups to share their answers with the class.

Exercise 2: Count / Non-Count Senses
- Have students complete the exercise. Go over the answers as a class.
- Call on students to explain why the answer is correct. For example: *a reading* is correct because it refers to a specific event.

Exercise 3: Non-Count Nouns Made Countable
- Have students complete the exercise individually. Then have them compare answers in pairs.
- Go over the answers as a class.
- ⏱ In pairs, have students write four to five more pairs of sentences similar to those in the exercise, but using different nouns. Then have pairs exchange papers and complete each other's sentences. Have them check their answers in groups of four. Call on students from each group to share their sentence pairs with the class.

Exercise 4: Personal Inventory (Past)
- Have students complete the exercise. Then have them work in groups to compare their answers.
- Call on students from various groups to share sentences about another person in the group. For example:
  The two best films that Rodrigo has seen in the last year are _____ *and* _____ . *The two funniest people he has ever met are* _____ *and* _____ .

Exercise 5: Editing
- Have students complete the exercise. Then have them work in pairs to check their answers.
- Call on pairs to explain each error and correction.

Go to **www.myfocusongrammarlab.com** for additional grammar practice.

Step 4: Communication Practice (pages 100–103)

See the general suggestions for Communication Practice on page 5.

Exercise 6: Listening
A
- Establish a purpose for listening. Have students read the question in Part A. Remind them to think about the question as they listen.

- Play the audio. Ask the class the question in Part A and go over the answer. Replay the audio if needed.

B
- Have students read the questions. Remind them to think about the questions as they listen. Play the audio again.
- Call on students to read and answer the questions in Part B.
- You may want to play the audio again to clarify any discrepancies in students' answers.
- (!) Provide copies of the audioscript. Have students practice reading the conversation in pairs. Then have one or two pairs role-play the conversation for the class.

Exercise 7: Pronunciation

A
- Have students listen to and read the Pronunciation Note.
- Have them repeat the examples several times as you say them.

B
- Play the audio once, pausing so students can repeat the sentences.
- Play the audio again. Pause after each sentence so students can circle their answers.
- Go over the answers as a class.

C
- Circulate as pairs practice saying the sentences. Make corrections as needed.

Exercise 8: Discussion

A
- If students have not done Exercise 4 first, have them complete the exercise now.
- Model the example with a student. Encourage students to give more information in their answer and to ask follow-up questions.
- Have students form groups and discuss their answers. Be sure the students do not work in the same groups as they did when they originally did Exercise 4.

B
- Call on students in each group to report answers to the class.
- In very large classes, you may want to have students report their answers to another group instead of the whole class.

Exercise 9: Personal Inventory

A
- Have students quickly read the survey questions. Answer any questions about vocabulary.

- Have students complete the survey individually.

B
- Call on students to share their answers from Part A. Make a tally chart on the board to record individuals' responses.
- Have students use the tally chart to analyze and discuss the trends that they see.

Exercise 10: Writing

A
- Have students read the example. Have students find examples of count and non-count nouns in the paragraph.
- Read the writing instructions. For each topic, brainstorm specific things students could write about.
- Have students write their paragraphs, either in class or as homework.

B
- Have students work in pairs to correct each other's work using the Editing Checklist. Have each student revise and rewrite as needed.
- (!) Have students post their papers in the classroom so the class can read them. You can also publish them together in a booklet or on a class website.

OUT OF THE BOX ACTIVITIES

Listening and Speaking
- Write this familiar American saying on the board: *You can't be too rich or too thin.* Explain to students that this is a common saying in the United States, but more and more Americans are becoming obese.
- Have students form teams of three or four. Pairs of teams will debate the benefits of different eating habits. One team will argue for the benefits of eating right and staying thin, stressing the physical, social, and economic benefits of being thin (e.g., *health, attractiveness, economic benefit, longer life*). The other team will argue for the benefits of people eating whatever they want, including convenience and junk food. These benefits can be psychological, practical (e.g., time), cultural, or economic.
- Give each team ample time to discuss the benefits for which they are arguing. Then have the pairs of teams have a debate for the class. Have class members vote for the team that they find most convincing, and have students share their reasons for voting the way they did.

Reading, Listening, and Speaking

- Bring in (or have students bring in) cookbooks or recipes from different sources.
- Have students work in small groups. Give each student a cookbook or a recipe. Have students choose a recipe to read and then list the ingredients in two columns, *Count Nouns* and *Non-Count Nouns*. Encourage students to use a dictionary to look up words they might not know.
- Have students put a check in front of all the ingredients they like. Have students discuss whether they would like to try the dish and support their answer by saying which ingredients they like and which they don't. Tell students they can also suggest replacing some of the ingredients with others they like better.

Listening, Speaking, and Writing

- Write this example on the board:
  There was so much snow on the road that we had to stop at a gas station. There we ate some cake, drank a cup of hot coffee, and filled the tank with gasoline. We had our skiing equipment in the trunk, and we couldn't wait to get to the ski resort!
- Have students work in pairs and write three simple stories (50 to 60 words) using non-count nouns. Point out that each story should contain at least five non-count nouns in uncountable or countable use. If needed, refer students to Appendices 5 and 6 on pages A-4 and A-5 as they work, and encourage them to be creative.
- Have pairs work together to share their stories and decide on one to read to the class.

Go to **www.myfocusongrammarlab.com** for additional listening, pronunciation, speaking, and writing practice.

Note:
- See the *Focus on Grammar Workbook* for additional in-class or homework grammar practice.

Unit 6 Review (page 104)

Have students complete the Review and check their answers on Student Book page UR-1. Review or assign additional material as needed.

Go to **www.myfocusongrammarlab.com** for the Unit Achievement Test.

UNIT 7 OVERVIEW

Grammar: DEFINITE AND INDEFINITE ARTICLES

Unit 7 focuses on the meanings and uses of definite and indefinite articles.

- Nouns that refer to unspecified people, places, or things are called *indefinite* nouns. Use the indefinite articles *a* and *an* before indefinite singular count nouns.
- Nouns are often indefinite the first time they are mentioned, but usually become definite at the next mention.
- Use no article (referred to as zero article) with indefinite plural count nouns, indefinite non-count nouns, names of people, names of most countries, and habitual places such as *home* or *work*.
- Generic nouns talk about things in general and represent all members of a class or category of persons, places, or things. There are three common ways to use nouns generically: indefinite article + count noun; zero article + plural count nouns; zero article + non-count noun. You can also use the definite article + an adjective to make a generic statement.
- A noun is definite when both speaker and listener know which person, place, or thing is talked about. Use the definite article *the* with non-count and singular and plural count nouns that are definite for you and your listener.
- Use the definite article with things that are unique. Sometimes an adjective can make a noun represent something unique.
- Use the definite article generically to talk about inventions, musical instruments, living things, and the parts of the body.
- The definite article can be used to talk about public places such as *the bank* or *the post office*. It is also used with geographical regions or features *(the Pacific Ocean, the Grand Canyon)*. It can also be used with the names of certain countries such as *the Netherlands* or *the United States* or with the names of ships such as *the Titanic*.

Theme: ENVIRONMENTAL CONCERNS

Unit 7 focuses on language that is used to talk about environmental issues and concerns.

Step 1: Grammar in Context (pages 105–107)

See the general suggestions for Grammar in Context on page 1.

Before You Read

- Have students work in small groups to discuss the questions.
- Call on students to share their answers with the class.
- You may also want to have students talk about environmental concerns that are specific to their areas of the world.

Read

- You may want to point out unfamiliar vocabulary. Write the words on the board and ask students what they think the words mean. Discuss the meanings as a class. For example:

gigantic	extremely large
cranes	tall machines used by builders for lifting heavy things
deforestation	the cutting or burning of all trees in an area
nutrients	chemicals or foods that provide what is needed for plants or animals to live and grow
scale	the size, level, or amount of something
shy away from	avoid because of worry, lack of confidence, or anxiety

- Write these questions on the board:
  1. What is the "real" mystery of Easter Island? *(Why did the ecology of Easter Island change so drastically?)*
  2. How did Easter Island get its name? *(It was discovered on Easter Sunday.)*
  2. What caused the environmental catastrophe on Easter Island? *(the deforestation caused by human beings)*
  4. What lesson can we learn from the decline of Easter Island? *(We may fail to recognize that we are destroying our environment until it is too late.)*
- Establish a purpose for reading. Call on students to read the questions to the class. Remind students to think about the questions as they read and listen to the text. Have students read the text and discuss the answers to the questions as a class.

After You Read

A. Vocabulary

- Have students complete the exercise and work in pairs to compare their answers.

- Go over the answers as a class, clarifying any discrepancies in answers among students.

B. Comprehension

- Have students complete the exercise individually and then compare answers in pairs or groups of three, sharing their corrected false sentences with each other.
- Have students share their corrected sentences with the class.

Go to **www.myfocusongrammarlab.com** for an additional reading, and for reading and vocabulary practice.

Step 2: Grammar Presentation (pages 108–110)

See the general suggestions for Grammar Presentation on page 2.

Grammar Charts

- Have students work in groups of three. Assign each group one of the three different sections of the grammar chart to look at. Have them come up with specific examples from the reading that apply to the section of the chart they are studying.
- Have students reform groups of three so that each new group has one person who has looked at a different section of the chart. Have students share information and examples with each other.
- Circulate as students are working. Provide assistance and clarification as needed.

Grammar Notes

Note 1

- The key to understanding the difference between the definite and indefinite article is the idea of what *definite* means. Similar objects of different colors and sizes (colored pencils, markers, apples) can be used to demonstrate this concept clearly. Place a number of these items on a table. Make sure that you have more than one of certain colors.
- Give students a command such as: *Take a red pencil.* On the board write:
  Take <u>a</u> _____ pencil.
  Ask students which colors they can use *a / an* with. *(They should identify the colors for which there is more than one item.)* Now write:
  Take <u>the</u> _____ pencil.
  Again, ask students which colors they can use with *the*. *(They should identify the colors for which there is only one item.)*
- Give students an opportunity to practice giving and responding to the commands with each other.

Note 2

- The concept of a noun becoming definite after the first mention is also nicely demonstrated with the use of objects such as colored pencils, crayons, or apples. Place groups of items on a table, with more than one each of various colors. You can also use groups of countable classroom objects such as books, pens, erasers, or pads of paper.
- Give students commands such as: *Pick up a yellow pencil and a red pencil. Give the yellow pencil to Francisco, and give the red pencil to Viktor.*
- Give students an opportunity to practice giving and responding to the commands with each other.

Note 3

- Have students form five different groups and assign each group one of the five categories given for the zero article. Have each group write more example sentences for the category. You may want to point out a few more "habitual locations" such as *church, downtown,* or *prison* since there are a limited number of these.
- Write the categories on the board and have students from each group write some of their sentences under the appropriate heading.

Note 4

- Have students label the examples in Note 4 as category *a, b,* or *c.* You may want to point out that plural count nouns (b) and non-count nouns (c) are the most common types of generic nouns in English.
- Brainstorm a variety of generic singular count, singular non-count, and plural nouns and write them on the board. Then do a quick oral drill. Say a noun from the board and have students say the correct article (or zero article) and the noun. You may also want to elicit some complete sentences using the nouns.
- **Note:** Since Notes 4 and 7 both deal with generic nouns, you may prefer to teach them together.

Note 5

- Set up groups of countable objects such as books, pens, pencils, or erasers on a table.
- Have a student take an object and then put it down. Have another student describe the action as you write on the board:
  Ivan took <u>a</u> yellow pencil and put it down.

- On the board, write:
  _____ pencil that Tran took is yellow.
  Elicit *the* from the students. Repeat this procedure with several other students. Have the class watch carefully so that pairs can later describe who took what. For example:
  S1: Maria took a book.
  S2: The book she took is blue.

Note 6

- Have a student read the note aloud. Then have students brainstorm a list of other unique things in groups (for example, *the sky, the moon, the earth, the ozone layer, the atmosphere, the world, the environment*).

Note 7

- Introduce the use of *the* with generic nouns. Start with singular nouns and point out that when generic reference is made to inventions or the names of musical instruments, it is more common to use *the* than *a / an.* For example, in the expression *play _____ piano / violin, the* is required.
- For plural forms, note that while the definite article is possible with people and animal and plant species, it is actually more common to use the zero article for generic use. Note also that the definite article is not used with most other plural generic nouns.

Note 8

- Have a student read the note aloud.
- Have students work in groups to brainstorm a list of other nouns for each category (for example, *the mall, the Indian Ocean, the United Kingdom*).

⏱ **Identify the Grammar:** Have students identify the grammar in the opening reading on pages 105–106. For example:
The other, greater **mystery** is what changed **the island** so drastically.
Easter Island, settled about **the year** 900 by Polynesians, lies in **the South Pacific** about 2,300 miles west of Chile, **the country** to which it belongs.
On landing, Roggeveen saw **the island** much as it is today: **a** rather desolate **place** covered mostly by grassland, with no trees taller than 10 feet. However, Easter Island was once much different: Most of it was **a** subtropical **forest**.

Go to **www.myfocusongrammarlab.com** for grammar charts and notes.

Step 3: Focused Practice (pages 110–114)

See the general suggestions for Focused Practice on page 4.

Exercise 1: Discover the Grammar

A
- Read the instructions and go over the example with the class.
- Have students complete the exercise individually. Then have them work in groups of three to compare their answers.
- Go over the answers as a group, clarifying any discrepancies among students' answers.

B
- Have students complete the exercise individually.
- Go over the answers as a class. Call on students to explain why each answer is correct.

Exercise 2: Articles
- Have students complete the exercise individually. Go over the answers as a class.
- Have students work in pairs to decide which Grammar Note applies for each answer.

Exercise 3: Articles
- Have students look over both paragraphs and underline unknown words. Have them work in pairs to share unknown words and assist each other with meanings. Circulate as students are working. Make note of any words that are still unfamiliar and go over these as a class.
- Have students complete the exercise individually. Then have them compare answers in pairs.
- Go over the answers as a class. Have students explain why each answer is correct.

Exercise 4: Generic Nouns
- Read the instructions and go over the example with the class. Point out the use of articles in the example.
- Have students complete the exercise individually and work in small groups to compare answers. If more than one answer is possible, elicit all possible answers.
- (⏱) Have each group think of three more inventions or musical instruments and write two sentences about each, using the example sentences as a model. Have students from each group share their ideas with the class.

Exercise 5: Editing
- Have students complete the exercise individually, then work in pairs to compare their corrections.
- Have students from each pair write their corrected sentences on the board and explain their corrections to the class.

Go to **www.myfocusongrammarlab.com** for additional grammar practice.

Step 4: Communication Practice (pages 115–118)

See the general suggestions for Communication Practice on page 5.

Exercise 6: Listening

A
- Establish a purpose for listening. Have students read the question in Part A. Remind them to think about the question as they listen.
- Play the audio and allow students time to answer the question.
- Go over the answer with the class.

B
- Have students read the statements. Remind them to think about them as they listen. Play the audio and have students complete the exercise.
- Go over the answers as a class. Have different students read the correct statements in Part B. You may want to play the audio again to clarify any discrepancies in students' answers.
- (⏱) Provide students with the audioscript. In pairs, have them practice the conversation twice, changing roles after the first practice.

Exercise 7: Pronunciation

A
- Have students read and listen to the Pronunciation Note.
- Have them repeat the examples (*the statue, the environment*) as you say them.

B
- Go over the example with the class. Play the audio and have students complete the exercise.
- Have students work in pairs to check their answers. Replay the audio as needed.

C
- Have students take turns saying the sentences for Part C. Have each pair practice the sentences twice, so that each person has the chance to say all of the sentences.

- Circulate as pairs practice the sentences. Make corrections as needed.

Exercise 8: Picture Discussion
- Read the instructions. Have students look at the picture and read the questions.
- Have students discuss the picture in small groups. Circulate and help as needed.
- Call on students from each group to share their ideas with the class.
- ⏱ Have students write a paragraph about the picture on page 116. Encourage them to use the target structures from this unit in their paragraphs. Then have students share their paragraphs in pairs.

Exercise 9: Game
- Have students read the answers in the chart. Point out that many of the written answers in the game come from the various texts and exercises in this unit.
- Read the instructions and model the example with a student. Divide the class into teams and have them ask and answer the questions. Have a student keep score on the board.
- **Note:** As a variation, you may want to establish a time limit for each team to come up with the question.

Exercise 10: Writing
A
- Have students read the instructions and the example. Point out that in this writing assignment, students will be expressing an opinion in the topic sentence of the first paragraph and providing reasons, facts, and evidence to support that opinion in the rest of the essay. Have students identify the topic sentence in the example and explain the writer's opinion.
- Have students read the list of possible issues. For each issue, have students brainstorm things they know about it and briefly share their views.
- Have students write their paragraphs, either in class or as homework.

B
- Have students work in pairs to correct each other's work using the Editing Checklist. Have each student revise and rewrite as needed.
- ⏱ Have students post their papers in the classroom so the class can read them. You can also publish them together in a booklet or on a class website.

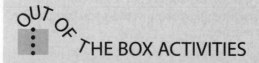

OUT OF THE BOX ACTIVITIES

Reading, Writing, Listening, and Speaking
- Bring in pamphlets (or have students bring them) from different kinds of environmental organizations. Alternatively, search environmental organizations on the Internet and print out information.
- Have students work in groups and give each group material about three environmental organizations. Have students read the material. Have them discuss the aims of the organizations and talk about whether they would like to join or contribute to any of them. Encourage students to support their views with specific reasons.
- Have each group choose one of the organizations and write a brief report about it. Remind them to pay particular attention to the use of articles as they write. The report should include the name and purpose of the organization and its core beliefs. Have groups exchange reports and correct each other's work using the Editing Checklist. Then have each group report to the class on the organization they wrote about. Discourage students from reading the reports they wrote. Have them use their reports as a guide instead.

Reading, Writing, Speaking, and Listening
- Have students use the information in the text about nuclear power in Exercise 5 on page 114 as the basis for an informal debate about alternative forms of energy. Divide the class into groups of three or four. Assign each group one of the alternative energy forms mentioned in the essay: geothermal, wind, or hydroelectric power.
- Have each group research the energy source and prepare a short oral presentation about the advantages of that particular energy source. Encourage students to deliver their presentation from notes rather than reading text that they have written.
- Allow time for questions at the end of each presentation. Then discuss which presentation students thought was most convincing and why.

Go to **www.myfocusongrammarlab.com** for additional listening, pronunciation, speaking, and writing practice.

Note:
• See the *Focus on Grammar Workbook* for additional in-class or homework grammar practice.

Unit 7 Review (page 119)

Have students complete the Review and check their answers on Student Book page UR-1. Review or assign additional material as needed.

Go to **www.myfocusongrammarlab.com** for the Unit Achievement Test.

UNIT 8 OVERVIEW

Grammar: QUANTIFIERS

Unit 8 focuses on the meanings and uses of a variety of quantifiers.

• Quantifiers can be single words or phrases. They specify the number or amount of something. They are used with nouns and pronouns and sometimes can be used alone.

• Quantifiers are used with different types of nouns: singular count nouns, plural count nouns, or non-count nouns.

• With singular count nouns, use quantifiers such as *one*, *each*, and *every*.

• With plural count nouns, use quantifiers such as *both*, *a couple of*, *a dozen*, *several*, *a few*, etc.

• With non-count nouns, use quantifiers such as *a little*, *little*, *much*, *a great deal of*, *a great amount of*, etc.

• With both plural count nouns and non-count nouns, use quantifiers such as *no*, *any*, *some*, *enough*, *a lot of / lots of*, *plenty of*, *most*, *all*, etc.

• Use *a few / few* with count nouns and *a little / little* with non-count nouns. *Few* and *little* are used to mean "hardly any" or "not much at all."

• Use *many* with count nouns and *much* with non-count nouns. *Much* is not often used in affirmative sentences but is common in questions and negative statements and in *too much*.

• Use *some* in affirmative statements and *any* in negative statements. For questions, use *some* to make offers. Use *any* in negative questions.

• You can often use a quantifier with *of + the* or another determiner to specify particular people or places. Example: *We saw many of her films*. When there is no specific person, place, or thing in mind, do not use *of*. Example: *Many restaurants take credit cards*.

Theme: MONEY

Unit 8 focuses on language that is used to discuss various forms of money that we use today to purchase a wide variety of goods and services.

Step 1: Grammar in Context (pages 120–122)

See the general suggestions for Grammar in Context on page 1.

Before You Read
• Have students work in small groups to discuss the questions or discuss them as a class.
• You may also want students to share what forms of payment are the most popular in their home countries.

Read
• You may want to point out unfamiliar vocabulary. Write the words on the board and ask students what they think the words mean. Discuss the meanings as a class. For example:

originate	to start or develop in a specific place or from a specific situation
balance	the amount of money in your bank account
huh?	an expression said as a response to a question to show lack of understanding or to ask for clarification
deduction	an amount that is subtracted from something
have little use for	dislike; prefer not to have or use

• Write these questions on the board:
  1. What gives paper money its value? *(trust in the government)*
  2. What is the most abstract type of money? *(electronic or e-money)*

3. How does the transfer of electronic money work? *(The balance in one account is increased, and the balance in the other account is correspondingly decreased.)*
4. According to the reading, what are some advantages of cash? *(universal acceptability, convenience, and "personal connection")*
5. What are some disadvantages of electronic money? *(It encourages people to spend more than they have. Mistakes are easily made and hard to correct.)*

- Establish a purpose for reading. Have students read the questions aloud. Remind students to think about these questions as they read and listen to the text.
- Have students read the text individually and discuss the questions in pairs or groups of three. Call on students from each group to share answers with the class.

After You Read

A. Vocabulary
- Have students complete the exercise individually.
- Go over the answers as a class.

B. Comprehension
- Have students complete the exercise individually. Then have them compare answers in pairs.
- Call on students to share their answers with the class. Have each student point out the place in the text where he or she found the answer to the question.

Go to **www.myfocusongrammarlab.com** for an additional reading, and for reading and vocabulary practice.

Step 2: Grammar Presentation (pages 122–125)

See the general suggestions for Grammar Presentation on page 2.

Grammar Charts
- Divide the class into enough groups so that each group has a different section of the chart to examine.
- Write these questions on the board:
  What is the meaning of each of the quantifiers in the section you are looking at?
  What types of nouns are the quantifiers used with: count, non-count, or both?
- Have groups read their assigned section of the chart and discuss the question. Have students from each group share answers with the class.

Grammar Notes

Note 1
- Point out that the following quantifiers are not used alone when answering a question; they need to be followed by a pronoun: _each_ of them, _every_ one (e.g., *How many of the bills did you pay? Every one.*). The following quantifiers can stand alone if *of* is dropped: *a couple, a great deal, a lot, lots, plenty* (e.g., *I found some scarves on sale and bought a couple.*). *No* becomes *none* (e.g., *How much time is left? None.*).

Note 2
- Point out that many quantifiers can be used with both count and non-count nouns. Some are limited to one or the other. Ask students: "Which quantifiers can be used for count nouns only? Which for non-count?" Then write these sentence frames on the board:
  He looked carefully at _____ coin. The travelers have _____ cash. She had _____ bills on her desk.
- Have students work in pairs to choose quantifiers to complete the sentences. Then have pairs share their ideas with the class.

Note 3
- Write these sentences on the board:
  They have a few problems.   They have few problems.
  They have a little money.   They have little money.
- Ask students how omitting *a* changes the meaning of the sentence. *(In the first set of sentences* a few *implies that they have some problems. The second sentence is more positive. It implies that they have almost no problems. In the second set of sentences, the first sentence is more positive. It implies that they have some money. The second sentence implies that they have almost no money.)*

Note 4
- Have students read the note. Read the example sentences aloud and have students repeat.
- Have students work in pairs to replace the nouns in each example sentence with others that are grammatically correct. For example, the first sentence, *He doesn't have many friends*, can be changed to *He doesn't have many relatives*. However, it cannot be changed to *He doesn't have many money*. Call on students to share their sentences with the class.

- Draw students' attention to the point about the use of *much* in affirmative statements. Brainstorm other quantifiers that can be used in these sentences instead of *much*. (Examples: *a great deal of, a large amount of, some*)
- Say the example sentences with *number* and *amount* and have students repeat them. You may want to point out to students that this is a point that many native speakers of English have trouble with.

Note 5

- Point out that although *some* and *any* are both used in questions, *any* is neutral, while *some* conveys a more positive expectation. It is thus usually more polite to make offers with *some*.
- Have students work in pairs to write four sentences: an affirmative statement, a negative statement, an offer, and a negative question.
- Call on several students to put their sentences on the board, leaving a blank for *some* and *any*. Have these students elicit the appropriate quantifier from the class and write it in the blank.

Note 6

- To make the point clear, it may be helpful to give students more examples. Write a few sentences on the board. Elicit which ones take *most of* and which take *most* and why. For example:
  1. _____ Americans have credit card debt. (*most*, because Americans *is a general group*)
  2. _____ the Americans I know have many credit cards. (*most of*, because the Americans I know *is a specific group*)
  3. _____ people are concerned about the economy. (*most*, because people *is a general group*)
  4. _____ the people in our class work very hard. (*most of*, because the people in our class *is a specific group*)
- Draw students' attention to the use of *the* in Sentences 2 and 4. Point out that if you use *of* after a quantifier, the next word should be *the* or another determiner such as *my, your, his,* etc.
- Have students work in groups to write more sentences with *most / most of, many / many of, few / few of,* and *all / all of.* Call on students from each of the groups to share their sentences with the class.

Identify the Grammar: Have students identify the grammar in the opening reading on pages 120–121. For example:

In the succeeding centuries, **many** other **items** came to be used as currency: e.g., jewelry, land, and even cattle.
One example is fiat money, i.e., paper currency issued by a government.
No actual **money** is transferred.
Does this mean that cash no longer has **any advantages**?

Go to **www.myfocusongrammarlab.com** for grammar charts and notes.

Step 3: Focused Practice (pages 125–129)

See the general suggestions for Focused Practice on page 4.

Exercise 1: Discover the Grammar

- Read the instructions. Point out that students need to consider two things. First, is it grammatically possible to rewrite the sentence with the words in parentheses? And second, if so, can you do so without changing the basic meaning? Students should write *Y* only if they can answer "yes" to both questions.
- To illustrate this, go over the first two items with students. Point out that the answer to Item 1 is *N* because it is grammatically incorrect to use *much* with the count noun *years*. For Item 2, it is grammatically possible to use *some,* but it changes the meaning of the question. Using *some* implies that there are probably advantages; using *any* implies that there might not be any.
- Have students complete the exercise and work in pairs to compare answers. Call on students from various pairs to share their answers with the class and explain why each answer is correct. Clarify any discrepancies in answers among groups.

Exercise 2: Quantifiers

- Have students complete the exercise. Go over the answers as a class.
- Have various students explain why the answer is correct. For example, for Item 1, *fewer* is correct because it precedes *countries,* a plural count noun. *Less* is used only with non-count nouns.

Exercise 3: Quantifiers

- Have students complete the exercise individually. Then have them work in pairs to compare answers.

- Have pairs practice reading the conversation twice, changing roles after the first practice.

Exercise 4: Numbers
- Have students look at the chart. Read the row headings aloud and have students repeat. Answer any questions about unfamiliar vocabulary such as *birth rate, per, death rate, life expectancy,* and *gross domestic product.* For each statistic, ask students if the figure from 2003 to 2009 is higher or lower than it was in 1960. You may want to point out that even though life expectancy is measured in years, the term *life expectancy* is non-count when used in a sentence. Example: *People who have unhealthy lifestyles have less life expectancy.*
- Read the instructions. Point out that one of the quantifiers will be used twice. Have students complete the exercise. Then have them work in groups to compare answers. Go over the answers as a class.

Exercise 5: Editing
- Have students complete the exercise and work in pairs to check their answers.
- Call on students to explain each error and correction.

Go to **www.myfocusongrammarlab.com** for additional grammar practice.

Step 4: Communication Practice (pages 130–132)

See the general suggestions for Communication Practice on page 5.

Exercise 6: Listening
A
- Establish a purpose for listening. Have students read the question in Part A. Remind them to think about the question as they listen.
- Play the audio. Ask the class the question in Part A and go over the answer. Replay the audio if needed.

B
- Have students read the questions. Remind them to think about the questions as they listen. Play the audio again.
- Call on students to read and answer the questions in Part B.
- You may want to play the audio again to clarify any discrepancies in students' answers.
- ⏱ Provide copies of the audioscript. Have students practice reading the conversation in pairs. Then have one or two pairs role-play the conversation for the class.

Exercise 7: Pronunciation
A
- Have students read and listen to the Pronunciation Note.
- If more practice is needed, say other words that use the schwa in unstressed syllables and have students repeat. Examples: *thousand, problems, television, syllable.*

B
- Play the audio once, pausing so students can repeat the sentences.
- Play the audio again. Pause after each sentence so students can circle their answers.
- Go over the answers as a class.

C
- Circulate as pairs practice saying the sentences. Make corrections as needed.

Exercise 8: Game
- Read the instructions and go over the example with the students.
- Divide the class into two teams and have them write the questions as a group. Have them check page G-AK 2 of the Student Book for the answers. (**Note:** You may want to assign this step for homework.)
- To play the game, have the teams take turns asking and answering questions. Keep score on the board.

Exercise 9: Personal Inventory
A
- Read the instructions and go over the example with the class. Read the quantifiers in the box and elicit example sentences students could make with each one.
- Have students write their sentences individually. Circulate and help as needed.

B
- Read the instructions. Elicit the definition of *trend (something that a lot of people are doing or is happening in a lot of places at the same time).* Give an example of this: "People spend more time online than they did five years ago."
- Have students discuss their answers in pairs.

C
- Call on pairs to share their answers with the class.
- Have students suggest trends based on the answers they hear.

Exercise 10: Writing

A

- Have students read the example. Read the topics and ask students: "Which topic goes best with the example?" *(a time when you ran out of money)*
- For each topic, brainstorm specific things students could write about.
- Have students write their paragraphs, either in class or as homework.

B

- Have students work in pairs to correct each other's work using the Editing Checklist. Have each student revise and rewrite as needed.
- (!) Have students post their papers in the classroom so the class can read them. You can also publish them in a booklet or on a class website.

OUT OF THE BOX ACTIVITIES

Listening, Speaking, Reading, and Writing

- Have students reread the article "What's Happening to Cash?" on pages 120–121.
- Have them work in groups to answer these questions:
  1. According to the article, what kind of purchases is cash generally used for? *(small purchases such as flowers and hot dogs, or for tips and gifts)*
  2. What other types of businesses do you know that prefer cash rather than credit cards? *(Some smaller, family-type restaurants or businesses prefer cash and certain kinds of labor are paid for with cash.)*
  3. What business do you know that will not take checks? *(Many smaller restaurants, dry cleaners, shoe repair shops, and gas stations will not take checks.)*
  4. What are some reasons you can think of that businesses prefer cash to credit cards or checks?
- Discuss each group's answers as a class.

Listening and Speaking

- Have students work in groups to brainstorm a list of things people take or bring back from a vacation or a trip. Then have groups share their answers with the class and write them on the board.

For example:

local currency	shaving cream
traveler's checks	toothpaste
photos	sunscreen
documentation	postcards
medications	souvenirs
film	gifts
art objects	jewelry

- Have students think of a specific trip or vacation and discuss with the group the things they packed and brought back. Encourage other group members to ask follow-up questions. Remind students to use quantifiers. You may want to model the activity with a student first.

Reading, Speaking, and Listening

- Bring in (or have students bring in) descriptions of holiday resort areas—for example, Cancún, Mexico, or Saint Moritz, Switzerland—with information about attractions, shopping, restaurants, nightlife, currency, language, etc.
- Have students work in small groups. Have each group choose one of the holiday resorts and discuss why they would or would not like to go there. Remind them to use quantifiers in their discussion. You may want to write these examples on the board: I wouldn't like Cancún in summer because most of the hotels are crowded. Also, there are only a few natural beaches.

  I think I'd like it because most hotels are first-rate. People who take a vacation in Cancún must spend a great deal of money!

Go to **www.myfocusongrammarlab.com** for additional listening, pronunciation, speaking, and writing practice.

Note:
- See the *Focus on Grammar Workbook* for additional in-class or homework grammar practice.

Unit 8 Review (page 133)

Have students complete the Review and check their answers on Student Book page UR-1. Review or assign additional material as needed.

Go to **www.myfocusongrammarlab.com** for the Unit Achievement Test.

Grammar: MODIFICATION OF NOUNS

Unit 9 focuses on the meanings and uses of noun, adjective, and compound modifiers as well as order of adjectives.

- Nouns can be modified by both adjectives and other nouns. These modifiers usually come before the noun they modify. When both an adjective and a noun modifier are used, the noun modifier is placed closer to the modified word.

- Participial adjectives are present and past participles that are used to modify nouns. A participial that ends in *-ing* describes someone or something that causes a feeling. A participial that ends in *-ed* describes someone who experiences a feeling.

- When a noun has more than one modifier, the modifiers generally occur in a fixed order. This order may be changed according to the emphasis a speaker or writer wants to give an adjective. Avoid using more than three adjective modifiers before a noun.

- When a noun has two or more modifiers in the same category, separate them by a comma. If the modifiers are in different categories, do not separate them with a comma.

- There are four common kinds of compound modifiers, or modifiers of more than one word. They are: number + noun; noun + present participle; noun + past participle; and adjective + past participle. When compound modifiers precede a noun, they are generally hyphenated.

- Plural nouns used as modifiers become singular when they come before the noun.

- Avoid using more than two noun modifiers together because it can be confusing.

Theme: EXPECTATIONS

Unit 9 focuses on language that is used to talk about unrealized expectations and unexpected outcomes.

Step 1: Grammar in Context (pages 134–136)

See the general suggestions for Grammar in Context on page 1.

Before You Read

- Read the questions aloud. To make them more concrete for students, you may want to model answers for each question based on your own ideas and experiences. In the third question, you may want to clarify what is meant by *positive* and *negative force*. In this context, the terms refer to whether expectations can influence outcomes.
- Have students work in pairs to discuss the questions.
- Call on students from each pair to share their answers with the class.

Read

- You may want to point out unfamiliar vocabulary. Write the words on the board and have students scan the text for each word. Have them read the entire sentence in which the word appears and ask students what they think each word means. Discuss the meanings as a class. For example:

syndrome	qualities, events, or behaviors that are typical of a particular type of problem
special effects	unusual images or sounds in a movie or television program that have been produced artificially
tedious	boring, tiring, and continuing for a long time
immense	extremely large
phenomenon	something that happens or exists in society, science, or nature, and often something that people discuss or study because it is difficult to understand

- Write these questions on the board (or prepare them as a handout):
1. Why did everyone expect Constantina Dita to hold the lead for just a short time? *(There were two other competitors that people expected might win.)*
2. What reenergized Dita as she entered the stadium? *(the roaring crowd)*
3. What is "the expectation syndrome"? *(a condition in which events do not turn out as we feel they will or ought to)*
4. What is "focal dystonia"? *(an abnormal muscle function caused by extreme concentration)*
5. What is Stevens's recommendation about expectations? *(It is better to hope for things than to expect them.)*

- Establish a purpose for reading. Have students read the questions. Remind students to think about the questions as they read and listen to the text.
- Have students read the text. Discuss the answers to the questions as a class.

After You Read

A. Vocabulary

- Have pairs look at the sentences on the left and identify what part of speech each boldfaced word is. For example: *surge* in the first sentence is used as a verb. Have them do the same for each of the definitions on the right. Point out that understanding how an unknown word is used in a sentence can often help readers get the meaning.
- Have pairs complete the exercise, discussing the part of speech for each boldfaced word and definition as an aid to selecting an answer.
- Have two pairs work together to check their answers. Go over the answers as a class.

B. Comprehension

- Have students complete the exercise individually and then compare answers in pairs or groups of three, sharing their corrected false sentences with each other.
- Call on various students to share their corrected sentences with the class.

Go to **www.myfocusongrammarlab.com** for an additional reading, and for reading and vocabulary practice.

Step 2: Grammar Presentation (pages 137–139)

See the general suggestions for Grammar Presentation on page 2.

Grammar Charts

- Write this sentence on the board and label it as shown:

  adj   noun   noun
They rave about its **superb color photography**
  compound modifier
  adj   pres participle   adj
and its **strange-looking, otherworldly** creatures.
- Use this sentence to generate new ones. Erase one word at a time and have students supply a new word of the same category. You might wind up with something like this: *extraordinary black-and-white cinematography and its odd-looking, extraterrestrial beings.*

- Have students compose group sentences following the Order of Adjective Modifiers chart. The first few times have them start and end with the phrases in the chart, changing only the adjectives.
- Have students look at the third chart. Ask: "Why are there three different ways to order the adjectives on the right but only one on the left?" *(The order with different modifier categories is fixed, while the order with the same categories is flexible.)*
- Have students look at the last chart. Point out the past and present participles in the compound modifiers. Have students generate a few other compound modifiers following the examples in the chart.

Grammar Notes

Note 1

- Have students read the note and the example sentence.
- Elicit noun and adjective modifiers that students can use instead of the ones in the example. (Examples: *Yao Ming is a great Asian basketball player. David Beckham is a handsome English soccer player.*)

Note 2

- *Milk chocolate* and *chocolate milk* illustrate the importance of word order in English. When the words are reversed, the meaning changes. If needed, give students other examples of this, such as *house pet, country home, piano player,* and *family dog.*
- Have students work in pairs for a minute or two to generate as many examples as they can think of in which a noun modifies another noun. (Examples: *soccer player, window seat, flower pot, vegetable seed, fruit basket, piano student, tennis teacher*)

Note 3

- It may take students some time to understand the principle that *-ing* causes a feeling and *-ed* experiences a feeling.
- Write these sentences on the board but draw a blank line for the adjective:
  The news was _____ .
  We were _____ by the news.
- Have students supply the correct participial forms of these words: *amaze, surprise, interest, frighten, astonish.*

Note 4

- As you go over the categories, elicit more examples of each from students. Point out that the "opinion" category also includes qualities such as *intelligent, funny, generous,* and so on.

- Have students work in pairs or small groups to create the longest descriptions they can think of. You can start them off with something like: *a beautiful, expensive antique, hand-finished 12-foot oak library table*
- (!) Point out that there are other participials that don't involve causing or experiencing feelings. For example: *boiled / boiling, rolled / rolling, carved / carving, written / writing, processed / processing*. They can be placed in various locations but are usually located between colors and origins. For example: *We bought a knife with a large, beautiful carved wooden handle*.

Note 5

- Point out that another option for two modifiers in the same category is to combine them with *and* if the words have a similar function. For example: *The dog is old and tired*. If they are contrastive, use *but*. For example: *The dog is old but energetic*.
- The comma reflects a pause between the adjectives when speaking. Read the example sentences in Note 5 aloud and have students repeat, pausing at the comma.

Note 6

- To help students understand how compound adjectives are formed, provide sentences based on the examples in Note 6 and point out how they have been converted to modifiers that precede the noun. For example:
  — The building where I work has ten stories. (*It's a ten-story building*.)
  — That film won a prize. (*It's a prize-winning film*.)
  — The problem relates to crime. (*It's a crime-related problem*.)
  — In the movie, the actor plays the part of a pirate with long hair and one arm. (*The actor plays the part of a long-haired, one-armed pirate in the movie*.)
  — Her daughter is 10 years old. (*She has a 10-year-old daughter*.)
- Write these examples on the board:
  It's a bag that weighs 40 pounds. (It's a
  _____ .)
  That diet reduces your weight. (It's a
  _____ .)
  The government controls that program. (It's a
  _____ .)
  That dog has long hair and three legs. (It's a
  _____ .)
  His house is 100 years old. (It's a
  _____ .)

- Have students work in small groups to change the sentences into sentences with compound modifiers. Go over the answers as a class.

Note 7

- Create a number of sentences with stacked noun modifiers and have students work in pairs to unstack them so that no more than two nouns occur in succession. For example, write on the board:
  She gave them a parent homework study guide.
- Students can change the sentence on the board into either of the following:
  She gave the parents a study guide to use for helping their children do homework.
  She gave the parents a study guide to help them help their children with homework.

- (!) **Identify the Grammar:** Have students identify the grammar in the opening reading on pages 134–135. For example:
  Picture the scene: It's the **29th Summer** Olympics in Beijing, China.
  The **Women's** Marathon is about at the **halfway** point when a **Romanian** runner, Constantina Dita, suddenly surges to the front of the pack.
  As she enters the stadium, Dita begins to slow a bit, but the **roaring** crowd reenergizes her and enables her to win the race with a time of two hours, 26 minutes, a **22-second** lead over the **silver** medalist.

Go to **www.myfocusongrammarlab.com** for grammar charts and notes.

Step 3: Focused Practice (pages 139–143)

See the general suggestions for Focused Practice on page 4.

Exercise 1: Discover the Grammar

- Have students complete the exercise. Review the answers as a class.
- (!) Have students look again at the opening text. In pairs, have them find three to five more sentences similar to the ones in the exercise. Have pairs exchange papers and circle the head nouns, underline adjective modifiers once, and underline noun modifiers twice.

Exercise 2: Multiple Modifiers

- Go over the example with students. Elicit why the modifiers go in this order. *(because when there are both adjective and noun modifiers, the noun modifier comes closer to the head noun; see Note 2)* Ask students: "Why isn't there a comma between *formal* and *office*?" *(because commas are only used to separate modifiers in the same category; see Note 5)* If students struggle with the example, you may want to have them review Notes 2, 4, and 5.
- Have students complete the exercise and work in groups of three to check their answers. Go over the answers as a class.
- ⏱ Have students practice reading the conversation in groups of three, changing roles after each practice.

Exercise 3: Compound Modifiers

- Go over the example with the class. Point out that students must form a compound modifier and put an article *(a, an, the)* before the modifier. You may also want to point out the use of hyphens.
- Have students complete the exercise. Go over the answers as a class.
- ⏱ Have students practice reading the text in pairs.

Exercise 4: Creative Sentences

- Have students complete the exercise individually and then work in groups of three to share their sentences with each other.
- Call on students from each group to share sentences with the class.

Exercise 5: Editing

- Have students complete the exercise individually.
- Have various students write their corrected sentences on the board. Have students explain their corrections to the class.
- ⏱ Have students practice reading the corrected text aloud to each other in pairs.

Go to **www.myfocusongrammarlab.com** for additional grammar practice.

Step 4: Communication Practice (pages 144–148)

See the general suggestions for Communication Practice on page 5.

Exercise 6: Listening

A

- Remind students that generally there are two purposes for listening: listening to get the *gist* or main idea and listening for *details*. Have students read the statements. Ask them what they will be listening for in Part A—the gist or details? *(details)*
- Play the audio and have students complete the exercise. Replay if needed. Go over the answers as a class.

B

- Have students read the sentences. Then play the audio, pausing as needed to give students enough time to write.
- Have students work in groups to check their answers.
- Review their responses as a class. You may want to play the audio again to clarify any discrepancies in students' answers.

Exercise 7: Pronunciation

A

- Have students read and listen to the Pronunciation Note.
- Have them repeat the examples several times after you say each one.

B

- Have students complete the exercise and work in pairs to compare answers.
- Have students from each pair read the sentences that they identified as needing commas and explain why.

C

- Have pairs work together to take turns reading the sentences. Have pairs read the sentences twice so that each person can practice saying every sentence.

Exercise 8: Story Discussion

A

- Have a student read the title of the story. Write the words *death* (lowercase) and *Death* (capitalized) on the board. Have a student explain the difference. *(Death is a personification of death; it is often a person or character in stories and movies)*. If possible, bring in photos depicting the figure of Death from movies or television.
- Write this question on the board: In the story, who is going to die? Where is he going to die? Have students read the story. Discuss the answer to the questions as a class. *(the servant, in Samarra)*

B

- Have students read the sentences. Explain any unfamiliar vocabulary, such as *personification* and *fate*.
- Have students complete the exercise individually.
- Go over the answers as a class. Call on students to point to the part of the story where they found the answer.

C

- Read the instructions. To help guide the discussion, write the following questions on the board:
  1. Why did the servant run away? What did he expect?
  2. What was Death's plan? Did the servant help Death's plan or prevent it?
  3. Do you think the servant could have done anything to avoid death?
  4. Do you believe in fate? Do you think people can avoid or change their fate?
- Have students discuss the questions as a class or, for large classes, in groups.

Exercise 9: Picture Discussion

A

- Have students describe the picture in small groups.
- Circulate and help as needed.

B

- You may want to have different groups focus on the expectations of the different groups of people involved in the sinking of the *Titanic*. For example, what were the expectations of the builders? the passengers? the crew? the company who owned the *Titanic*?
- **Note:** As an alternative or extension to this exercise, you may want to have groups do a round-robin writing activity. One person in the group writes a sentence describing the picture (or what the picture suggests about expectations) and passes the paper to the next person. That person writes another sentence and passes the paper to the next person. The activity continues until each member of the group has written one or two sentences. Have two groups share their writing with each other and select two sentences to share with the class.

Exercise 10: Writing

A

- Review the structure of an essay. For this assignment, students will most likely have an introductory paragraph, one or two body paragraphs, and a concluding paragraph. Point out that in this writing assignment, students will be writing a narrative about something that occurred in the past. Point out that the topic sentence in the first paragraph of the example clearly identifies a specific situation. Elicit that the second sentence states the expectation.
- Have students brainstorm a list of situations that they could write about and have them each select one. Have them jot down a list of details associated with that event and eliminate any of the details that are not directly related to the topic: describing a situation that did not turn out as expected.
- Have students write their paragraphs, either in class or as homework.

B

- Have students work in pairs to correct each other's work using the Editing Checklist. Have each student revise and rewrite as needed.
- ⏱ Have students post their papers in the classroom so the class can read them. You can also publish them together in a booklet or on a class website.

OUT OF THE BOX ACTIVITIES

Listening and Speaking

- Have students work in groups to consider these questions about the Olympics:
  1. What is it about the Olympics that makes them so special and different from all other sports events?
  2. Why do you think that people who are not usually interested in sports watch the Olympics?
- Have groups talk about an Olympic moment that was exciting for them. What person or event was the most thrilling? Why?

Reading, Speaking, Listening, and Writing

- Bring in (or have students bring in) a wide variety of magazine advertisements for different kinds of products. Make sure half of the advertisements contain modifiers. The other half should be pictures only.
- Have students work in small groups and give each group two or three advertisements with text. Have students discuss them, identifying the adjective, noun, and/or compound modifiers that are used to describe the advertised products.
- Give each group one or two of the ads without text. Have the group work together to write text that describes the product in the pictures. Have each group make a poster with their ads and text and post them around the room.

Go to **www.myfocusongrammarlab.com** for additional listening, pronunciation, speaking, and writing practice.

Note:
- See the *Focus on Grammar Workbook* for additional in-class or homework grammar practice.

Unit 9 Review (page 149)

Have students complete the Review and check their answers on Student Book page UR-2. Review or assign additional material as needed.

Go to **www.myfocusongrammarlab.com** for the Unit Achievement Test.

From Grammar to Writing (pages 150–153)

See the general suggestions for From Grammar to Writing on page 9.

Go to **www.myfocusongrammarlab.com** for an additional From Grammar to Writing Assignment, Part Review, and Part Post-Test.

PART IV OVERVIEW

NOUN CLAUSES

UNIT	GRAMMAR FOCUS	THEME
10	Noun Clauses: Subjects, Objects, and Complements	Humor
11	Direct and Indirect Speech	Communication and Misunderstanding

Go to **www.myfocusongrammarlab.com** for the Part and Unit Tests.

Note: PowerPoint® grammar presentations, test-generating software, and reproducible Part and Unit Tests are on the *Teacher's Resource Disc*.

UNIT 10 OVERVIEW

Grammar: NOUN CLAUSES: SUBJECTS, OBJECTS, AND COMPLEMENTS

Unit 10 focuses on the meanings and uses of noun clauses as subjects, objects, and complements.

- Noun clauses are dependent clauses that have the same functions as regular nouns. They can be subjects, objects, subject complements, or adjective complements. Noun clauses begin with *that, whether, if,* or question words.
- *That* introduces certain noun clauses and has no concrete meaning in these cases. It is often omitted when it introduces an object or complements a noun clause, especially in speaking. *That* is never omitted when it introduces a subject noun clause. Subject noun clauses beginning with *that* are formal.
- Unlike the word *that*, the word *what* refers to something definite and serves as the object in the noun clause. It cannot be omitted.
- In subject noun clauses, *the fact that* is sometimes used in place of *that*. In noun clauses that are objects of prepositions, *the fact that* must be used in place of *that*.

- When a question is changed to a noun clause, it is an embedded question. Embedded questions use statement word order. An embedded question is more polite than a direct question. An embedded question can occur within a statement or another question. When an embedded question occurs within a statement, it is followed by a period. When it occurs within a question, it is followed by a question mark.
- *Wh-* question words introduce embedded *wh-* questions. The subject of an embedded *wh-* question takes a singular verb. Do not use *do, does,* or *did* in embedded questions.
- Use *if* and *whether* to introduce embedded *yes / no* questions. *If* and *whether* are similar in meaning and are often used interchangeably. Do not use *if* to introduce a subject noun clause. *Whether . . . or not* can replace *whether* in all noun clauses. *If . . . or not* can replace *whether* in all but subject noun clauses.

Theme: HUMOR

Unit 10 focuses on language that is used to tell funny stories.

Step 1: Grammar in Context (pages 156–158)

See the general suggestions for Grammar in Context on page 1.

Before You Read
- Have students work in small groups to discuss the questions or discuss them as a class.
- If students discuss the questions in groups, have students from each group share their ideas with the class.

Read
- Write these questions on the board:
  1. Did the mother have a favorite son? (*No, she loved each one for his own uniqueness.*)
  2. Why was their rivalry so intense? (*Each brother wanted to be number one in his mother's affection.*)
  3. Even though the brothers spent a lot of money buying their mother expensive gifts, what did the mother need? (*nothing*)
  4. What did the mother suggest doing with the mansion and the chauffeured car? (*selling them*)
  5. Why did she appreciate the trained parrot? (*She thought it was a delicious chicken.*)

- Establish a purpose for reading. Call on several different students to read each of the questions. Remind students to think about these questions as they read and listen to the text.
- Have students read the text or play the audio and have students follow along in their books. Have students discuss the questions in pairs or groups of three. Then have students from each group or pair share answers with the class.

After You Read
A. Vocabulary
- Have students complete the vocabulary exercise individually. Then have them compare answers in pairs. Circulate as students compare answers.
- Have different students read their answers aloud.

B. Comprehension
- Have students complete the exercise individually. Then have them compare answers in pairs.
- Have different students share their answers and corrected false statements with the class. Have each student point out the place in the text where he or she found the answer for the question.

Go to **www.myfocusongrammarlab.com** for an additional reading, and for reading and vocabulary practice.

Step 2: Grammar Presentation (pages 159–161)

See the general suggestions for Grammar Presentation on page 2.

Grammar Charts
- Write these sentences on the board (or prepare them as a handout):
  1. The boys realized that their mother's final days were approaching.
  2. That the boys were intensely competitive had always bothered the lady, but she didn't know what to do about it.
  3. The store owner told him this was a specially trained parrot.
  4. I don't know if you believed me, though, when I said I didn't need anything.
  5. Plus, the fact that the chauffeur doesn't speak English is a problem.
  6. Curly was pleased that he had finally risen to the number-one spot in his mother's affections.
  7. All I know is that the chicken you gave me was delicious.

- Have students study the grammar charts in pairs or small groups. Have them look at the previous sentences, underlining the noun clauses and circling the word that begins each noun clause. Then have them identify the function of noun clause(s) in each sentence (*subject—2, 5; object—1, 3, 4; subject complement—7; adjective complement—6*) Have them identify the sentences in which *that* is optional or has been omitted (*optional—1, 7; omitted—3*)

Grammar Notes

Note 1
- Have students read the explanation and the examples.
- If students do not understand how objects and complements differ, read the example sentence *You can see that I am easily amused.* Point out that *see* has an object: the fact that I am easily amused. Then read the example sentence *The question is whether people will laugh.* Point out that the verb, *is*, does not take an object. *Whether people will laugh* is the complement; it gives more information about the subject.

Note 2
- Have students read the note aloud.
- Read the example sentences with *that* and (where possible) those with *that* omitted and have students repeat.
- Say (or write on the board) a few sentences with subject and object noun clauses using *that*. Have students tell you if *that* can be omitted.

Note 3
- Help students develop fluency with *the fact that* and *it's* + adjective + noun clause.
- Have students find example sentences in Note 2 where *the fact that* could be used and say these aloud. For example: *The fact that she was a funny person was apparent. The fact that Joe has a good sense of humor is obvious.* Point out that *the fact that* is less formal than the word *that* to introduce the clause.
- On the board, write:
  It's <u>funny</u> that you should say that.
  Erase *funny*, eliciting other adjectives from students, each time erasing the old adjective and writing in the new one. Then erase the noun clause and elicit several substitutions for it. For example:
  It's interesting <u>(that) you should ask that question.</u>

Note 4
- Point out that embedded questions are more polite than direct questions.
- Point out that embedded questions are used for a wide range of purposes—when we really don't know the answer, when we are unsure of the answer, when we want to say something without being very direct about it, and when we want to be polite. For example, when requesting information from a stranger, embedded questions are expected: *Excuse me, do you know / could you tell me / I wonder if you could tell me* (note double embedded question) *where the post office is.*
- Look at the example sentences in Note 4 and have students tell you what the original questions were. Write them on the board.
  1. Is she from around here?
  2. Who is she?
  3. What does *incongruous* mean?
  4. How far is it to the nearest town?
- On the board, write:
  I'm not sure. Who is she?
  Have students combine the sentences to make an embedded question. (*I'm not sure who she is.*) Ask them what has changed in the question. (*the word order and punctuation*)

Note 5
- Draw attention to the punctuation of examples in Note 5. Ask students: "Why is there a question mark after the first one?" (*because the embedded question is embedded in a question*)
- Write some *wh-* questions with *do, does,* or *did*. For example: *Where does she live? When does he finish work?* Have students make embedded questions starting with *Do you know.* (*Do you know where she lives? Do you know when he finishes work?*) Once again, ask students what has changed from the original question. (*As with the preceding examples, word order and punctuation changed. In these examples, as the word order is changed,* does *disappears.*)

Note 6
- On the board write:
  Is she from around here? I don't know.
  Have students make an embedded question. (*I don't know if / whether she is from around here.*) Ask: "What has changed?" (*word order, punctuation, and the addition of* if *or* whether)

- Have students work in pairs to look at Note 6 to find the expressions that are used to introduce embedded questions. Have different students write these on the board. (*Do you know, who knows, I have no idea, we're not sure, it is difficult to say*) Ask if they can think of any others and write them on the board. (Examples: *Could you [please] tell me, do you happen to know, it's hard to say / see, I can't imagine, can you guess, I wonder*)
- Have students practice forming embedded questions in pairs. One student says a *yes / no* question and the other changes it to an embedded question, using the expressions on the board.

Note 7

- Point out that when *whether* is used, *or not* can appear in two places: *We don't know whether or not she got the job. We don't know whether she got the job or not.* When *if* is used, the only position for *or not* is at the end of the sentence: *We don't know if she got the job or not.*
- On the board write:
  <u>Whether</u> she received it isn't known.
  Ask: "Can *or not* be added?" (*Yes, but only after* whether: <u>Whether or not</u> she received it isn't known.)

⏱ **Identify the Grammar:** Have students identify the grammar in the opening reading on pages 156–157. For example:
  What wasn't so admirable was their rivalry, for a spirit of one-upmanship had always characterized their relationship.
  Each brother constantly tried to figure out **how he could outdo the other two**.
  What the sons wanted was a secure place in their mother's affections.

Go to **www.myfocusongrammarlab.com** for grammar charts and notes.

Step 3: Focused Practice (pages 162–167)

See the general suggestions for Focused Practice on page 4.

Exercise 1: Discover the Grammar

A
- Have students complete the exercise individually.
- Have students compare answers in pairs. Then go over the answers as a class.

B
- Have students complete the exercise individually and compare answers in small groups.

- Call on students from various groups to share their answers with the class. Discuss and clarify any discrepancies in answers among groups.

Exercise 2: Embedded Questions

- Have students read the instructions, the conversations in the chart, and the example answer. Make sure students understand how the example answer is based on the conversations.
- Have students complete the exercise. Go over the answers as a class.
- ⏱ Have students read the story aloud to each other in pairs.

Exercise 3: Embedded Questions

A
- Have students read the instructions, the example, and the questions below. Tell students to answer as though they don't know the answers to the question, even if they do. (Or, alternatively, model ways to answer using an embedded question such as *I know what a pun is. It's a joke based on words that sound the same.*)
- Explain that students will learn the answers to these questions in the next part of the exercise.
- Have students ask and answer the questions. Circulate and provide help as needed.

B
- Have students read the text and look for the answers to the questions in Part A. Then have students ask and answer the questions in Part A again.
- Go over the answers to the questions as a class.
- ⏱ For more advanced classes, have pairs choose one of the six types of humor and write a short story that exemplifies it. Have pairs share their humorous stories with the class.

Exercise 4: Noun Clauses

- You may want to discuss these words and their definitions:
  eschew　　　to deliberately avoid doing, using, or having something
  obfuscation　deliberately making something unclear or difficult to understand
- Have students complete the exercise, then have them work in groups to compare their answers. Call on students from various groups to share their sentences with the class.

- ⏱ Have groups work together to create a bumper sticker (or talk about one they have seen). Have each group present the bumper sticker to the class. Have students from the class explain what each one means and discuss any differences between the group's intended meaning and what the students in the class say.

Exercise 5: Editing

- You may want to write these words and their definitions on the board:

vulgar	dealing with or talking about sex and body wastes in a way people think is disgusting and not socially acceptable
punch line	the last few words of a joke or story that make it funny or surprising
animated	showing a lot of interest and energy

- Have students complete the exercise and work in pairs to check answers. Then call on students to explain each error and correction.

Go to **www.myfocusongrammarlab.com** for additional grammar practice.

Step 4: Communication Practice (pages 168–171)

See the general suggestions for Communication Practice on page 5.

Exercise 6: Listening

A

- Establish a purpose for listening. Have students read the question in Part A. Remind them to think about the question as they listen.
- Play the audio. Ask the class the question in Part A and go over the answer. Replay the audio if needed.

B

- Have students read the questions. Remind them to think about the questions as they listen.
- Play the audio again. Allow students time to write their answers.
- Call on students to read and answer the questions in Part B. You may want to play the audio again to clarify any discrepancies in students' answers.

Exercise 7: Pronunciation

A

- Have students read and listen to the Pronunciation Note.
- Have students repeat the example questions several times as you say them.

B

- Play the audio, pausing so students can mark their answers.
- Replay the audio. Pause after each item and go over the correct answer.

C

- Play the audio and have students repeat.
- Have students practice saying the questions. Circulate and make corrections as needed.

Exercise 8: Pair Discussion

A

- Have students read the article and underline unfamiliar vocabulary. Write these items on the board and ask students what they think the words mean. Discuss the definitions. Some of these might be:

aviation	the science or practice of flying aircraft
controller	someone at an airport who gives instructions to pilots by radio about where and when they can leave the ground or come down to the ground
cargo	the goods being carried in a ship, airplane, truck, etc.
handler	someone whose job it is to deal with a particular type of object, especially to move it or lift it
cargo hold	the part of a ship or a plane where goods are stored
pound	a place where dogs and cats that are found on the street are kept until someone comes to get them
cockpit	the part of an airplane in which the pilot sits
gauge	an instrument for measuring the amount, size, or speed of something

B

- Go over the example with the class.
- Have students complete the exercise. Call on students to share the jokes they found the funniest with the class.

Exercise 9: Class Discussion

A

- Read the instructions. You may want to assign this for homework or suggest websites where students can find jokes in English.
- Have students work in pairs to practice their jokes with each other. Circulate and help as needed.

B

- Have students tell their joke or story to the class.
- For large classes, have students tell their jokes or stories in groups.

C

- After each joke, have students turn to a partner and tell each other what they think the joke means.
- Call on students to share their ideas with the class.

Exercise 10: Writing

A

- Have students look at the example and identify the topic sentence. Point out that the writer begins by briefly setting the scene of the situation in the topic sentence. The next two sentences add details about the situation, and the last sentence begins the narrative or story.
- Remind students that this will be a narrative essay—one that tells a story. Point out that in this three- to five-paragraph essay, students will describe the situation in the first paragraph. In the next one to three paragraphs, they will give the details of the story, and in the final paragraph they will reveal what happened at the end.

B

- Have students work in pairs to correct each other's work using the Editing Checklist. Have each student revise and rewrite as needed.
- Have students post their papers in the classroom so the class can read them. You can also publish them together in a booklet or on a class website.

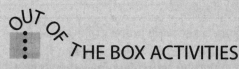

OUT OF THE BOX ACTIVITIES

Reading, Listening, and Speaking

- Bring in (or have students bring in) newspaper or magazine cartoons, jokes from magazines, or jokes and cartoons from websites on laughter and humor.
- Have students work in groups to discuss the jokes. Write this useful language for this discussion on the board:
  What I like / don't like about this joke is . . .
  What I think is funny is . . .
  What isn't so funny is . . .
  It's amusing that . . .
  What I don't understand about this joke is . . .
  Can you explain what / why . . .
  I wonder why . . .
  What makes me laugh is . . .

Reading, Listening, Speaking, and Writing

- Do a search on the Internet (or have pairs or groups of students do the search) for funny bumper stickers.
- Have students work in groups or pairs. Give each group two or three bumper stickers.
- Have each group write a short explanation of what the bumper sticker means. Remind students to use noun clauses in their writing. Post the bumper stickers and explanations around the room and give students an opportunity to look at them. As a class, discuss which ones the students thought were the best and the worst and why.

Go to **www.myfocusongrammarlab.com** for additional listening, pronunciation, speaking, and writing practice.

Note:
- See the *Focus on Grammar Workbook* for additional in-class or homework grammar practice.

Unit 10 Review (page 172)

Have students complete the Review and check their answers on Student Book page UR-2. Review or assign additional material as needed.

Go to **www.myfocusongrammarlab.com** for the Unit Achievement Test.

Grammar: DIRECT AND INDIRECT SPEECH

Unit 11 focuses on the forms, meanings, and uses of reporting verbs and direct and indirect speech for questions and statements. It also addresses changes in other types of words that take place when speech is reported.

- We report speech in two ways: direct speech and indirect speech. Direct, or quoted speech, is the exact words a person spoke or thought and is enclosed in quotation marks. Direct speech is often introduced by reporting verbs.

- Indirect speech, or reported speech, is someone's report of what another person said or thought. It is not the exact words of a speaker and not enclosed in quotation marks. Indirect speech reports what a person said in a noun clause or phrase introduced by a reporting verb.

- If a statement is reported, *that* can be used to introduce it. If a question is reported, the noun clause is introduced by *if, whether (or not)*, or a *wh-* question word.

- *Say* and *tell* are the most common reporting verbs, and we usually use their simple past forms with both direct and indirect speech.

- We normally use the simple past form of *ask* to report indirect questions. For *yes / no* questions, use *if* or *whether (or not)* to introduce the question and use statement word order. Do not use *do* or *did* in indirect questions, and end them with a period, not a question mark.

- Use question words to introduce indirect *wh-* questions. Use statement word order to report indirect questions about the predicate. Use question word order to report indirect questions about the subject.

- If the reporting verb is in the past, the verb in the noun clause often changes. We sometimes do not change verbs in a noun clause in spoken English, especially if what we are reporting happened a short time ago. If general truths are reported, we often do not change verbs in the noun clause.

- Certain modals often change in indirect speech. Certain other words change as well.

Theme: COMMUNICATION AND MISUNDERSTANDING

Unit 11 focuses on language that is used to talk about effective communication and potential misunderstandings during communication.

Step 1: Grammar in Context (pages 173–175)

See the general suggestions for Grammar in Context on page 1.

Before You Read
- Have students work in groups to discuss the questions.
- Have students from each group share their answers with the class.

Read
- Write these questions on the board (or prepare them as a handout):
  1. What does Ellen Sands say that she wants to talk about? *(ways to avoid verbal conflict)*
  2. What did she see at a restaurant in New York City? *(She saw an Asian couple talking to their server.)*
  3. Why was the couple upset? *(because the service was slow)*
  4. According to Sands, what mistake did the waitress make? *(She didn't listen actively and never answered the couple's question.)*
  5. What is one other way Sands thinks we can avoid conflict? *(by stating things positively rather than negatively)*
- Establish a purpose for reading. Have students read the questions aloud. Remind students to think about the questions as they read and listen to the text.
- Have students read the text individually. Then have them discuss their answers in pairs.

After You Read
A. Vocabulary
- Have students cover the definitions in the right-hand column. Have students read the sentences in the left-hand column and try to guess the meanings of the expressions in bold. Then have students work in pairs to discuss what they mean and write a brief definition for each one.
- Have students complete the exercise. Then go over the answers as a class. Have students compare the definitions they wrote with the correct answers.

B. Comprehension
- Have students complete the exercise individually and then compare answers in pairs or groups of three.
- Have various students share answers with the class. Clarify any discrepancies in students' answers. Have students point to the part of the text where they found each answer.

Go to **www.myfocusongrammarlab.com** for an additional reading, and for reading and vocabulary practice.

Step 2: Grammar Presentation (pages 176–180)

See the general suggestions for Grammar Presentation on page 2.

Grammar Charts

- Have students look at the first two charts. Ask: "Can the verb *said* in the first chart be replaced by *told*?" (*No.*) "Why not?" (*The verb* tell *is followed by a person. You* tell *someone something.*)
- Have students look at the charts that show formation of indirect questions. Ask: "In the first set of examples, are the words *if / whether* required?" (*Yes.*) "What about the examples that report *wh-* questions—are the *wh-* question words needed?" (*Yes.*)
- Elicit that changing direct to indirect speech is essentially forming noun clauses and embedded questions, which was studied in Unit 10.
- Tell students that there are some additional complications with reported speech, and turn their attention to the next two charts. Have pairs of students read aloud the direct and indirect versions of each sentence in the charts. Ask: "What is different in the indirect version?" (*The pronoun changes from* I *to* he. *The verb expresses an earlier time.*)
- Look at the last chart. Ask students what other words change. (*pronouns, possessives,* this, here, ago, now, today, yesterday, *and* tomorrow)

Grammar Notes

Note 1

- Have students read Note 1.
- Write the first two example sentences of direct speech on the board without punctuation and invite different students to punctuate them properly. Point out that the final punctuation goes inside the closing quotation marks.

Note 2

- Have students read the explanation and example sentences. Draw students' attention to the usage note and the *Be Careful!* notes that precede and follow it.
- Write some sentences based on the opening reading on the board (or prepare them as a handout). Have students work in pairs to change the sentences from direct to indirect speech using the reporting verbs *say* and *tell*. For example:

"Hello, everyone. My name is Brad Ness," said the reporter. (*The reporter told everyone that his name was Brad Ness.* OR *The reporter said that his name was Brad Ness.*)

"The service was very slow," the man said to the waitress. (*The man told the waitress that the service was very slow.* OR *The man said that the service was very slow.*)

"The waitress didn't listen carefully, Brad," said Ellen Sands. (*Ellen Sands told Brad that the waitress didn't listen carefully.* OR *Ellen Sands said that the waitress didn't listen carefully.*)

- Have students from different pairs share their answers with the class.

Note 3

- Have students look at the three indirect questions in Note 3.
- Have students write the original questions from which the indirect questions were made.
- Have them work in pairs to compare answers and identify the changes in the other words when the questions were transformed from direct to indirect questions. Then go over their answers as a class. For example:

"Mary, are you going to resign?" asked Mrs. Mason. (*The change to an indirect question includes the use of* if *changing* Mary *to* she, *and changing the verb from* are . . . going *to* was going.)

Note 4

- With the class, develop a list of *wh-* question words and write them on the board.
- Have students work in small groups to write one direct question with each word. Have groups exchange questions and transform the direct questions into indirect questions.
- Call on students from each group to share their direct and indirect questions with the class and explain the changes they made. For example:

"Where is Tony?" he asked.	He asked where Tony was.
"What are you eating?" Tom asked Martha.	Tom asked Martha what she was eating.
"Sit down!" her mother said.	Her mother told her to sit down.

Note 5

- Have students read the explanation. Read the examples aloud and have students repeat.
- Say a question (or write it on the board) and have students change it into an indirect question. Repeat until you have practiced each of the transformations mentioned in the note.

Note 6

- Write the following chart on the board or prepare it as a handout.

Direct Speech	Indirect Speech
"The sun <u>sets</u> earlier here in winter."	Jeong said that the sun <u>sets</u> earlier here in winter.
"I <u>arrived</u> late this morning."	Sara has just told me she <u>arrived</u> late this morning.
"I<u>'m going</u> home."	Tulu says he<u>'s going</u> home.
"I<u>'m tired</u>."	Jared is saying that he<u>'s tired</u>.

- Have students discuss in pairs why it is not necessary to change the verbs in each reported statement.

Note 7

- Have students work in pairs to compare the examples of direct and indirect speech in Note 7. Have them underline changes in verbs and circle changes in pronouns and other words. Have students from each pair share their answers with the class.
- To give students practice discriminating among modals that change and those that don't change in reported speech, write the following sentence on the board. Then have a student transform it into indirect speech:
Ana said, "We can go out for dinner." (*Ana said they could go out for dinner*.)
  - Replace *can* with *could* and elicit the indirect version. (*Ana said they could . . . [no change].*)
- Have students work in pairs to write sentences with direct speech for each of the remaining modals in Note 7. Then have pairs exchange sentences and transform the sentences into indirect speech. Have various pairs share their sentences with the class.

Note 8

- Have students read the example sentences aloud and note the changes in pairs. Then have two pairs work together to compare their changes.
- Write sentences on the board with words that change in indirect speech. Then have students change the sentences into reported speech. For example:
Tomiko asked, "Have you been to this restaurant?" (*Tomiko asked if I had been to that restaurant*.)

She said, "I ate here three days ago." (*She said she had eaten there three days before*.)
"I told my parents about it yesterday," she explained (*She explained that she had told her parents about it the day before*.)

🕐 **Identify the Grammar:** Have students identify the grammar in the opening reading on pages 173–174. For example:
When the waitress brought the check, the man said, **"The bill seems very high. Did you include the service in it? How much is the service?"**
When the waitress brought the check, the man said **the bill seemed very high**.
He asked **how much the service was**.

Go to **www.myfocusongrammarlab.com** for grammar charts and notes.

Step 3: Focused Practice (pages 181–185)

See the general suggestions for Focused Practice on page 4.

Exercise 1: Discover the Grammar

A
- Read the instructions and go over the example with students.
- Have students complete the exercise. Then go over the answers as a class. If needed, have students find the direct speech in the text so they can see how the verbs changed.

B
- Have students complete the exercise individually. Then have them compare answers in pairs.
- Have various pairs share and explain their answers to the class. Call on students to correct the incorrect sentences.

Exercise 2: Direct Speech to Indirect Speech

- Read the instructions and go over the example with the class. Have students quickly check the headlines for unfamiliar vocabulary. Explain any new terms.
- Have students complete the exercise individually. Go over the answers as a class.
- 🕐 Have students create two or three headlines about their classes, the school, or their classmates in small groups. Then have them write the headlines on the board. Have students change the headlines to indirect speech. Then go over the changes as a class.

Exercise 3: Indirect Speech to Direct Speech

- Have students complete the exercise individually.

- Call on students to write their direct speech questions on the board. Review the answers as a class.

Exercise 4: Multiple Changes to Indirect Speech
- Have students complete the exercise. Go over the answers as a class.
- Have students rewrite the indirect speech account from Sally's point of view in small groups. For example: *I asked my dad if he could help me with my homework. He said he could and asked me what I needed.* Have various groups write their sentences on the board and review them as a class.

Exercise 5: Editing
- Have different students write their corrected sentences on the board. Then have them explain their corrections to the class.
- Have students practice reading the text aloud in pairs.

Go to **www.myfocusongrammarlab.com** for additional grammar practice.

Step 4: Communication Practice (pages 186–189)

See the general suggestions for Communication Practice on page 5.

Exercise 6: Listening
A
- Establish a purpose for listening. Have students read the question in Part A. Remind them to think about the question as they listen.
- Play the audio and allow students time to answer the question. Go over the answer as a class.

B
- Have students read the questions. Remind students to think about the questions as they listen. Play the audio. Allow students time to write their answers.
- Go over the answers as a class. You may want to play the audio again to clarify any discrepancies in students' answers.
- Provide students with the audioscript. Have them underline the examples of direct speech and change them into indirect speech individually. Then have them compare their sentences in pairs. Go over the answers as a class.

Exercise 7: Pronunciation
A
- Have students read and listen to the Pronunciation Note.
- Have them repeat the examples several times as you say them.

B
- Have students read the sentences.
- Play the audio. Pause as needed so students can underline the words that use consonant blending. Then replay the audio and have students write the letter that represents the /y/ sound.
- Have students work in pairs to check their answers. Go over the answers as a class.

C
- Have students form new pairs and practice saying the sentences.
- Circulate and provide correction as needed.

Exercise 8: Group Reporting
- If your class is large you might want to have students work in three or four groups so that they are more involved. At the end have the directors of each group write the original messages on the board next to the final messages and, if there was a change, explain how it occurred.
- **Note:** As a variation, students in each group can take turns being the director.

Exercise 9: Picture Discussion
A
- Divide the class into groups. Have students look at the picture and imagine what the people are saying.
- Call on a student from each group to report their answers to the class.

B
- Read the instructions. You may need to teach the term *objective*.
- Elicit a list of people in the photo. Write the list on the board. Have the class give reasons why each person would or would not be objective. Write the reasons on the board.
- Have the class vote on who is most likely to give the most objective report.
- Have students discuss in pairs an accident they were involved in or witnessed. Encourage them to use reported speech.

Exercise 10: Writing
A
- Have students read the instructions and the example.
- Point out that a summary is shorter than the original event or story and must be in the students' own words.

B
- Have students use the Editing Checklist to revise and rewrite as needed, or have them correct each other's work in pairs.

- 🕐 Have students post their papers in the classroom so the class can read them. You can also publish them in a booklet or on a class website.

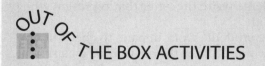

OUT OF THE BOX ACTIVITIES

Reading, Speaking, and Listening

- Bring in (or have students bring in) magazine interviews with famous people.
- Have students work in small groups. Give each group an interview to read and discuss. Then have students in each group underline interesting pieces of information and select some things they would like to share with the class. Have each person in the group tell the class at least one piece of information. Point out that for each piece of information, students should report both the question and the answer. Encourage students to use a variety of reporting verbs.

Reading, Writing, Speaking, and Listening

- Have students work in pairs to write a conversation similar to the one in Exercise 4 on page 184. Tell them that the conversation can have two or three speakers.
- Have two pairs work together to exchange conversations and write an account of their partners' conversation using indirect speech.
- Have various groups share an original conversation and the account of it with the class.

Listening, Speaking, Writing, and Reading

- Bring in (or have students bring in) magazine or personal pictures that lend themselves to discussion and speculation.
- Have students work in groups. Give each group a picture and have them discuss what happened and what the people said to each other. Have them write their ideas as direct speech.
- Have groups exchange pictures and papers and rewrite the sentences using indirect speech.
- Have each group show the picture and tell the class about it using indirect speech. If you have a large class, have two groups share their pictures and ideas with each other.

Go to **www.myfocusongrammarlab.com** for additional listening, pronunciation, speaking, and writing practice.

Note:
- See the *Focus on Grammar Workbook* for additional in-class or homework grammar practice.

Unit 11 Review (page 190)

Have students complete the Review and check their answers on Student Book page UR-2. Review or assign additional material as needed.

Go to **www.myfocusongrammarlab.com** for the Unit Achievement Test.

From Grammar to Writing (pages 191–193)

See the general suggestions for From Grammar to Writing on page 9.

Go to **www.myfocusongrammarlab.com** for an additional From Grammar to Writing Assignment, Part Review, and Part Post-Test.

PART V OVERVIEW

ADJECTIVE CLAUSES

UNIT	GRAMMAR FOCUS	THEME
12	Adjective Clauses: Review and Expansion	Personality Types
13	Adjective Clauses with Prepositions; Adjective Phrases	Movies

Go to **www.myfocusongrammarlab.com** for the Part and Unit Tests.

Note: PowerPoint® grammar presentations, test-generating software, and reproducible Part and Unit Tests are on the *Teacher's Resource Disc.*

Grammar: ADJECTIVE CLAUSES: REVIEW AND EXPANSION

Unit 12 focuses on the meanings and uses of adjective clauses. It addresses placement of adjective clauses, relative pronouns as subjects and objects, *whose* + noun to indicate possession, and *where* and *when* in adjective clauses. Identifying and nonidentifying adjective clauses are also presented and explained.

- Sentences with adjective clauses combine two sentences. The adjective clause is a dependent clause that modifies a noun in the main clause of the sentence. Adjective clauses can occur after or inside of a main clause. Adjective clauses often begin with relative pronouns such as *who, whom, which,* or *that.* Adjective clauses can also begin with *whose, when,* or *where.* The word that begins the adjective clause usually comes after the noun or pronoun that the clause modifies.

- Use *who, which,* or *that* as the subjects of verbs in adjective clauses. *Who* and *that* refer to people. *Which* and *that* refer to things. *That* is less formal than *who* or *which.*

- The verb in the adjective clause agrees with the noun or pronoun that the clause modifies. Be careful not to use double subjects in adjective clauses.

- Use *who, whom,* or *that* as objects of verbs in adjective clauses. *Whom* is formal; *who* and *that* are less formal and are used in conversation and informal writing. To refer to things, use *which* or *that* as objects of verbs in adjective clauses. *Which* is more formal.

- If the relative pronoun is an object, you can sometimes omit it in speech and informal writing.

- The verb of an adjective clause agrees with the subject of the clause, not the object.

- Use *whose* to introduce an adjective clause that indicates possession. An adjective clause with *whose* can modify people or things. *Whose* cannot be omitted.

- Use *where* to modify a noun of place. Use an adjective clause with *where* only if you can restate the location with the word *there.*

- Use *when* or *that* to begin an adjective clause that modifies a noun of time. *When* and *that* can be omitted in less formal language.

- An adjective clause that distinguishes one person or thing from another is an *identifying* adjective clause. It is not enclosed in commas. If the adjective clause adds extra information but does not make a distinction between people or things, it is *nonidentifying.* It is enclosed in commas. Object relative pronouns can be omitted only from identifying adjective clauses. Don't use *that* as a relative pronoun in a nonidentifying clause.

- You can use *which* to refer to an entire previous idea in speech or informal writing. In formal writing, use a noun at the beginning of a *which* clause.

Theme: PERSONALITY TYPES

Unit 12 focuses on language that is used to talk about various types of personality traits.

Step 1: Grammar in Context (pages 196–198)

See the general suggestions for Grammar in Context on page 1.

Before You Read

- Have students complete the sentence in the first question individually and compare answers in pairs. Then have students report about their partners to the class using the sentence frame.

- Have groups discuss the second question. Then have students from various groups share their ideas with the class.

Read

- Write these questions on the board (or prepare them as a handout):
  1. How does the reading define *introvert* and *extrovert*? *(An introvert is a person whose energies are activated by being alone. An extrovert is a person whose energies are activated by being with others.)*
  2. How many different personality types does the article discuss? *(four)*
  3. What are the types? What is a characteristic of each one? *(Type A: competitive and have no-nonsense approach to life; Type B: socializers who love the spotlight; Type C: love details; Type D: like routine)*

- Establish a purpose for reading. Have students read each of the questions silently. Remind students to think about these questions as they read and listen to the text.

- Have students read the text, or play the audio and have students follow along in their books. Discuss the answers to the questions as a class. Have students identify the specific place in the text where they found each answer.

After You Read

A. Vocabulary
- Have students highlight the sentences in the text that contain each of the boldfaced words or phrases. Have them work in pairs to guess at the meaning of each word by using context clues. Have them write the words and their meanings in their notebooks.
- Have students complete the exercise individually. Then have them compare answers in pairs.
- Have different students read their answers aloud. Then have them look at the meanings they wrote in their notebooks and compare them with the definitions in the exercise.

B. Comprehension
- Have students complete the exercise individually. Then have them compare answers in pairs.
- Have different students share their answers and corrected false statements with the class. Have each student point out the place in the text where he or she found the answer to the question.

Go to **www.myfocusongrammarlab.com** for an additional reading, and for reading and vocabulary practice.

Step 2: Grammar Presentation (pages 199–202)

See the general suggestions for Grammar Presentation on page 2.

Grammar Charts
- Divide the class into five groups and assign each group a section of the chart to examine. If you have a large class, more than one group might examine the same section.
- Have each group write a grammar rule for their section and give two examples that illustrate the rule: one from the chart and one from the opening reading or of the group's own invention.
- Have each group write their rules and examples on the board. Leave these rules and examples posted as you work through the Grammar Notes.
- **Note:** The rules that students will write are essentially the rules explained in the Grammar Notes on Student Book pages 200–202.

Grammar Notes

Note 1
- Have students read the explanation and the examples aloud.
- Have students find an example of an adjective clause from the opening reading on Student Book pages 196–197. Then have them tell you the two sentences that are combined in the example. (Example: *The hosts have a new party game that involves comparing each person to a flower.* = *The hosts have a new party game. The game involves comparing each person to a flower.*)

Note 2
- Have students read the explanation and examples aloud.
- Have students look at the opening reading on Student Book pages 196–197 and find adjective clauses that begin with *who, whom, which, that, whose, when,* or *where.* For each example, ask students: "Is the adjective clause after the main clause or inside it?"

Note 3
- Read the note aloud. Read the examples aloud and have students repeat.
- Have students say the examples again, this time substituting another relative pronoun that is possible. (Examples: *The Ings are the people that bought the house. Sam is the man who lives next door to me. Math is the subject that is the easiest for me.*)

Note 4
- Have students read the example sentences in this note and in Note 3. Ask: "How are the sentences different?" (*In Note 3, the relative pronouns are the subjects of the verbs in the adjective clause, but in Note 4 they are objects.*)
- Read the example sentences with *who* and *whom* aloud. Have students repeat, substituting *whom* for *who* and vice versa. Ask: "Can you use *whom* as the subject of an adjective clause?" (*No.*)
- Have students read the information about omitting the relative pronoun. Choose an example sentence from the note that can have its relative pronoun omitted and read it aloud. Have students repeat twice, first with the relative pronoun then without it. (Example: *Mr. Pitkin was the person who I mentioned. Mr. Pitkin was the person I mentioned.*)

Note 5
- Have students read the explanation and examples.

- Write the third example sentence on the board:
  Harvey, whose house we're renting, is a lawyer.
  Have students give you the two sentences that are combined in this sentence. *(Harvey is a lawyer. We're renting his house.)*
- 🕐 Have students find the *whose* sentence in the opening reading and break it into two sentences. *(An extrovert is basically a person whose energies are activated by being with others. = An extrovert is basically a person. His or her energies are activated by being with others.)*

Note 6

- Have students read the note. Draw their attention to the *Be Careful!* note. You may want to give more examples to help students understand this point. Write sentences such as the following on the board and have students break them into two sentences using *there* at the end of the second sentence:
  This is the place where I live. *(This is the place. I live there.)*
  We passed the restaurant where we had our wedding. *(We passed the restaurant. We had our wedding there.)*
- Have students read the note about *which* or *that* + preposition. Say sentences that use *which / that* + preposition and have students change them into *where* sentences. *(Example: This is the park that we play soccer at. = This is the park where we play soccer.)*

Note 7

- Read the note and the examples aloud. Elicit other nouns of time that can appear in the structure. *(Examples: day, year, hour, decade, moment, instant)*
- Write on the board:
  The day _____ was the happiest day of my life.
  Read the sentence aloud, completing the blank with information that is true for you. *(Example: The day my daughter was born was the happiest day of my life.)* Call on students to give more examples. Write them on the board.

Note 8

- Have students read the first part of the note and the first two example sentences. Elicit how the use of commas changes the meaning of the sentence. *(In the first sentence, there is more than one man and the speaker is identifying the one that the sentence is about. In the second, it is already understood which man the sentence is about.)*

- Have students find more identifying and nonidentifying adjective clauses in the opening reading. Have students explain why each one is identifying or nonidentifying and how it affects the meaning.
- Have students read the rest of the note. Have them find examples of each point in the opening reading.

🕐 **Identify the Grammar:** Have students identify the grammar in the opening reading on pages 196–197. For example:
  Imagine you're at a party **where you know several people well**.
  The hosts have a new party game **that involves comparing each person to a flower**.
  Are you the kind of person **who resembles a daisy**, open to the world most of the time?
  Or are you more like a morning glory, **which opens up only at special moments**?

Go to **www.myfocusongrammarlab.com** for grammar charts and notes.

Step 3: Focused Practice (pages 202–206)

See the general suggestions for Focused Practice on page 4.

Exercise 1: Discover the Grammar

A

- Read the instructions and go over the example answer with the class. You may also want to go over the second item as a class. Ask students: "Why can't *which* be replaced by *that* in the second item?" *(because you can't use* that *as a relative pronoun in a nonidentifying clause—see Grammar Note 8b)*
- Have students complete the exercise individually and compare answers in pairs.
- Call on students from various pairs to share their answers with the class. For *no* answers, have students explain why the relative pronoun in the sentence cannot be replaced by the one in parentheses.

B

- Have students complete this part and work in groups to compare answers.
- Go over the answers with the class. Then ask: "What is one important clue that tells us whether the clause is identifying or nonidentifying?" *(Nonidentifying clauses are enclosed in commas.)*

Exercise 2: Relative Pronouns
- Have students complete the exercise. Go over the answers as a class.
- ⏱ As students provide their answers, have them explain which of the Grammar Notes cited applies to that item.

Exercise 3: Identifying / Nonidentifying Clauses
- Read the instructions and go over the example answer. Draw students' attention to the instruction to use the first sentence in each pair as the main clause in the combined sentence.
- Have students complete the exercise. Call on several students to write one of their sentences on the board.
- Go over the answers as a class. Ask the other students whether the use of commas in the sentences on the board is correct or incorrect and why.

Exercise 4: Formal / Informal
- Have students complete the exercise in groups of four.
- Have pairs of students in each group share and discuss their answers for the spoken report. Then have them create different pairs to compare their answers to the written report.

Exercise 5: Editing
- Have students complete the exercise.
- Call on several students to write the corrected sentences on the board and explain each error and correction.

Go to **www.myfocusongrammarlab.com** for additional grammar practice.

Step 4: Communication Practice (pages 206–209)

See the general suggestions for Communication Practice on page 5.

Exercise 6: Listening
A
- Establish a purpose for listening. Have students read the comprehension question. Remind them to think about the question as they listen.
- Play the audio. Ask the class the question and go over the answer. Replay the audio if needed.

B
- Have students read the pairs of sentences. Point out that for many sentence pairs, students will have to decide if there is one or more than one of something. Ask: "If there is only one of something, will you hear an identifying or nonidentifying clause?" *(nonidentifying)* "How can you tell if a clause you hear is nonidentifying?" *(The speaker will pause where there are commas enclosing the clause; nonidentifying clauses don't use* that *as a relative pronoun.)*
- Remind students to think about the sentences as they listen. Play the audio again.
- Call on students to give their answers. You may want to play the audio again to clarify any discrepancies in students' answers.
- ⏱ Provide copies of the audioscript. Have students practice reading the conversation in groups, emphasizing the pauses where there are commas enclosing nonidentifying clauses. Call on a group to role-play the conversation for the class.

Exercise 7: Pronunciation
A
- Have students read and listen to the Pronunciation Note. Then have students repeat the example sentences several times as you say them.

B
- Play the audio, pausing as needed as students mark their answers. Have students work in pairs to compare answers.
- Go over the answers as a class and clarify any discrepancies among students' answers.

C
- Circulate as pairs practice saying the sentences. Make corrections as needed.
- ⏱ Have different students choose sentences from each pair at random and read them to the class. Have the other students explain the meanings of the sentences.

Exercise 8: Pair Discussion
A
- Read the instructions and the questions.
- To help start the discussion, you may want to give an example of a conflict you have dealt with (real or fictional).
- Have students discuss the question in pairs. Circulate, helping as needed.

B
- Call on students from each pair to report their answers to the class.

- **Note:** As a variation, you may want to have students in each pair report about each other to the class.

Exercise 9: Class Activity

A
- Write the name of each student on a separate piece of paper. Put the papers in a bag or box and have students pick a name at random.
- Read the instructions and the examples. Point out that the sentences should not say the student's name.
- Brainstorm a list of the relative pronouns students learned about in the grammar charts and notes. Write the list on the board. Encourage students to use a variety of relative words in their sentences, not just *who* or *that*.

B
- Have students read their sentences aloud. Have students listen and guess who each sentence describes.
- Call on students to read the sentences they thought were the most creative.

Exercise 10: Writing

A
- You may want to review the definition and structure of a paragraph. *(A paragraph is a group of sentences that discuss one topic. The topic sentence expresses the main idea of the paragraph, and the remaining sentences provide details about the main idea.)*
- Have students look at the example and identify the topic sentence. Ask students: "What is the purpose of this paragraph?" *(to introduce the main idea)* Then ask: "What do you think the writer will do in the next three paragraphs?" *(give details and examples that support the main idea)* "What will the writer do in the last paragraph?" *(restate what was said in the first paragraph in a different way)*
- Have students write topic sentences for each of their paragraphs. Have them compare topic sentences in pairs. Call on a few students to share their topic sentences. Correct the sentences as needed. Then have students write their paragraphs, either in class or as homework.

B
- Have students work in pairs to correct each other's work using the Editing Checklist. Have each student revise and rewrite as needed.
- ⏱ Have students post their papers in the classroom so the class can read them. You can also publish them together in a booklet or on a class website.

OUT OF THE BOX ACTIVITIES

Speaking, Listening, and Writing
- Have students work in pairs to discuss whether they are extroverts or introverts and provide reasons and examples.
- Have students in each pair write one or two paragraphs about whether their partner is an introvert or extrovert and why.
- ⏱ Publish students' writing by making copies of the paragraphs and putting them in a booklet.

Reading, Writing, Speaking, and Listening
- Have students search the Internet for various types of personality tests and bring one or two to class.
- Have students take one of the tests.
- Have students form pairs to discuss the results of the test. Remind them to use adjective clauses in their discussions.

Reading, Writing, Speaking, and Listening
- Have students work in pairs. Each pair will use a dictionary to find eight nouns with definitions that use adjective clauses. Encourage students to find definitions of interesting words and to make sure the definitions they choose include a variety of relative pronouns.
- Have two pairs work together to take turns reading the definitions aloud and guessing each other's words.

Go to **www.myfocusongrammarlab.com** for additional listening, pronunciation, speaking, and writing practice.

Note:
- See the *Focus on Grammar Workbook* for additional in-class or homework grammar practice.

Unit 12 Review (page 210)
Have students complete the Review and check their answers on Student Book page UR-2. Review or assign additional material as needed.

Go to **www.myfocusongrammarlab.com** for the Unit Achievement Test.

Grammar: Adjective Clauses with Prepositions; Adjective Phrases

Unit 13 focuses on the forms, meanings, and uses of adjective clauses used as objects of prepositions, and various patterns that are used in adjective clauses. The unit also addresses reducing adjective clauses to adjective phrases and changing adjective clauses to adjective phrases.

- The relative pronouns *who(m)*, *that*, *which*, and *whose* can all be used as objects of prepositions in adjective clauses. When the preposition is at the beginning of the clause, the language is more formal. A preposition at the end of the clause is informal. When the clause begins with *that*, the preposition cannot be at the beginning.

- After a preposition, we can omit *who(m)*, *that*, and *which*. The preposition then moves to the end of the clause. *Whose* cannot be omitted.

- Some adjective clauses have the pattern quantifier + *of* + relative pronoun. Quantifiers occur only in clauses with *whom*, *which*, and *whose* and can refer to people or things. These types of clauses are formal. If the clause occurs within the main clause, it is enclosed in commas. If the clause is after the main clause, it is preceded by a comma.

- Some adjective clauses have the pattern noun + *of which*. These clauses refer only to things. If the clause occurs within the main clause, it is enclosed in commas. If the clause is after the main clause, it is preceded by a comma.

- We sometimes shorten, or reduce, adjective clauses to adjective phrases, but they have the same meaning. To reduce an adjective clause with a *be* verb, omit the relative pronoun and the *be* verb. Adjective clauses with *be* verbs can be reduced only when *who*, *which*, or *that* is the subject pronoun of the clause. If an adjective clause needs commas, the corresponding phrase also needs commas.

- In an adjective clause with a verb other than *be*, you can often change the clause to a phrase by omitting the relative pronoun and changing the verb to its *–ing* form. You can do this only when *who*, *which*, or *that* is the subject pronoun of the clause.

Theme: Movies

Unit 13 focuses on language that is used to talk about various types of movies.

Step 1: Grammar in Context (pages 211–213)

See the general suggestions for Grammar in Context on page 1.

Before You Read

- Have students work in pairs or groups to discuss the questions.
- Have various students share their answers with the class.

Read

- You may want to discuss these words and their meanings:

decade	a period of 10 years
apartheid	a system formerly used in South Africa to separate different people there based on race, with privileges given to those who were descendants of Europeans
persist	to continue in spite of problems or difficulties
inhabitant	a person or animal that lives in a certain area
exploiter	a person who takes unfair advantage of a person or situation, usually to benefit him or herself

- Write these questions on the board (or prepare them as a handout):
  1. What is the purpose of the article? *(to give readers a list of the best movies of the decade)*
  2. What five films does the author recommend? *(Julie and Julia, Invictus, Avatar, Babel, and Slumdog Millionaire)*
  3. Who is the real-life political leader that the author mentions? *(Nelson Mandela)*
  4. Which film is the author's favorite? *(Slumdog Millionaire)*

- Establish a purpose for reading. Have students read each of the questions silently. Remind students to think about these questions as they read and listen to the text. Have students read the text, then discuss the questions as a class.

After You Read

A. Vocabulary

- Have students cover the definitions in the right-hand column. Have students read the sentences in the left-hand column and try to guess the meanings of the boldfaced expressions. Then have students work in pairs to discuss what they mean and write a brief definition for each one.

- Have students complete the exercise and go over the answers as a class. Have students compare the definition they wrote with the correct answers.

B. Comprehension
- Have students complete the exercise individually and compare answers in pairs or groups of three.
- Have various students share their answers with the class. Clarify any discrepancies in students' answers. Have students refer to the text to defend their answers if needed.

Go to **www.myfocusongrammarlab.com** for an additional reading, and for reading and vocabulary practice.

Step 2: Grammar Presentation (pages 214–216)
See the general suggestions for Grammar Presentation on page 2.

Grammar Charts
- Write these sentences on the board:
  1. The movie stars Morgan Freeman and Matt Damon as Mandela and Pienaar, both of whom play their roles to near perfection.
  2. An American couple, played by Brad Pitt and Cate Blanchet, are traveling in Morocco when the wife is wounded by a stray bullet.
  3. Science-fiction films, a compelling example of which is *Avatar*, continue to be popular.
  4. Mandela reaches out to François Pienaar, the captain of the mostly-white national rugby team, with whom he develops an enduring friendship.
  5. Jamal recounts events in his life, illustrating how he knew the answers to the questions.
- Have students work in pairs or groups to match the sentences on the board with the chart that shows their structures. *(Sentence 1— adjective clause with quantifier; Sentence 2— reducing adjective clauses to adjective phrases; Sentence 3—adjective clause with noun; Sentence 4— adjective clause with preposition; Sentence 5—changing adjective clauses to adjective phrases)*
- Have students work in pairs to select one or two more sentences from the text and identify which of the charts show their structure. Then have pairs share their sentences with the class.

Grammar Notes

Note 1
- Have students label the example sentences as formal or informal and then work in pairs to compare answers.
- Have them transform the sentences from formal to informal and vice versa, omitting the relative pronoun where possible.
- Point out the last two example sentences. Ask: "In which one of these it is possible to omit the relative pronoun and move the preposition to the end?" *(only the identifying clause)* Review identifying and nonidentifying clauses if necessary.

Note 2
- Ask: "Which of the relative pronouns can refer both to people and things?" *(whose)* "Which refers only to people?" *(whom)* "Which refers only to things?" *(which)*
- Write a few sentences with this pattern on the board, some with the clause in the middle and some with the clause at the end, leaving out the commas for students to supply. Then have students expand the sentences into two sentences. For example: *The students in this class, most of whom are present today, are advanced.* (*The students in this class are advanced. Most of them are present today.*)
- Write these sentence frames on the board (or prepare them as a handout):
  I have two _____, both of whom _____.
  I have two _____, both of which _____.
  I have several _____, three of whom _____.
  I have many _____, none of whom _____.
  I have lots of _____, some of which _____.
- Have students complete the sentences on the board with true information about themselves. (Example: *I have two brothers, both of whom are living abroad.*)

Note 3
- Point out that this structure is formal and is generally reserved for writing or formal speaking.
- Have students look at the example sentences and notice the nouns that come before *of*. *(example, occurrences).* Then ask: "Why is *example* singular? Why is *occurrences* plural?" (Example *refers to one musical.* Occurrences *refers to more than one strike.*)

Note 4
- Have students read the examples.
- Ask: "Is any information lost when the adjective clause is shortened to a phrase?" *(No.)*

Note 5

- Have students read the explanation and the example sentences. Ask: "When can you shorten an adjective clause?" (*when it contains* who, which, *or* that *as the subject pronoun* + be.)
- Have students look at the grammar chart titled "Reducing Adjective Clauses to Adjective Phrases." Have them read the example sentences aloud.

Note 6

- Have students read the note. Divide the class into pairs and have them explain the rule to each other in their own words.
- Have students look at the grammar chart titled "Changing Adjective Clauses to Adjective Phrases." Have them read the example sentences aloud.

⏱ **Identify the Grammar:** Have students identify the grammar in the opening reading on pages 211–212. For example:

The trouble is, I've seen a lot of movies since 2000, **many of which are outstanding in their own way**.

To narrow down my list I'll start with five pictures that anyone **interested in cinema should revisit** . . .

Anyone **having even the slightest interest in food** should see this one.

Clint Eastwood, **whose films I'm always impressed with**, directed with great skill.

Meanwhile, the American couple's Mexican housekeeper, **to whom they've entrusted their children**, takes the kids to her son's wedding in Mexico, where unfortunate events occur.

Go to **www.myfocusongrammarlab.com** for grammar charts and notes.

Step 3: Focused Practice (pages 217–221)

See the general suggestions for Focused Practice on page 4.

Exercise 1: Discover the Grammar

A

- Have students complete the exercise and work in pairs to check their answers.
- Call on pairs to share and explain their answers to the class.

B

- Have students complete the exercise individually and work in pairs to compare answers.
- Go over the answers as a class.

- ⏱ Point out the adjective phrases in Items 3 and 8 that use the *-ing* form of the verb. Ask: "Why do these phrases use the *-ing* form of the verb?" (*because when there is no* be *verb in an adjective clause, the reduced phrase uses the* -ing *form of the verb*)

Exercise 2: Adjective Clauses with Quantifiers

- Have students complete the exercise. Go over the answers as a class.
- ⏱ Have students discuss these questions in pairs:
  1. What are the two relative pronouns that you used in your answers? (*whom, which*)
  2. What rule helped you decide which one to use? (Whom *refers to people;* which *refers to things.*)

Exercise 3: Adjective Phrases

- Read the instructions and go over the example. Point out that the adjective phrase comes from the first sentence except in Item 4, where it comes from the second sentence.
- Have students complete the exercise and work in pairs to check their answers.
- Have students from various pairs share their answers with the class.

Exercise 4: Clause to Sentence

- Have students complete the exercise. Go over the answers as a class.
- ⏱ In pairs, have students decide which original sentences that contain adjective clauses could be reduced to adjective phrases. (*none of them*) Why? (*Adjective clauses with quantifiers and the noun + preposition pattern cannot be reduced.*)

Exercise 5: Personal Inventory

- Read the instructions and go over the examples. Brainstorm one or two additional sentences that use the words in the box and the clauses and phrases taught in this unit.
- Have students complete the exercise and work in pairs to compare sentences.
- Have them exchange papers and report about their partners to the class.

Exercise 6: Editing

- Have students complete the exercise individually.
- Call on students to write their corrected sentences on the board. Discuss the corrections as a class. Then have pairs work together to read their corrected letters to each other.

Go to **www.myfocusongrammarlab.com** for additional grammar practice.

Step 4: Communication Practice (pages 222–227)

See the general suggestions for Communication Practice on page 5.

Exercise 7: Listening

A

- Establish a purpose for listening. Have students read the question in Part A. Remind them to think about the question as they listen.
- Play the audio and allow students time to answer the question.

B

- Have students read the statements. Remind them to think about them as they listen. Play the audio and have students complete the exercise.
- Have students work in pairs to check their answers and correct the false statements.
- Have various pairs share their corrected statements with the class.

Exercise 8: Pronunciation

A

- Have students read and listen to the Pronunciation Note, then have them repeat the example sentences several times as you say them.

B

- Play the audio, pausing as needed as students circle their answers. Have students work in pairs to compare their answers.
- Go over the answers as a class. Replay the audio as needed to clarify any discrepancies among students' answers.

C

- Have students practice saying the sentences. Have students switch roles after the first practice so each person has a chance to say each sentence.
- Circulate and make corrections as needed.

Exercise 9: Information Gap

- Divide students into pairs, with one person Student A and the other Student B. Have Student B turn to page 227. Explain that they are looking at the same movie review, but each person is missing information that his or her partner has. They should ask and answer questions to find the information.

- Have a pair read the example conversation aloud. Make sure everyone understands that the information Student A asks for is in Student B's text, and vice versa.
- Have students complete the activity in pairs. Circulate and help as needed.
- ⏱ Show the movie *A Beautiful Mind* in class (or have students watch it at home). Have them write a letter (or email) about the film. Point out that the message should include the title, the actors' names, the setting, a brief summary of the story, and an opinion about the film. Encourage students to use different types of adjective clauses and phrases. Students can use the opening reading as a model for their writing.

Exercise 10: Group Discussion

- Have students read the chart. Explain any unfamiliar vocabulary. If students are familiar with American movies, brainstorm examples of movies that have each of the ratings.
- Have students complete the questionnaire individually. Then have them compare answers in groups. Circulate, helping as needed.
- Call on students from each group to share their ideas with the class.
- ⏱ Have students discuss the following questions in pairs or small groups:
  1. Is there a movie rating system in your home country?
  2. If so, how does it compare to the system in the United States? If not, do you think there should be one? Why or why not?

Exercise 11: Picture Discussion

A

- Have students look at the picture and briefly describe what they see. Write key words and phrases they use on the board.
- Go over the examples. Point out the use of adjective clauses and phrases in the example. Have students work in pairs to discuss the picture. Encourage them to use adjective clauses or phrases whenever possible.

- ⏱ Have students work in pairs. Using the picture, have Student A describe a person (or group of people) to Student B. Student B locates that person in the picture and then describes someone else for Student A to locate. For example:
  - S1: I'm looking at someone who has just stepped on a piece of chewing gum.
  - S2: (points to woman in the aisle in lower right-hand corner) I'm looking at someone throwing something on the floor.

B

- Have students read the questions and the example.
- Have students discuss the questions as a class. Encourage them to give reasons for their opinions and ask follow-up questions.
- **Note:** If you have a large class, as a variation you may want to have students discuss the questions in groups.

Exercise 12: Writing

A

- Read the instructions. Have students look at the example and identify the topic sentence. Brainstorm other movies (old or recent) that students might want to review.
- Have students write their reviews, either in class or as homework.
- **Note:** As a variation, you may want to have students bring in a movie review they read in a newspaper, magazine, or online. Have students analyze the structure of the review and then work in pairs to discuss what they noted. Then have students write their own reviews.

B

- Have students use the Editing Checklist to revise and rewrite as needed. As an alternative, have them work in pairs to correct each other's work.
- ⏱ Have students post their papers in the classroom so the class can read them. You can also publish them together in a booklet or on a class website.

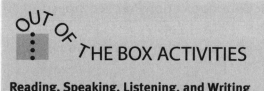

OUT OF THE BOX ACTIVITIES

Reading, Speaking, Listening, and Writing

- Bring in film reviews (or have students bring them in) of big movie hits. Have students work in groups. Give each group a review for students to read. (**Note:** You may want to have all groups work with photocopies of the same review.)
- Have students imagine that the sequel to the movie has been released and turned out to be an even more successful film. Have students decide on the setting, plot, main actors, and director of the sequel.
- Have each person in the group write his or her own imaginary review, using the reviews they read as a model. Remind students to complete the reviews with their own ideas and make any changes they think are necessary. Then have groups reconvene and share their reviews with each other.

Speaking and Listening

- Bring in (or have students bring in) photos that suggest an event that has just happened or is about to happen. Each photo should include several people.
- Give each student a photo. Then have students work in pairs to describe the people and events to each other. Remind students to use adjective clauses and phrases in their descriptions.
- Call on a few students to show their photos and share their descriptions with the class.

Go to **www.myfocusongrammarlab.com** for additional listening, pronunciation, speaking, and writing practice.

Note:
- See the *Focus on Grammar Workbook* for additional in-class or homework grammar practice.

Unit 13 Review (page 228)

Have students complete the Review and check their answers on Student Book page UR-2. Review or assign additional material as needed.

Go to **www.myfocusongrammarlab.com** for the Unit Achievement Test.

From Grammar to Writing (pages 229–232)

See the general suggestions for From Grammar to Writing on page 9.

Go to **www.myfocusongrammarlab.com** for an additional From Grammar to Writing Assignment, Part Review, and Part Post-Test.

PART VI OVERVIEW

PASSIVE VOICE

UNIT	GRAMMAR FOCUS	THEME
14	The Passive: Review and Expansion	Unsolved Mysteries
15	The Passive to Describe Situations and to Report Opinions	Legends and Myths

Go to **www.myfocusongrammarlab.com** for the Part and Unit Tests.

Note: PowerPoint® grammar presentations, test-generating software, and reproducible Part and Unit Tests are on the *Teacher's Resource Disc*.

UNIT 14 OVERVIEW

Grammar: THE PASSIVE: REVIEW AND EXPANSION

Unit 14 focuses on the forms, meanings, and uses of the passive voice and the passive causative.

- We say that the subject of a passive voice sentence is acted upon because the object in an active voice sentence most commonly becomes the subject in the passive voice. The subject of an active sentence becomes the agent or disappears in a passive sentence. Only transitive verbs, those that can be followed by an object, can have a passive form.

- Passive sentences can occur in past, present, or future form. They are formed with *be* + a past participle. To make a passive sentence negative, place *not* after the first verb word. Use the present and past progressive passive to show that an action is not finished at a certain time.

- Use the passive voice (a) when you don't know who performed the action or it is not important to know who performed the action, (b) when you want to avoid mentioning the agent, or (c) when you want to focus on the receiver or the result rather than the agent.

- Use a *by* phrase with the passive voice (a) to introduce new information about the agent, (b) to give someone credit for something, or (c) when the agent is surprising. Omit the *by* phrase if you feel it is unnecessary or undesirable to mention the agent.

- An indirect object may sometimes be the subject of a passive sentence.

- We often use modals and modal-like auxiliaries in the passive voice. To form the present passive with a modal, use the modal + *be* + past participle. To form the past passive with a modal, use the modal + *have been* + past participle.

- Use *have got, had better, had to, must, ought to,* and *should* in passive sentences to express advisability, necessity, and obligation. Use *can* and *could* to express present and past ability. Use *will* and *be going to* to talk about future events. Use *can't, could, may,* and *might* to talk about possibility or impossibility in the future.

- The *get* passive is formed with *get* and is more informal than the passive with *be*. It is used in conversation and informal writing. The *get* passive can be used only with action verbs.

- The passive causative is formed with *have* or *get* + object + past participle. There is little difference in meaning between these two forms. The passive causative is used in past, present, and future and with modals. Use the passive causative to talk about services or activities that people arrange for someone to do. Although the passive causative can occur with a *by* phrase, this phrase is often omitted. Use a *by* phrase only when it is necessary to mention the agent.

Theme: UNSOLVED MYSTERIES

Unit 14 focuses on language that is used to talk about unsolved criminal mysteries.

Step 1: Grammar in Context (pages 234–236)

See the general suggestions for Grammar in Context on page 1.

Before You Read

- Have students work in groups to discuss the questions, or discuss them as a class. If students discuss the questions in groups, have students from each group share their ideas with the class.
- You may want to have students talk about famous unsolved mysteries or crimes in their home countries.

Read

- You may want to discuss these words and their meanings:

parachute   a piece of equipment fastened to the back of people who jump out of airplanes which makes them fall slowly and safely to the ground

proceed   to move in a particular direction

cockpit   the part of an airplane in which the pilot sits

- Write these questions on the board:
  1. Cooper threatened to blow up the plane unless he received three things. What were they? *($200,000, four parachutes, and a plane that would fly to Mexico)*
  2. What did the bills look like after eight and a half years of being buried in the ground? *(They had decayed so much that only the picture and serial numbers were visible.)*
  3. Why do people think Cooper could not have survived the jump? *(a combination of the weather conditions and the impact of his fall: the temperature was too cold—7 degrees below zero—and he wore no survival gear)*
  4. Why did Cooper become a legend? *(His story has been told in books, articles, and a movie, and it is believed that he got away with the crime.)*

- Establish a purpose for reading. Call on several different students to read each of the questions aloud. Remind students to think about these questions as they read and listen to the text.
- Have students read the text, or play the audio and have students follow along in their books. Have students discuss the questions in pairs or groups of three. Then go over the answers as a class.

After You Read

A. Vocabulary

- Have students complete the exercise individually. Then have them compare answers in pairs.
- Go over the answers as a class.

- ⏱ Point out that in this type of exercise all the answer choices are the same part of speech as the target word. In this case, looking at the context (words and sentences around the target word) can help to determine meaning. One way to do this is to replace the target word in the sentence with the word choice that they think is correct. If the sentence makes sense, it is likely that the choice is correct.

B. Comprehension

- Have students read the statements. You may want to explain the meaning of *denominations* in Item 3.
- Have students complete the exercise individually. Then have them work in pairs to check answers.
- Have different students write their corrected false statements on the board and indicate where in the text they found the information that prompted their correction.

Go to **www.myfocusongrammarlab.com** for an additional reading, and for reading and vocabulary practice.

Step 2: Grammar Presentation (pages 237–240)

See the general suggestions for Grammar Presentation on page 2.

Grammar Charts

- Have students look at the first two sections of the chart that show the transformation of active voice to passive voice. Have students explain the change in verb forms for the two example sentences. (Example: Cooper hijacked the plane—*The verb is simple past. The plane was hijacked (by Cooper)—The verb becomes simple past* be + *past participle.*)
- Write this sentence on the board:
  Someone makes a movie about Cooper and this mysterious crime.
- Have students work in pairs or small groups to examine the rest of the grammar charts. Have them look at the above sentence and change it from active voice to each of the passive forms shown in the charts. For example:
  A movie is made about Cooper and this mysterious crime.
  A movie is being made about Cooper and his mysterious crime.

Grammar Notes

Note 1

- You may want to review transitive and intransitive verbs. Point out that in a passive-voice sentence, it is the object from the active-voice sentence that becomes the subject. Therefore, if a verb is intransitive and cannot take an object, a transformation to the passive voice is impossible.

Note 2

- Emphasize that all passive-voice sentences (except the passive causative and passives with *get*) include some form of *be*. Then have students look back at the example sentences in the grammar charts (except the last one), circle any forms of *be*, and then identify them. (Example: *The plane was hijacked by Cooper—* was *is the form of* be *in the simple past*.)
- Have students identify the tense and aspect of the verbs used in the examples. Elicit transformations of a few of them into the active voice using *they*. Have students identify the tense and aspect, making sure that they see the parallel, for example:
Cooper <u>has</u> not <u>been</u> caught. *(present perfect)*
They <u>have</u> not <u>caught</u> Cooper. *(present perfect)*
- Have students work in pairs to practice transforming active sentences into passive ones. Have them look through the reading for ideas. (Example: *Cooper ordered the flight attendant to go to the cockpit. = The flight attendant was ordered to go to the cockpit by Cooper.*)

Note 3

- Point out that in most cases, the active voice is considered stronger than the passive, and it is generally preferred. However, there are occasions when the passive is needed.
- Go over the three categories listed in the note. Perhaps the most interesting of these is the second: to avoid mentioning the performer when it is inappropriate to do so. (Example: *We were told not to use the photocopy machine for personal use— The speaker doesn't want to say who told them this.*)

Note 4

- Students may find Note 4 contradictory. If so, ask them which of the uses of the passive pointed out in Note 3 apply here. *(c)* Point out that *by* phrases occur quite naturally in many contexts: books or plays *written by* an author, music *sung / written / composed by* someone, paintings *painted by* an artist, inventions *invented by* a person, and so on.

- ⏱ In small groups, have students make two lists. One list is names of inventions, paintings, book titles, song titles, and so on. The other list is the *by* phrase that goes with each item on the name list. Have groups cut the names and the *by* phrases into individual strips, mix them up, and place them in an envelope. Have groups exchange envelopes, place the strips on a flat surface, and then match the title items with the appropriate *by* phrases. (Examples: *The light bulb was invented by Thomas Edison.* Don Quixote *was written by Cervantes.*)

Note 5

- Review the distinction between direct and indirect objects. Tell students that a direct object receives the action of the verb. Have students read the first example sentence *(The police arrested the suspect.)*. Ask: "Who did the police arrest?" *(They arrested the suspect.)* Explain that for this reason, *suspect* is the direct object of the verb. Explain that an indirect object shows to whom / what or for whom / what the action occurred. Have students read the second example sentence *(The FBI gave Cooper the money)*. Ask: "What did the FBI give?" *(the money)* "To whom did they give the money?" *(Cooper)* "What is the direct object?" *(money)* "What is the indirect object?" *(Cooper)*
- Place an object on each of several students' desks when students are out of the room. When they return, have students make sentences in the active voice and identify the parts of the sentence:

             indirect   *direct*
subject   *object*   *object*
Someone gave Maria a set of keys.

             indirect   *direct*
subject   *object*   *object*
Someone gave Jaime a cell phone.

Then have students transform each sentence into two types of passive-voice sentences. For example:

Maria was given a set   Jaime was given a
  of keys.   cell phone.
A set of keys was given   A cell phone was
  to Maria.   given to Jaime.

- Make sure students notice where those sentence parts went from the first set of sentences to the second set. (Maria, *the indirect object, became the subject in the first sentence. A set of keys, the direct object, became the subject in the second one.*)

Note 6

- Have students work in small groups to test which modals can be used in each of the example sentences in the note. Write these categories on the board: advisability, obligation, necessity, ability, certainty, possibility / impossibility.
- Have each group choose a different example sentence from the note. Have them rewrite the sentence to express each of the categories on the board. For example:
  The criminal should be arrested. *(advisability)*
  The criminal must be arrested. *(obligation, necessity)*
  The criminal has got to be arrested. *(obligation, necessity)*
  The criminal had better be arrested. *(obligation, necessity)*
  The criminal can be arrested. *(ability)*
  The criminal might (or may) be arrested. *(possibility)*
  The criminal is going to be arrested. *(future certainty)*
- Have students write some of their sentences on the board. As a class, decide which ones could be expressed in the past and write those forms.

Note 7

- Point out that the *get* passive is often used to emphasize action and to suggest that someone or something is subjected to another force.
- Do a quick oral drill, calling on different students to substitute the appropriate form of *get* for *be* in the example sentences in Note 6. For example: *The criminal got arrested.*

Note 8

- Point out that passive causatives express the idea that someone causes something to happen. The example "You should have your car serviced" is similar in meaning to "Someone should service your car." Have students change the remaining examples to sentences with active verbs. *(Someone just dry-cleaned my suit. Someone washed the windows. Someone tunes up my car twice a year. Someone is going to cut her hair.)*

Note 9

- Conduct a drill with the example sentences in Notes 8 and 9. Sit in a circle with students. Begin by substituting *get* for *have*. Address one student, saying, for example: *Tomiko, you should get your car serviced.* Tomiko addresses another student with her sentence: *José, I just had my car serviced. You should get your car washed.* Continue around the circle, alternating between *get* and *have*.
- When students finish this round, continue the drill, this time transforming the sentences to reflect a different time period. For example, *We had the windows washed* becomes *We are going to have the windows washed*.
- Have students work in pairs or small groups to personalize the practice by asking each other questions such as the following:
  S1: Where do you get your car repaired?
  S2: I get it repaired at a garage near my office. Do you cut your own hair or have it cut?
  S1: I don't have it cut. I cut it myself.

🕐 **Identify the Grammar:** Have students identify the grammar in the opening reading on pages 234–235. For example:
  Some crimes never **get solved**, and the case of Dan Cooper is one that **hasn't been**.
  Late in November of 1971, on a short flight between Portland and Seattle, a flight attendant **was handed** a note . . .
  The plane proceeded to Seattle with none of the other passengers even aware it **was being hijacked**.
  They got off the plane, and "Cooper" got what he was demanding: $200,000, all in $20 bills that **had been photocopied** by FBI agents so they **could** easily **be identified**.

Go to **www.myfocusongrammarlab.com** for grammar charts and notes.

Step 3: Focused Practice (pages 240–244)

See the general suggestions for Focused Practice on page 4.

Exercise 1: Discover the Grammar

- Have students complete the exercise and compare their answers in small groups.
- Call on students from different groups to share their answers with the class. Discuss and clarify any discrepancies in answers among groups.

Exercise 2: Transitive / Intransitive

- Have students complete the exercise. Go over the answers as a class.

- ⏱ In pairs, have students transform the passive-voice sentences into active-voice sentences. Have different students write their transformed sentences on the board. Then go over them as a class.

Exercise 3: Progressive Passives
- Have students complete the exercise. Then have them work in pairs to check answers.
- Have different students share their answers with the class. As students share, have them identify the clues in the text that helped them decide whether to use the present or past progressive passive.

Exercise 4: Various Passives
- You may want to point out and discuss the following vocabulary items:

sight	to see something from a long distance away or for a short time
in order	as it should be
perplexing	puzzling and difficult to understand

- Have students complete the exercise. Go over the answers as a class.
- ⏱ Have students take turns reading the article aloud in pairs.

Exercise 5: Passive Causative

A
- Have students complete the exercise. Have them work in pairs to check their answers.
- Circulate as students are working together, noting any particular items that were problematic for students. Go over the problematic items as a class. Have students explain why each answer is correct.

B
- Have students complete the exercise individually and work in groups to check answers.
- Have students from each group share their answers with the class. Have students explain why each answer is correct.
- ⏱ Have students practice reading the text aloud in groups.

Exercise 6: Editing
- You may want to write the following words and their definitions on the board:

extraterrestrial	a living creature that people think may live on another planet
speculation	the act of guessing without knowing all the facts about something

- Have students complete the exercise. Have them work in pairs to check their answers. Then call on students to explain each error and correction.

Go to **www.myfocusongrammarlab.com** for additional grammar practice.

Step 4: Communication Practice (pages 245–248)

See the general suggestions for Communication Practice on page 5.

Exercise 7: Listening

A
- Establish a purpose for listening. Have students read the question. Remind students to think about the question as they listen. Ask: "What will you be listening for—a main idea or details " (*main idea*)
- You may also want to write the following words on the board and discuss their meanings:

sustain	to experience an injury, loss, or defeat
massive	large in comparison to what is typical or usual

- Play the audio and have students complete the exercise. Replay as needed. Go over the answers as a class.

B
- Establish a purpose for listening. Have students read through the questions. Remind students to think about these questions as they listen. Ask: "What will you be listening for—a main idea or details?" (*details*)
- Play the audio and have students complete the exercise. Go over the answers as a class.
- **Note:** Since students' ability to understand this listening exercise and to answer the questions correctly depends on their understanding of the meaning conveyed by the passive voice, it provides an excellent opportunity for them to understand the importance of learning the grammatical content of this unit. It is also an excellent opportunity for you to assess their level of mastery of it. You may want to play the audio another time to give students the opportunity to comprehend what they are hearing.

Exercise 8: Pronunciation

A

- Have students read and listen to the Pronunciation Note. Tell students to listen as you say the two example sentences, pronouncing the verb in the contracted form. For example: *The subject's been questioned. / The subject's being questioned.*
- Have students listen again and raise their hands if they think the action has already happened. Repeat the sentences randomly several times. Go over the correct answer for each sentence.

B

- Play the audio and have students complete the exercise.
- Go over the answers as a class. You may want to play the audio again to clarify any discrepancies in students' answers.

C

- Circulate as pairs practice saying the lines. Make corrections as needed.

Exercise 9: Information Gap

- Divide students into pairs with one person as Student A and the other Student B. Have Student B turn to page 248. Have students look at the list of partial sentences. Explain that their partner has the other half of the sentences. They should read their halves to each other to put together the sentences.
- If needed, model the activity with a student to show how the first sentence is formed.
- Have students complete the activity in pairs. Circulate and help as needed. Go over the identity of the mystery object with the class (*a sandwich*).
- ⏱ In small groups, have students research different kinds of sandwiches in the United States and other countries. Examples: *cheese steak, po'boy, panino* (Italy); *bahn mi* (Vietnam). Have groups describe the sandwich using passive forms. What is it called? Where was it first created? When was it created? How is it made?

Exercise 10: Survey and Discussion

A

- Have students read the questions. If needed, explain the meanings of the following words:
  juvenile   young; in some countries, after a certain age, a person can no longer be considered a juvenile

indict   to formally charge someone with a crime
incarcerate   to put someone in prison or jail

- Have students complete the survey with their own opinions. Then have them discuss the questions in groups. Circulate, helping as needed. Encourage students to give reasons for their opinions.

B

- Call on students from each group to share their ideas with the class.
- ⏱ Have students use the survey to interview two or three people from outside of the classroom. Then have them discuss their findings in small groups.

Exercise 11: Picture Discussion

A

- Have students look at the photos and describe what they see. Write any key vocabulary words on the board.
- Have students read the questions and go over the example. Divide the class into groups and have them discuss. Circulate, helping as needed.

B

- Have each group compare answers with another group.
- Call on students from each group to share ideas with the class.

Exercise 12: Writing

A

- Read the instructions and have students read the example.
- Point out that this is essentially a cause-effect essay. In it, students will describe an effect (the mysterious incident) and then speculate about possible causes. Explain that in this essay students will describe the incident in the first paragraph. In the next paragraphs, they will offer possible causes, and the final paragraph will be a summary paragraph or conclusion.
- Have students write their essays, either in class or as homework.

B

- Have students use the Editing Checklist to revise and rewrite as needed.
- **Note:** As an alternative, have students use the checklist to correct each other's work in pairs.

OUT OF THE BOX ACTIVITIES

Reading, Listening, and Speaking

- Have students do an Internet search for *unsolved mysteries*. Have each student choose one mystery to research and make notes about. Some well-known unsolved mysteries are "The Babushka Lady," "The Voynich Manuscript," and "The Taos Hum."
- Have students work in pairs to tell each other about their mysteries. Remind students to focus on use of the passive voice in their conversations.

Writing, Reading, Speaking, and Listening

- Have students use Part B of Exercise 5 on Student Book pages 243–244 as a model to write a short narrative about an unpredictable day of their own, either real or imagined. Remind them to focus on the passive and the passive causative in their writing.
- Have students work in pairs, exchange papers, and correct each other's work using the Editing Checklist on page 248. Have students share their feedback with each other orally and revise their narratives.
- Have students form new pairs and read their revised papers to each other. Encourage them to ask questions about the events of the narrative and then guess whether it was real or imagined.

Go to **www.myfocusongrammarlab.com** for additional listening, pronunciation, speaking, and writing practice.

Note:

- See the *Focus on Grammar Workbook* for additional in-class or homework grammar practice.

Unit 14 Review (page 249)

Have students complete the Review and check their answers on Student Book page UR-2. Review or assign additional material as needed.

Go to **www.myfocusongrammarlab.com** for the Unit Achievement Test.

Grammar: THE PASSIVE TO DESCRIBE SITUATIONS AND TO REPORT OPINIONS

Unit 15 focuses on the forms, meanings, and uses of the stative passive and the passive in clauses with *it* and phrases with *to*.

- Stative passives are common in English. They can be used to describe states or situations. Unlike other passive-voice sentences, most stative passives do not have a corresponding active-voice sentence and usually do not include a *by* phrase. In the stative passive, there is normally no action taking place.
- The stative passive is formed with *be* and a past participle. The past participle functions as an adjective and is often followed by a prepositional phrase.
- Passive constructions are commonly used to report ideas, beliefs, and opinions. They often occur in the form *it* + *be* + past participle + *that* clause. This type of passive sentence does have a corresponding active-voice sentence. These structures can be used only with verbs that can be followed by a *that* clause. A *by* phrase in these types of passives is optional.
- Another passive construction that is used to report ideas, beliefs, or opinions is subject + *be* + past participle + *to* phrase.
- Passives with *that* clauses or *to* phrases (infinitive phrases) are often used in academic discourse and reporting the news. They provide a more objective impression by creating "distance" between the author and the idea.

Theme: LEGENDS AND MYTHS

Unit 15 focuses on language that is used to talk about legends and myths in different societies.

Step 1: Grammar in Context (pages 250–252)

See the general suggestions for Grammar in Context on page 1.

Before You Read

- Have pairs discuss the questions. Call on a few students to share their ideas with the class.

Read

- Write these questions on the board (or prepare them as a handout):
  1. Where do the Nacirema live? *(between Mexico and Canada)*
  2. What do the Nacirema spend a great deal of time on? *(the appearance and health of their bodies)*

3. What are some things the Nacirema do to preserve their bodies and appearance? *(They have a "shrine room" where they use magical creams and use sticks with paste on their teeth.)*

4. What is the author really writing about? *(the importance of appearance and health in American culture; "Nacirema" is "American" spelled backward.)*

- Establish a purpose for reading. Call on different students to read the questions to the class. Remind students to think about the questions as they read and listen to the text.
- Have students read the text. Then have them work in pairs to discuss their answers.

After You Read

A. Vocabulary

- Have students complete the exercise and go over the answers as a class.
- ⏱ Have students choose four or five of the vocabulary words from the exercise and write original sentences for each one. Then have them discuss their sentences in pairs.

B. Comprehension

- Have students complete the exercise individually and compare answers in pairs or small groups.
- Have different students share their answers with the class. Clarify any discrepancies in students' answers. Have students refer to the text to defend their answers if needed.

Go to **www.myfocusongrammarlab.com** for an additional reading, and for reading and vocabulary practice.

Step 2: Grammar Presentation (pages 253–255)

See the general suggestions for Grammar Presentation on page 2.

Grammar Charts

- Divide students into four groups and assign each group one of the grammar charts. (For larger classes, divide the class into more groups and assign each chart to more than one group).
- Have groups read the chart and the examples. Then have them find more examples of the structure in the opening reading on Student Book pages 250–251.
- Call on students from each group to write their examples on the board.

Grammar Notes

Note 1

- Have students read the explanation and the examples.
- Say a few passive sentences and have students say if they are examples of the stative passive. (Examples: *A lot of coffee is grown in South America—not stative passive. The house is located near the beach—stative passive.*)

Note 2

- Point out the examples of stative passives found at the end of this note.
- Have students work in small groups to describe their hometowns and/or countries using these stative passives.

Note 3

- Do a simple substitution drill to help students become comfortable with the *it + be +* past participle + *that* construction. Write this sentence on the board:
  It is assumed that this culture is very old.
- Erase *assumed* and have a student write a replacement verb into the sentence. For example:
  It is <u>thought</u> that this culture is very old.
  This student selects the next student, who substitutes a third verb, and so on, until all the verbs listed in the note have been used.
- Have students look at the examples in the note and notice the way the passive sentence that they practiced has been transformed into an active one *(Scholars assume . . .)*. Have them similarly transform the other example sentences into active ones.

Note 4

- Have students look at the first two examples and notice how the first sentence has been transformed from the active into the passive voice in the second sentence. Have them do the same for the other examples in the note, using *people* as a subject.
- Point out the note about the use of *consider*. Ask: "Are there any examples of the passive in this note where *consider* could be used in place of the existing verb?" *(all of them)* Ask: "Are there are any sentences where the infinitive phrase could be dropped after *consider*?" *(He is <u>considered</u> [to be] the author.)*
- Point out the note about the need to follow *regard* by *as*. Have students substitute *regard* in as many of the examples in Note 4 as possible and write the resulting sentences. *(He is regarded as the author. Native Americans are regarded as the real discoverers.)*

Note 5
- If students need more practice using passives with *that* clauses or infinitive phrases, have them transform the example sentences into different passive constructions.
- **Note:** You may want to point out that knowing when to use passive constructions is as important as knowing how to form them and the information presented in this note about achieving formality and distance through the use of these particular grammatical forms will be valuable to students in their academic work. You might also want to point out that an element of good writing is sentence variety. Even in situations that call for the use of the passive, students will need to vary their writing to include active sentences as well; in fact, as a rule they will want to use considerably more active than passive sentences in their writing.

🕐 **Identify the Grammar:** Have students identify the grammar in the opening reading on pages 250–251. For example:

The territory of the Nacirema **is located** between the Canadian Cree and the Tarahumara of Mexico.

On the southeast their territory **is bordered** by the Caribbean.

In Nacirema culture the body **is** generally **believed** to be ugly and likely to decay.

Go to **www.myfocusongrammarlab.com** for grammar charts and notes.

Step 3: Focused Practice (pages 256–260)

See the general suggestions for Focused Practice on page 4.

Exercise 1: Discover the Grammar

A
- Have students complete the exercise individually.
- Go over the answers as a class.

B
- Have students complete the exercise individually and compare answers in small groups. Then have groups rewrite the sentences with a *by* phrase or in the active voice if possible.
- Have different groups share and explain their sentences to the class.

Exercise 2: Stative Passives
- Have students complete the exercise individually and compare answers in groups. Then go over the answers as a class.

- 🕐 Have students work in pairs to write three to five more sentences based on the map. Then have pairs share their sentences with the class.

Exercise 3: Beliefs / Thoughts / Opinions

A
- Have students complete this part individually and compare answers in groups. Then have the groups share their answers with the class.

B
- Have different students write their sentences on the board and discuss them as a class.

Exercise 4: Personal Inventory
- Have students read the instructions, the words in the box, and the example. Brainstorm some other sentences that could be written using the words in the box and the target grammar.
- Have students write their sentences individually. Circulate, helping as needed. Then have them work in groups to share their sentences.
- 🕐 Have students from different groups share with the class information about someone else in the group by changing the passive structure in that person's sentence. For example:

S1 writes: Jorge Amado **is considered** one of the greatest Brazilian writers.

S2 reports: In Paolo's country, Jorge Amado **is regarded as** one of the greatest Brazilian writers.

Exercise 5: Editing
- Have different students write their corrected sentences on the board. Then have students explain their corrections to the class.
- Have students work in pairs to practice reading the corrected text aloud to each other.

Go to **www.myfocusongrammarlab.com** for additional grammar practice.

Step 4: Communication Practice (pages 261–264)

See the general suggestions for Communication Practice on page 5.

Exercise 6: Listening

A
- Establish a purpose for listening. Have students read the question. Remind them to think about the question as they listen.

- Play the audio and allow students time to answer the question. Go over the answer as a class.
- (🕐) Have students note down any information that they recall from the listening in their notebooks.

B
- Have students read the statements. Remind them to think about them as they listen. Play the audio, pausing as needed so students can mark their answers.
- Go over the answers as a class. You may want to play the audio again to clarify any discrepancies in students' answers.
- (🕐) Have students look at the information they noted after the first listening. It is likely that they will not have remembered too much. If so, ask students why they think this is true. *(In Part A, they are listening for a very specific piece of information that was given toward the end of the listening. For this reason, they may have missed hearing much of the other information.)*

Exercise 7: Pronunciation

A
- Have students read and listen to the Pronunciation Note.
- Say the example sentences and have the students watch how your lips change as each vowel is pronounced. Then say the examples again and have students repeat.

B
- Play the audio and have students complete the exercise.
- Go over the answers as a class. You may want to play the audio again to clarify any discrepancies in students' answers.

C
- Circulate as pairs practice saying the sentences. Make corrections as needed.

Exercise 8: Game
- Read the instructions and go over the example with students.
- Divide the class into teams and have them work together to write the questions. Then have students find the answers to the questions. (Many of the answers can be found in Exercises 2, 3, and 5 on Student Book pages 257–258 and 260.) You may want to assign this portion as homework, or you can provide each team with the following answers:

Team A
1. Which island is composed of the nations of Haiti and the Dominican Republic? *(Hispaniola)*
2. Which Central American country is bordered by Panama and Nicaragua? *(Costa Rica)*
3. Which people are considered by some to be descendants of Atlanteans? *(the Basques)*
4. Which legendary creature is thought to live in the Himalayas? *(the yeti, or Abominable Snowman)*
5. Which individual is claimed to be the assassin of U.S. President John F. Kennedy? *(Lee Harvey Oswald)*
6. Which individuals are regarded as great humanitarians? *(Mother Teresa and Albert Schweitzer)*

Team B
1. Which Caribbean nation is composed of many islands? *(The Bahamas)*
2. Which Caribbean nation is located about 90 miles south of Florida? *(Cuba)*
3. Which forest creature is said to live in the Pacific Northwest? *(Bigfoot)*
4. Which lost continent is thought to be located in the Atlantic Ocean? *(Atlantis)*
5. What planet was thought to be the center of the universe before Copernicus? *(the earth)*
6. Which presidents are regarded by many as the greatest American presidents? *(George Washington and Abraham Lincoln)*

- Have students play the trivia game. Keep score on the board. If your class is large, you might want to have students work in groups of four or six. Then divide each of those groups into two teams.

Exercise 9: Picture Discussion

A
- Have students look at the pictures. Brainstorm what students know about each person. Write key words on the board.
- Go over the instructions and the example. Elicit another sentence or two about the pictures that use passive constructions.
- Have students continue describing the pictures in groups. Call on groups to share their sentences with the class.

B
- Have students read the questions and the example.
- Have students discuss the questions in groups. Encourage students to take notes during their discussion.

- Call on students from each group to share their ideas with the class.

Exercise 10: Writing

A

- Have students read the instructions and the example.
- Review the features of a summary. (*It should be shorter than the original and written in the students' own words.*)
- Brainstorm some legends or myths students could write about. Then have students write their summaries, either in class or as homework.

B

- Have students use the Editing Checklist to revise and rewrite as needed.
- **Note:** As an alternative, have students work in pairs to correct each other's work using the checklist.

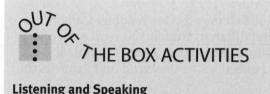

OUT OF THE BOX ACTIVITIES

Listening and Speaking

- Have students work in small groups to discuss the following questions:
  1. What was the author's purpose in writing the opening reading on Student Book pages 250–251? How do you know?
  2. What evidence does the author provide to support his or her criticism of American ideas about appearance and health? Do you agree or disagree with the author's criticism? Why or why not?
- Have groups share their ideas with the class.

Listening, Speaking, Writing, and Reading

- Bring in information about the Nazca lines in Peru from different sources—for example, books about archaeological mysteries, encyclopedias, travel magazines, or websites.
- Have students work in small groups. Hand out the material and have students read about this mystery of pre-Colombian archaeology. Have students discuss what they read and express their views about the Nazca lines.
- Have each group share information with the class. Remind students to use the passive to describe situations and report opinions.

Go to **www.myfocusongrammarlab.com** for additional listening, pronunciation, speaking, and writing practice.

Note:

- See the *Focus on Grammar Workbook* for additional in-class or homework grammar practice.

Unit 15 Review (page 265)

Have students complete the Review and check their answers on Student Book page UR-2. Review or assign additional material as needed.

Go to **www.myfocusongrammarlab.com** for the Unit Achievement Test.

From Grammar to Writing (pages 266–268)

See the general suggestions for From Grammar to Writing on page 9.

Go to **www.myfocusongrammarlab.com** for an additional From Grammar to Writing Assignment, Part Review, and Part Post-Test.

PART VII OVERVIEW

GERUNDS AND INFINITIVES

UNIT	GRAMMAR FOCUS	THEME
16	Gerunds	Friendship
17	Infinitives	Procrastination

Go to **www.myfocusongrammarlab.com** for the Part and Unit Tests.

Note: PowerPoint® grammar presentations, test-generating software, and reproducible Part and Unit Tests are on the *Teacher's Resource Disc.*

Grammar: GERUNDS

Unit 16 focuses on the meanings and uses of gerunds.

- A gerund is a noun made from a verb by adding -ing to the base form of the verb. Gerunds and gerund phrases perform the same functions as nouns: subjects, objects, or complements in sentences. Gerunds can also be objects of prepositions. To make a negative statement with a gerund, add *not* before the gerund.

- Gerunds function as objects after many verbs and verb phrases in English. Some of these are *avoid, consider, enjoy, keep,* and *mind.*

- In writing and formal speaking, use a possessive noun or pronoun before a gerund to show possession. In informal speech, it is acceptable to use a noun or object pronoun before a gerund to show possession.

- Gerunds can occur in simple or past form. We use simple gerunds to make generalizations. To form a past gerund, use *having* + a past participle. Past gerunds indicate an action that occurred before the main verb of the sentence. Past gerunds are also used to emphasize a difference in time between two actions.

- Gerunds can also occur in the passive form. For present passive gerunds, use *being* + past participle. For past passive gerunds, use *having been* + past participle.

Theme: FRIENDSHIP

Unit 16 focuses on language that is used to talk about friendship and the various types of friendships one experiences in life.

Step 1: Grammar in Context (pages 270–272)

See the general suggestions for Grammar in Context on page 1.

Before You Read

- Have students discuss the first question in pairs. Brainstorm a list of important qualities and traits in friendship.
- Have students discuss the second question in pairs. Brainstorm a list of kinds of friends. Write these words on the board.

Read

- You may want to discuss the following words and definitions as a class:

  long since   if something has "long since" happened, it happened a long time ago

  awfully   very

- Write the following questions on the board:
  1. Why doesn't the author like the traditional description of friends as either true or false? *(He recognizes at least six types.)*
  2. What are the author's six types of friends? *(convenience friends, special-interest friends, long-term friends, cross-generational friends, part-of-a-couple friends, "best" friends)*
  3. Why is Bill important to the author? *(He is a father figure and mentor.)*
  4. Who are Amanda and Gretta? *(the author's wife and the wife of a friend)*
  5. Who is Ken? *(one of the author's two "best" friends)*

- Establish a purpose for reading. Call on several different students to read each of the questions. Remind students to think about these questions as they read and listen to the text.

- Have students read the text, or play the audio and have students follow along in their books. Have students discuss the questions in pairs or groups of three. Call on students from each group or pair to share answers with the class.

After You Read

A. Vocabulary

- Have students complete the vocabulary exercise individually. Then have them compare answers in pairs.
- Circulate as students compare answers.
- Call on students to read their answers aloud.

B. Comprehension

- Have students complete the exercise individually. Then have them compare answers in pairs.
- Call on students from each pair to share their answers with the class. Have each student point out the place in the text where he or she found the answer to the question.

Go to **www.myfocusongrammarlab.com** for an additional reading, and for reading and vocabulary practice.

Step 2: Grammar Presentation (pages 273–275)

See the general suggestions for Grammar Presentation on page 2.

Grammar Charts

- Have students work in seven groups to examine the grammar charts. Have each group look at one section of the charts.
- Have students come up with a rule for forming the gerund in the section of the chart they are examining and find an example sentence of that type in the opening reading (or their own example). **Note:** There is no example of a past passive gerund in this text.
- Have students in each group explain their section to the class.

Grammar Notes

Note 1

- Have students make lists of their hobbies and what they like to do in their free time. Then have them work in groups of four to talk about the items on their lists.
- Have students from each group share their lists. How many of the items on their lists included gerunds?

Note 2

- Have groups from the Note 1 activity divide into pairs.
- Have pairs work together to find out from each other what they enjoy doing and how much time they spend in an average week or month practicing or doing what they like. Then have them ask each other about things they don't mind doing or avoid doing.
- Write the following verbs on the board: *enjoy, spend time, practice, don't mind, avoid.*
- Have the students in each pair report to the class about their partners. Have them use the verbs on the board as they report.

Note 3

- Have students work in pairs to make up new sentences using the verb and preposition combinations shown in the examples.
- Have students from each pair share some of their sentences with the class.

Note 4

- Do a quick oral drill, eliciting substitutions for the nouns, pronouns, and gerunds in the example. For example:
  Pete's dominating . . . (Maria's dominating . . . , her dominating . . . , their dominating . . . , their controlling . . .)
- Elicit a few personal examples from the class using the same sentence frame or a variation.

Note 5

- Have students break down the second example sentence into two sentences and label them to show the sequence:

  1

  I met Jane in my first week of college.

  2

  This helped me throughout my college career.
- Write the example sentence on the board (*Having met Jane . . .*). Then write the following sentence frame on the board:
  Having _____ helped me _____ .
  Give students one to two minutes to write as many sentences using the frame as they can. Then have students share their sentences.
- To practice gerunds in passive constructions, you may want to write structures such as the following on the board and elicit others from the students, encouraging them to use other verbs:
  I hate / dislike being . . . / I hate getting . . .
  I like / enjoy being . . . . / I like getting . . .
- If you want to give students some practice with the past passive, write a frame such as the following on the board:
  Having been (past participle) is one of the best things that ever happened to me.
  Then elicit sentences in which they talk about their personal experiences.

⏱ **Identify the Grammar:** Have students identify the grammar in the opening reading on pages 270–271. For example:

I was having difficulty **finding** a subject for this month's column . . .

I've long since stopped **thinking** in these terms.

I didn't have a way of **getting** to the practices . . .

. . . but Bill supported **my becoming** a writer . . .

Our having gone through difficult experiences has bonded us for life.

Go to **www.myfocusongrammarlab.com** for grammar charts and notes.

Step 3: Focused Practice (pages 275–280)

See the general suggestions for Focused Practice on page 4.

Exercise 1: Discover the Grammar

A

- Have students read the instructions. If needed, have students refer to the Grammar Notes for the definitions of subject, object, object of a preposition, and complement.

- Have students complete the exercise. Go over the answers as a class.

B
- Have students complete the exercise. Then have them compare their answers in small groups.
- Call on students from various groups to share their answers with the class. Discuss and clarify any discrepancies in answers among groups. As students share their answers from Part B, have them explain what function the -*ing* word has if it is not a gerund. (3—kayaking *is a participle (adjective) that describes* club; 6—writing *is a participle (adjective) that describes* class)

Exercise 2: Simple Gerunds

A
- Have students complete the exercise. Go over the answers as a class.
- ⏱ Have students practice the conversation in pairs twice, changing roles after each practice.

B
- Have students complete the exercise individually. Have pairs continue to work together to check their answers.

Exercise 3: Simple / Past Gerunds
- Have students complete the exercise and work in pairs to check their answers. Then go over the answers as a class. Have students explain why they chose a simple or past gerund for each answer.
- ⏱ Have pairs continue to read the text about Martha to each other.

Exercise 4: Active / Passive Gerunds

A
- Have students complete the exercise individually.
- Go over the answers as a class.

B
- Divide the class into pairs. Read the instructions and model the example conversation with a student.
- Have students take turns asking and answering the questions. Circulate and help as needed.
- Call on a few students to share their partners' answers.

Exercise 5: Editing
- You may want to write the following words on the board and discuss their definitions:

jerk	someone who does things that annoy or hurt other people
wilderness	a large area of land that has never been built on or changed by humans
chauffeured	driven by someone

- Have students complete the exercise and work in pairs to check their answers. Then call on students to explain each error and correction.

Go to **www.myfocusongrammarlab.com** for additional grammar practice.

Step 4: Communication Practice (pages 281–283)

See the general suggestions for Communication Practice on page 5.

Exercise 6: Listening

A
- Read the instructions. You may want to remind students that they learned about orienteering in Exercise 2 on Student Book page 277.
- Establish a purpose for listening. Have students read the questions. Remind students to think about the questions as they listen.
- Play the audio and have students complete the exercise. Replay as needed. Go over the answers as a class.

B
- Establish a purpose for listening. Have students read the statements. Remind students to think about these statements as they listen.
- Play the audio and have students complete the exercise.
- Have students work in groups to compare their answers. Then go over the answers as a class. As students share their answers in Part B, have them correct the false statements.
- ⏱ Provide copies of the audioscript. Have students practice reading the conversation in pairs. Have one pair role-play the conversation for the class.

Exercise 7: Pronunciation

A
- Have students read and listen to the Pronunciation Note. Have them repeat the examples several times as you say them.

B
- Have students read the sentences and predict which syllables will be stressed.
- Play the audio, pausing as needed so students can circle their answers.

- Go over the answers as a class. Replay the audio as needed.

C
- Circulate as pairs practice the sentences. Make corrections as needed.

Exercise 8: Personal Inventory

A
- Have students read the phrases that start each item. Read the example aloud and brainstorm other ways to complete the sentence with gerunds. (Examples: *I especially enjoy sleeping in on weekends. I especially enjoy not having to commute so far to my new job.*)
- Have students complete the exercise individually.

B
- Have students compare answers in pairs. Encourage them to add extra information and ask follow-up questions.
- **Note:** If you have a large class or for variation, have two or three pairs work together to complete this part. Have partners report about each other's inventories.

Exercise 9: Group Discussion

A
- Have students read the chart and the ratings scale. Call on a few students to say how they would rate the items in the chart.
- Have students complete the chart individually with their own opinions.

B
- Divide the class into groups of four and have them compare answers. Circulate, helping as needed.
- Call on a student from each group to share their scores and any interesting information they learned. If possible, keep track of scores on the board and calculate an average score for each item.
- ⏱ Have students survey two or three people outside the class. Then have them report their findings in small groups.

Exercise 10: Writing

A
- For this essay, have students use a typical writing process: brainstorm ideas, select, organize, and write.
- For the brainstorming stage in this process, use the following questions to generate ideas and elicit vocabulary:
  Who are four or five of your friends and how did you meet them?
  How long have you known them?

How often do you see or talk to them?
What do you do when you are together?
What are some interesting experiences you have had with them?
- Have students select one person from their brainstorm lists to write about. Have them choose which category of friendship this person fits into. Have them organize their ideas in outline form. Then have them write a first draft, using the outline as a guide.

B
- Have students work in pairs to correct each other's work using the Editing Checklist. Have each student revise and rewrite as needed.
- ⏱ Have students post their papers in the classroom so the class can read them. You can also publish them together in a booklet or on a class website.

OUT OF THE BOX ACTIVITIES

Writing and Reading
- Have students write sentences expressing their own views about friendship. You may want to use the following prompts and have students complete them:
  A good friend should be grateful for _____ .
  Appreciating _____ is very important.
  It is worth _____ .
  _____ with a friend is very enjoyable.
  Not _____ is a big mistake.
  A good friend looks forward to _____ .
  It's important not to get angry at _____ .
  A good friend doesn't mind _____ .
- Have students work in pairs to share their sentences. Then post students' papers around the room and give students time to read them. Have students discuss the sentences in small groups.

Reading, Speaking, and Listening
- Have students bring in a favorite short story about friendship. Have them exchange and read each other's stories.
- Make up some discussion guide questions using the grammar in this unit. Then have pairs discuss their stories with each other.
- You may want to have some students tell the class about the stories they read and share a lesson they learned about friendship from reading the story.

Go to **www.myfocusongrammarlab.com** for additional listening, pronunciation, speaking, and writing practice.

Note:
• See the *Focus on Grammar Workbook* for additional in-class or homework grammar practice.

Unit 16 Review (page 284)

Have students complete the Review and check their answers on Student Book page UR-3. Review or assign additional material as needed.

Go to **www.myfocusongrammarlab.com** for the Unit Achievement Test.

UNIT 17 OVERVIEW

Grammar: INFINITIVES

Unit 17 focuses on the forms, meanings, and uses of infinitives in the simple, past, and passive forms.

• An infinitive is *to* + the base form of the verb. Infinitives often have the same functions as nouns. They can act as subjects, objects, or object complements. To make an infinitive negative, place *not* before *to*.

• Certain verbs are followed only by infinitives. Some verbs are followed by a noun or pronoun + an infinitive. Still other verbs are followed by an optional noun or pronoun + an infinitive, depending on the meaning of the verb.

• Certain adjectives can be followed by infinitives. These adjectives usually describe people rather than things. Some of these adjectives are *afraid, amazed, excited, fortunate, glad, happy, important, likely, proud, reluctant, sorry,* and *willing.*

• When a noun is followed by an infinitive, the infinitive gives information about the noun. A noun + infinitive often expresses advisability or necessity.

• Some verbs can be followed only by infinitives and others only by gerunds. There are some verbs that can be followed by either an infinitive or a gerund. Sometimes there is no change in meaning between the use of an infinitive or a gerund, but at other times there is a significant change in meaning.

• The words *too* and *enough* often occur before infinitives. The use of *too* implies a negative result.

• Infinitives occur in simple, past, and passive forms. Use a simple infinitive to indicate an action in the same general time frame as the action in the main verb. Use a past infinitive to show an action that occurred before the action of the main verb. Passive infinitives can be either present or past forms. Use a past passive infinitive to indicate an action that occurred before the action of the main verb.

Theme: PROCRASTINATION

Unit 17 focuses on language that is used to talk about putting things off until a later time.

Step 1: Grammar in Context (pages 285–287)

See the general suggestions for Grammar in Context on page 1.

Before You Read
• Have students work in groups to discuss the questions.
• Have students from various groups share their answers with the class.

Read
• Write the following questions on the board (or prepare them as a handout):
  1. What is the difference between *procrastinate* and *postpone*? (Postpone *means to reschedule for a later time.* Procrastinate *means to avoid doing something.* Postpone *has a neutral sense.* Procrastinate *has a negative connotation.*)
  2. According to the author, what is the reason for procrastination? *(fear of failure)*
  3. What three principles does Dr. Stevens recommend for his clients who want to stop procrastinating? *(never put things off, do not avoid painful or difficult things, and* carpe diem—*do not put off living)*
• Establish a purpose for reading. Have students read the questions silently. Remind them to think about the questions as they read and listen to the text.
• Have students read or listen to the text. Go over the answers to the questions as a class.

After You Read

A. Vocabulary

- Have students cover the definitions in the right-hand column. Have them read the sentences in the left-hand column and try to guess the meanings of the boldfaced expressions. Then have students work in pairs to discuss what they mean and write a brief definition for each one.
- Have students complete the exercise and go over the answers as a class. Have students compare the definition they wrote with the correct answers.
- ⏱ Remind students that when they guess at meaning by reading the words and sentences around a word or phrase they don't know, they are using *context* to get meaning. One important way to guess at meaning is to understand the function the unknown word has in the sentence. Have students identify the part of speech for each of the definitions on the right.

B. Comprehension

- Have students complete the exercise individually and then compare answers in pairs or groups of three.
- Have various students share their answers and the corrected false statements with the class. Clarify any discrepancies in students' answers. Have students refer to the text to defend their answers if needed.

Go to **www.myfocusongrammarlab.com** for an additional reading, and for reading and vocabulary practice.

Step 2: Grammar Presentation (pages 288–291)

See the general suggestions for Grammar Presentation on page 2.

Grammar Charts

- Have students work in nine groups and assign one section of each chart to each group. Have students study their section of the chart and then write one or two more example sentences that use the structure they are examining.
- Have students from each group write their example sentences on the board and explain their section of the chart. Discuss the examples as a class.
- If you have a class that has fewer that 18 students, have students work in groups and assign each group an appropriate number of sections of the chart to examine.

Grammar Notes

Note 1

- Have students read the explanation and the example sentences. Read the first two and last two example sentences aloud and have students repeat. For each example, ask: "What is the infinitive? Is it a subject, object, or complement?"
- Point out the *it* + infinitive example sentences and have students read them aloud. Brainstorm other adjectives students could use to replace *advisable* and *important* in the examples. Have students say the sentences again and substitute these adjectives.
- The elliptical use of *to* is a very useful structure. Write the following conversation on the board and have students practice it in pairs. Then have them think of other questions that can be answered with the elliptical use of *to*.
  A: Are you going to the party?
  B: I'm planning to.
  A: Why did you take a second job?
  B: I had to. I've got a lot of expenses
- ⏱ Have students look at the opening reading on pages 285–286 and find examples of infinitives as subjects, as objects, as complements, and in *it* + infinitive structures.

Note 2

- Have students read the note. Then have them turn to Appendix 17 on page A-8.
- Have students make one list of the verbs that require a noun or pronoun before the infinitive. Then have them write a list of the verbs after which an object is optional.
- ⏱ Have students work in pairs. Student A, looking at his or her lists, gives Student B, who is not looking at the lists, a verb, and Student B makes a sentence. If it is a verb that does not require a pronoun / noun object, Student B says, "optional." Student A tells Student B if he or she is right. Then have them reverse roles and repeat the activity.

Note 3

- Have students look at the example sentences. For each example, ask: "Which of the common adjectives followed by infinitives listed in the note could replace the ones in the examples?"
- Have students read Appendix 18 on page A-8.

- Do a whole-class oral substitution drill. Have students sit in a circle. Write the example sentence from the Appendix on the board. Call on a student to change the sentence with an adjective from the list. For example: *I was amazed to hear about that.* Continue around the circle, having each student change the sentence with a different adjective from the list.

Note 4
- Have students read the explanation and the examples. Brainstorm other nouns and infinitives that often go together. Write them on the board. (Examples: *a good person to know, a nice / mean thing to say, an important skill to have, a good time to visit*)
- Write the example sentences and others on the board, replacing the nouns with blanks. For example:

  _____ is a good place to spend a vacation.

  _____ is a good trait to have.

  _____ is a good person to know.

  _____ is the best time to visit my hometown.

  When you're in (place), _____ is the thing to do.
- Have students work in pairs to complete the sentences with their own ideas and opinions. Call on a few pairs to share their sentences with the class.

Note 5
- Have students read the explanation and example sentences. Have students say the examples aloud, then have them say the examples again and substitute other verbs from the appropriate list. (Example: *They managed to find new jobs. They decided to find new jobs.*)
- Read the example sentences in (d). Have students work in pairs to explain in their own words how the meaning changes when an infinitive is used instead of a gerund.
- ⏱ Have students look at the additional verbs in Appendices 14 and 15 on page A-7.

Note 6
- Go over the examples and elicit sentences from the class using the same patterns. For fun you might suggest students talk about what they think about English or gerunds and infinitives in particular. For example:

  English is too _____ to _____ .

  There are too many _____ to _____ .

  We learned enough to understand the basics of gerunds and infinitives.

  There's not enough time (for us) to learn it all.

Note 7
- Have students practice past and passive infinitives by adding past participles and completing sentences such as the following:

  When I started high school I expected to have . . .

  The paper is supposed to be . . .

  By the time people are twenty-one years old, they are expected to have . . .

⏱ **Identify the Grammar:** Have students identify the grammar in the opening reading on pages 285–286. For example:

  It's written in longhand, but it **has to be typed**.

  I can't **stop to type** your paper now.

  But Steve, you **have to.**

  Steve, you**'ve got to do** it, or I'll flunk.

  No, Alice, there's not **enough time to do** it now.

Go to **www.myfocusongrammarlab.com** for grammar charts and notes.

Step 3: Focused Practice (pages 292–295)
See the general suggestions for Focused Practice on page 4.

Exercise 1: Discover the Grammar
A
- Read the instructions and go over the example with the class. If needed, review the information about infinitives as subjects, objects, and complements in Note 1 on Student Book page 289.
- Have students complete the exercise individually and compare answers in pairs.
- Go over the answers as a class.

B
- Have students complete the exercise. Go over the answers as a class.
- Have students work in pairs to correct the false statements.
- Have various pairs share and explain their corrected statements to the class.

Exercise 2: Verbs / Nouns / Infinitives
- Have students complete the exercise. Then have them work in pairs to check their answers.
- Have pairs take turns reading the completed text to each other.

Exercise 3: Past Infinitives
- Have students complete the exercise. Go over the answers as a class.

- Have students explain why their answers are correct. For example, *to have cleaned* is correct because the cleaning should have been completed before the parents called their son and daughter.

Exercise 4: Passive Infinitives

A
- Have students complete the exercise.
- Go over the answers as a class.

B
- Model the example conversation with a student. Then model it again with another student, but this time read B's line yourself and add a reason or extra information to the answer.
- Have students take turns asking and answering the questions in pairs. Circulate and help as needed. Encourage students to give reasons, add extra information, and ask follow-up questions.
- Call on a few pairs to share their answers with the class.

Exercise 5: *Too / Enough / Infinitives*
- Have students complete the exercise and work in groups of three to compare answers.
- Have students from each group share their answers with the class.

Exercise 6: Editing
- Read the instructions and go over the example with the class.
- Have students complete the exercise individually. Call on a few students to write their corrected sentences on the board. Have students explain their corrections to the class.
- ⏱ Have students practice reading the text aloud in pairs.

Go to **www.myfocusongrammarlab.com** for additional grammar practice.

Step 4: Communication Practice (pages 296–301)

See the general suggestions for Communication Practice on page 5.

Exercise 7: Listening

A
- You may want to review the following vocabulary with the class:

inmate	someone who is kept in a prison or mental hospital
break-out	an escape from prison
install	to put a piece of equipment somewhere and connect it so that it is ready to be used
head	to go in a particular direction
sheriff	the highest-ranking law officer of a county in the United States

- Establish a purpose for listening. Have students read the question. Remind them to think about the question as they listen.
- Play the audio and allow students time to answer the question. Go over the answer as a class.

B
- Have students read the questions. Remind them to think about them as they listen.
- Play the audio. Students may need some time to write complete sentences. Allow them to concentrate first on the content of their answers by just jotting down key words. Then have them go back and construct full sentences using passive infinitives.
- Go over the answers as a class. You may want to play the audio again to clarify any discrepancies in students' answers.
- ⏱ Provide copies of the audioscript. Have students underline the examples of infinitive structures. Then have them compare their answers in pairs. Review their answers as a class and have students say if each infinitive is a present, past, or passive infinitive.

Exercise 8: Pronunciation

A
- Have students read and listen to the Pronunciation Note.
- Have them repeat the examples several times as you say them.
- Brainstorm other familiar words that use each of the vowel sounds. (Examples: /æ/: *mad, glad;* /ɑ/: *lot, odd;* /ʌ/: *but, hug*)

B
- Read the instructions and play the audio for the first item. Go over the example answer. Replay as needed so students understand why the example answer is correct.

- Play the rest of the audio and have students complete the exercise. Then have them work in pairs to check their answers.
- Go over the answers as a class. Replay the audio to clarify any discrepancies in students' answers.

C
- Have students practice saying the sentences, switching roles after the first practice. Circulate and help as needed.
- ⏱ Have students form new pairs and write a list of three or four words that have the same vowel sound as each of the examples. Have each pair exchange lists with another pair and write an original sentence using each of the words. Have pairs return the lists and give their sentences to the original pair. Then have them take turns reading the sentences to each other.

Exercise 9: Personal Inventory
A
- Read the instructions and have students read the topics for each item. Answer any questions about vocabulary or meaning.
- Brainstorm possible sentences for a few of the topics and write them on the board.
- Have students complete the exercise individually.

B
- Have students discuss their personal responses. Then have them report about each other to the class.
- ⏱ Have students interview people outside the class and note their responses to the items in Part A. Then have them report their findings in pairs.

Exercise 10: Group Discussion
A
- Read the instructions and the example. Have students read the sayings. Answer any questions about vocabulary. You may want to review the following words and their definitions with the class:

err   to make a mistake
divine   coming from God or a god;
           supremely good
seek   to look for something (in this case,
           something spiritual) you need

- Have students complete the exercise individually.
- Have students compare answers in pairs or groups. Call on groups to share their answers with the class.

B
- Divide students into groups of four. Read the instructions and have students read the example aloud.
- Have students discuss each saying. Circulate and help as needed. Call on groups to share their ideas with the class.
- ⏱ Have students share any similar sayings they can think of with the class, either in English or in another language.

Exercise 11: Picture Discussion
- Have students discuss in groups. Call on students from each group to share their ideas with the class.
- ⏱ Have students write a memo in pairs to the person in the picture. The memo should include a list of specific instructions that will determine how the office area is to be organized. Encourage students to use as many different types of infinitive structures as possible. Have pairs read their memos to the class.

Exercise 12: Writing
A
- Review the structure of a narrative essay. Point out that in this writing assignment students will be writing about a specific event.
- Have students read the example. Brainstorm other specific events students could write about.
- Have students write their essays, either in class or as homework.

B
- Have students use the Editing Checklist to revise and rewrite as needed. As an alternative, have them work in pairs to correct each other's work.
- ⏱ Have students post their papers in the classroom so the class can read them. You can also publish them together in a booklet or on a class website.

OUT OF THE BOX ACTIVITIES

Listening, Speaking, and Writing

- Bring in the movie *Dead Poets Society*. Have students watch the part of the film in which Professor John Keating (Robin Williams) encourages his students to live their lives to the fullest and says, among other things, "*Carpe diem*, lads! Seize the day. Make your lives extraordinary!"
- Have students discuss Professor Keating's advice. On the board, write the following questions (or prepare them as a handout):
  1. What does Professor Keating advise his students to do?
  2. What does he advise them not to do?
  3. What are some good reasons to "seize the day"?
  4. How do the students react?
  5. Are Professor Keating's ideas too revolutionary for them to understand? Are they reluctant or willing to follow his advice? Why?
  6. Do you think Professor Keating expects to be admired by his students? What motivates him to talk to his students the way he does?
- Have students work in groups to discuss the questions and then discuss them as a class.
- You may want to have students use the questions as a guide to writing a paragraph about the movie scene they watched. Remind students that they should pay particular attention to their use of infinitives. Have them correct their work using the Editing Checklist on page 301.

Speaking and Listening

- Write the following questions on the board:
  1. Do you think most people procrastinate?
  2. Do you tend to procrastinate?
  3. What kinds of things do you generally put off doing?
  4. What are some of the reasons you (or people you know) procrastinate?
  5. What are the consequences?
  6. Did your (or someone else's) procrastination ever lead to something good? What was it?
  7. Did it ever have a very dramatic consequence? What was it?
- Have students work in groups to discuss the questions on the handout.

Go to **www.myfocusongrammarlab.com** for additional listening, pronunciation, speaking, and writing practice.

Note:
- See the *Focus on Grammar Workbook* for additional in-class or homework grammar practice.

Unit 17 Review (page 302)

Have students complete the Review and check their answers on Student Book page UR-3. Review or assign additional material as needed.

Go to **www.myfocusongrammarlab.com** for the Unit Achievement Test.

From Grammar to Writing (pages 303–306)

See the general suggestions for From Grammar to Writing on page 9.

Go to **www.myfocusongrammarlab.com** for an additional From Grammar to Writing Assignment, Part Review, and Part Post-Test.

PART VIII OVERVIEW

ADVERBS

UNIT	GRAMMAR FOCUS	THEME
18	Adverbs: Sentence, Focus, and Negative	Controversial Issues
19	Adverb Clauses	Sports
20	Adverb and Adverbial Phrases	Compassion
21	Connectors	Memory

Go to **www.myfocusongrammarlab.com** for the Part and Unit Tests.

Note: PowerPoint® grammar presentations, test-generating software, and reproducible Part and Unit Tests are on the *Teacher's Resource Disc*.

Grammar: ADVERBS: SENTENCE, FOCUS, AND NEGATIVE

Unit 18 focuses on the form, meaning, and placement of sentence adverbs, focus adverbs, and negative adverbs.

- Adverbs modify verbs, adjectives, and other adverbs. Some adverbs modify whole sentences. These are called sentence or viewpoint adverbs because they express an opinion or view about a whole sentence. Sentence adverbs can be used in various places in a sentence. If the adverb comes first or last in the sentence, separate it from the rest of the sentence by a comma. Within the sentence, an adverb usually comes after *be* or before other verbs and is not set off by commas.

- Simple adverbs do not modify the whole sentence. They modify single words within the sentence. Some adverbs can be simple or sentence adverbs.

- Focus adverbs focus attention on a particular word or phrase and usually precede the word or phrase they are focused on. Changing the position of a focus adverb will often change the meaning of the sentence.

- Negative adverbs include such words as *hardly, in no way, little, neither, never, not only, only, rarely,* and *seldom.* When a negative adverb begins a sentence or clause, place the verb or auxiliary before the subject to emphasize the negative meaning.

- *Here* and *there* are adverbs that force inversion of the subject when they occur at the beginning of a sentence and the subject is a noun (rather than a pronoun).

Theme: CONTROVERSIAL ISSUES

Unit 18 focuses on language that is used to discuss controversies.

Step 1: Grammar in Context (pages 308–310)

See the general suggestions for Grammar in Context on page 1.

Before You Read

- You may want to discuss the following words and their meanings:

voluntary   done willingly, without being forced or without being paid

combat   organized fighting, especially in a war

- You may also want students to share what they know about the military in their own countries. Is it voluntary or required? Are women allowed in the military? Can they serve in combat positions?

Read

- Write the following questions on the board:
  1. What is Jerry Burns' opinion of the military in general? *(Service should be voluntary. A lot of evil things have been done by military forces. Maybe we shouldn't even have them.)*
  2. Does Burns think that women are too weak to serve? *(No, he doesn't think fighting is feminine.)*
  3. What does Sarah Lopez think about voluntary military service? *(She thinks military service should be required.)*
  4. What is Lopez's reason for supporting required military service? *(It's the only way to ensure fair treatment for all.)*
  5. Does Sarah Lopez believe that combat is feminine? *(Yes.)*

- Establish a purpose for reading. Have various students read each of the questions. Remind students to think about these questions as they read and listen to the text.

- Have students read the text, or play the audio and have students follow along in their books. Then have students discuss the questions in pairs or groups of three. Call on students to share answers with the class.

After You Read

A. Vocabulary

- Have students complete the vocabulary exercise individually. Then have them compare answers in pairs.

- Have pairs work together to take turns asking each other for the definitions of the vocabulary words in the box. For example:
  S1: What does uncensored mean?
  S2: Unrestricted.

B. Comprehension

- Have students complete the exercise individually. Then have them compare answers in pairs.

- Call on students to share their answers with the class. Have each student point out the place in the text where he or she found the answer to the question.

Go to **www.myfocusongrammarlab.com** for an additional reading, and for reading and vocabulary practice.

Step 2: Grammar Presentation (pages 311–313)

See the general suggestions for Grammar Presentation on page 2.

Grammar Charts

- Elicit from students some of the basic facts about adverbs. *(They often end in -ly; they can modify verbs, adjectives, or other adverbs.)* Then point out that this unit provides a more detailed examination of adverbs.

- Have students look at the sentences in the first chart. Ask: "What word does the adverb *clearly* modify in these sentences?" *(In these examples, clearly is a sentence adverb. It modifies the entire sentence rather than a single word.)*

- Have students look at the next two charts. Ask: "Does the placement of adverb in any of the examples change the meaning of these sentences?" *(In the second chart [focus adverbs], in each set of examples, moving the adverb changes the meaning of the initial sentence. The ideas are opposite—or nearly opposite. In the third chart [negative adverbs], the meaning doesn't change.)* Then ask: "What changes in the example sentences in the last chart when the adverb moves?" *(The position of the subject and verb is inverted and an auxiliary verb is added. The meaning does not change, but there is more emphasis on the meaning of the adverb.)*

Grammar Notes

Note 1

- Have students read the note and the examples. Then have students work in groups of four to come up with a clear explanation of the rule in their own words. Call on various groups to share their explanation with the class.

- Have students read the two example sentences that contrast sentence adverbs and simple adverbs. *(Clearly, he is a very good speaker. / He speaks clearly.)* Have students work in groups again to explain the difference in their own words.

- Point out that when *be* follows a modal verb, the adverb comes after the modal (Example: *Nuclear weapons can hopefully be eliminated.*)

- ⏱ Have students circle the adverbs in the opening reading on pages 308–309. For each adverb ask: "Is it a sentence adverb or a simple adverb?"

Note 2

- Have students read the note and the examples. Have students work in groups to explain in their own words how the meaning differs in each pair of example sentences. Call on a few groups to give their explanation.

- Students may need additional practice. Write the following sentence frames on the board and have students practice them in pairs or groups:

  Only kids like to eat _____ .
  Kids only like to eat _____ .
  Even my grandmother knows how to _____ .
  My grandmother even knows how to _____ .

- Call on a few groups to share their sentences and explain how the meaning is different. Then have groups try to write one or two pairs of sentences in which the position of *even, just, only,* or *almost* changes the meaning.

Note 3

- Have students read the explanation and the examples. Read each example aloud several times and have students repeat.

- Point out that sentences beginning with negative adverbs other than *neither* sound more formal in English.

- Do a quick transformation drill. Say a few sentences with negative adverbs in the middle of the sentence and have students change them so the sentence begins with the negative adverb. (Example: *I never wake up early on Saturdays. / Never do I wake up early on Saturdays.*)

Note 4

- Divide the class into groups. Have students go over the note and come up with a clear explanation of it and some original sentences that exemplify the point. Circulate as students are working and provide help as needed.

- Call on students from each group to share their explanations and examples.

⏱ **Identify the Grammar:** Have students identify the grammar in the opening reading on pages 308–309. For example:

Basically, I think military service should be voluntary.
And I'm **definitely** against women in combat.
Maybe we shouldn't **even** have them.
I'm a pretty accepting guy, but **even** I find that suggestion extreme.

Go to **www.myfocusongrammarlab.com** for grammar charts and notes.

Step 3: Focused Practice (pages 314–317)

See the general suggestions for Focused Practice on page 4.

Exercise 1: Discover the Grammar

- Have students complete the exercise individually and compare answers in small groups.
- Call on students from various groups to share their answers with the class.
- ⏱ In groups, have students rewrite the sentences with focus or negative adverbs, changing their position. Go over the rewritten sentences as a class. Discuss how the changes influenced the meaning or the structure of the sentences.

Exercise 2: Sentence Adverbs

- Have students complete the exercise. Call on different students to write their sentences on the board.
- As you discuss each sentence, ask: "Where else can we place these adverbs? Will that placement affect the punctuation in the sentence?"

Exercise 3: Focus Adverbs

- Have students complete the exercise individually and work in pairs to check their answers.
- Go over the answers as a class.
- ⏱ Have students in pairs write three more sentences with blanks and answer choices similar to those in the exercise. Then have pairs exchange papers and complete each other's sentences. Have them check their answers in groups of four. Call on students from each group to share their sentence pairs with the class.

Exercise 4: Negative Adverbs

- Read the instructions and go over the examples. You may want to point out to students that in most items they will keep the two sentences separate, but for one item they will need to combine the sentences. Have students quickly read the negative adverbs in parentheses and tell you the item that will need to be combined. *(Item 5, because the adverb* not only *+ subject + verb does not create an independent clause)*
- Have students complete the exercise. Then have them work in groups to compare answers.
- Call on students from different groups to write their sentences on the board. As you go over the sentences, have students decide if the adverb could be moved. Have them explain how moving the adverb would affect the structure of the sentence.

Exercise 5: Negative / Focus Adverbs

- Read the instructions and have students look at the chart. Answer any questions about vocabulary. You may want to define terms such as *retired*, *drafts*, *allows*, and *combat*.
- Have students complete the exercise. Explain that in this exercise students should think only about the countries in the chart, not other countries whose policies they know about. Go over the answers as a class.
- ⏱ Have students discuss how these policies compare to those in their home countries. Encourage them to use focus and negative adverbs.

Exercise 6: Editing

- Have students complete the exercise and work in pairs to check their answers. Then call on students to explain each error and correction.

Go to **www.myfocusongrammarlab.com** for additional grammar practice.

Step 4: Communication Practice (pages 318–321)

See the general suggestions for Communication Practice on page 5.

Exercise 7: Listening

A

- **Note:** The listening is a continuation of the opening conversation on Student Book pages 308–309. You may want to have students reread the opening conversation first, then complete the listening exercises.
- Establish a purpose for listening. Have students read the question. Remind students to think about the question as they listen.
- Play the audio. Have students work in small groups to compare answers. Then go over the answer as a class.

B

- Have students read the questions. Answer any questions about vocabulary. Remind students to think about the questions as they listen.
- Play the audio and have students complete the exercise. Replay the audio as needed. Have students compare answers in pairs.
- Go over the answers as a class. You may need to replay the audio to clarify any discrepancies in students' answers.

- 🕐 Provide copies of the audioscript. Have students underline the adverbs in pairs and discuss what type each one is. Have pairs practice the conversation twice, changing roles after each practice.

Exercise 8: Pronunciation

A
- Have students read and listen to the Pronunciation Note. Then have them repeat the examples several times as you say them. Make sure students understand how the change in stress affects the meaning in the examples. Point out that the word after a focus or negative adverb is stressed, not the adverb itself.
- Play the audio, pausing after each sentence so students can write their answers.
- Go over the answers as a class. Replay the audio if needed.

B
- Circulate as pairs practice saying the sentences. Make corrections as needed.

Exercise 9: Personal Inventory

A
- Read the instructions and have students read the adverbs. For each adverb, give an example sentence that is true for you. Brainstorm others with the students and write them on the board.
- Have students complete the exercise individually.
- **Note:** To help focus students, you may want to give them a topic to think about as they write their sentences. For example, ask them to write about their opinions about women serving in combat.

B
- Have students compare sentences in pairs. Call on various students to tell the class about their partners' answers.
- **Note:** If you have a large class, you may want to have two pairs work together to report their examples.

Exercise 10: Pros / Cons

A
- Have students read the list of topics. You may want to review the definitions of the following items:

capital punishment	execution of or killing a person who has been convicted of committing a crime
cloning	a scientific process in which a plant, animal, or other organism that is genetically identical to its parent is created

- Explain that for each issue there are two "sides." For example, regarding capital punishment, one side believes it should be used and the other side believes it should not be used. Brainstorm the sides or positions for each of the topics. Write them on the board and leave them up for the next exercise.
- Have students choose a topic they want to discuss and find a partner who has chosen the same topic.

B
- Read the instructions. Remind students that different sides or positions for each issue were written on the board in Exercise A.
- Have students think of facts and arguments that support each side of the issue. Circulate, helping as needed.
- Call on pairs to share their ideas with the class. Write their ideas on the board and leave the information there for the next exercise.

Exercise 11: Debate

- Read the instructions. Have the class vote on a topic to debate (or choose the topic yourself). Divide the class into teams and give them time to research their opinions.
- You may want to establish some basic rules for the debate. For example, each side can take turns speaking for two minutes, no interruptions are allowed, and each side is allowed (or not) to ask the other questions.
- Set a time limit and have the class debate.
- **Note:** As a variation, you may want students to work in groups of four for this activity: two students who will debate one side of the issue and two who will debate the other side.

Exercise 12: Writing

A
- Read the instructions. As you explain each step of preparing and organizing the composition, you may want to give the students examples of how you would do this for a specific topic or point of view.

- Brainstorm some topics that students can write about. Point out that students can write about a topic they discussed or debated in Exercise 11.
- Have students research, plan, and write their essays, either in class or as homework.
- **Note:** As a variation, you may want to have students use the information about organizing their essay to create a simple outline first. Have them read each other's outlines in pairs and make suggestions for changes. Then have students write their essays.

B

- Have students work in pairs to correct each other's essays using the Editing Checklist. Then have students revise and rewrite their essays.
- (!) Post the essays around the room. Have students circulate and read each essay. Have students choose one essay that has a viewpoint opposite to their own but also has a convincing argument. Then discuss them as a class.

OUT OF THE BOX ACTIVITIES

Listening and Speaking

- Have students work in pairs. Write several controversial topics on individual slips of paper. You can use the ones that have been presented in the unit or have students brainstorm a list of topics they think are controversial.
- Put the slips of paper in a hat or a basket and have each pair draw a topic. Tell students that they are candidates for an important government position, and their success in being elected depends on a debate that will be broadcast on national TV.
- Give pairs ample time to prepare their arguments about the issue. Have students make notes to assist them in their debate. Have teams present their debates to the class. Hold an "election" and have class members vote for the candidates they thought were the most convincing.

Writing, Reading, Listening, and Speaking

- Have students work in groups to create a talk show of their own. It can be similar to or different from the one in the opening conversation on Student Book pages 308–309. Have each group decide on a topic and decide who will be the host and the guests. Remind students that guests should have opposing views about the issue.
- Have students write a script. They can use the opening conversation as a model. Remind them to focus on using various types of adverbs in their conversations.
- Have each group present the show to the class. At the end of the show, class members can be callers who ask specific questions of the guests and/or host about their positions on the issue.

Go to **www.myfocusongrammarlab.com** for additional listening, pronunciation, speaking, and writing practice.

Note:
- See the *Focus on Grammar Workbook* for additional in-class or homework grammar practice.

Unit 18 Review (page 322)

Have students complete the Review and check their answers on Student Book page UR-3. Review or assign additional material as needed.

Go to **www.myfocusongrammarlab.com** for the Unit Achievement Test.

Grammar: ADVERB CLAUSES

Unit 19 focuses on the meanings and uses of various types of adverb clauses, as well as their placement and punctuation.

- Adverb clauses are dependent clauses. Unlike independent clauses, they cannot stand alone; they need another clause to be fully understood. Adverb clauses indicate how, when, why, where, or under what conditions things happen. They may also introduce a contrast.

- Adverb clauses begin with subordinating conjunctions, which may be single words or phrases. Adverb clauses may occur before or after an independent clause and sometimes occur within the independent clause.

- Adverb clauses of time indicate when something happens. They are introduced by a variety of words and expressions that signal time.

- Adverb clauses of place indicate where something happens, and adverb clauses of reason indicate why something happens. Adverb clauses of condition indicate under what conditions something happens.

- Adverb clauses of contrast make a contrast with the idea expressed in the independent clause.

Theme: SPORTS

Unit 19 focuses on language that is used to talk about sports, athletes, and sporting events.

Step 1: Grammar in Context (pages 323–325)

See the general suggestions for Grammar in Context on page 1.

Before You Read

- Have students work in small groups to discuss the questions.
- Call on students to share their answers with the class.
- You may also want to have students talk about the significance of sports and sporting events in their countries.

Read

- You may want to point out unfamiliar vocabulary. Write the words on the board and have students say what they think the words mean. Discuss the meanings as a class. For example:

  endorsement   saying in an advertisement that people should buy a particular product

  excesses   actions that are socially or morally unacceptable because they are too extreme

  javelin throw   an event in which competitors throw a light spear to see who can throw it the farthest

  rival   a person, group, or organization that you compete with

  also-ran   someone who has failed to win a competition or an election

- Write the following questions on the board (or prepare them as a handout):
  1. What has the author identified as the three excesses in sports today? *(misplaced focus on fame, money, violence)*
  2. According to the author, why is the focus on breaking records a problem in today's Olympic games? *(because it's difficult to say who a champion is when the difference in their performances is just 1/10 of a second)*
  3. Who are the two athletes that the author uses as examples of excesses in money? *(Kobe Bryant and Alex Rodriguez)*
  4. According to the author, how do we show we value people? *(by what we pay them)*
  5. Why did hockey player Steve Moore have to be hospitalized? *(because another player hit him in the head with his stick)*

- Establish a purpose for reading. Call on some students to read the questions to the class. Remind students to think about the questions as they read and listen to the text. Have students read the text, or play the audio as students follow along in their books. Discuss the answers to the questions as a class.

After You Read

A. Vocabulary

- Have students complete the exercise and work in pairs to compare answers.
- Go over the answers as a class, clarifying any discrepancies in answers among students.
- ⏱ Have students practice pronouncing these words.

B. Comprehension

- Have students complete the exercise individually and compare answers in pairs or groups of three.
- Go over the answers as a class. As students share answers, have them identify where in the text they found the answers to the questions.

Go to **www.myfocusongrammarlab.com** for an additional reading, and for reading and vocabulary practice.

Step 2: Grammar Presentation (pages 326–329)

See the general suggestions for Grammar Presentation on page 2.

Grammar Charts

- Have the class work in seven different groups and assign each group one chart to examine. Have students look at the example sentences in their assigned charts and say if the sentences are simple, compound, or complex. *(All of the examples sentences are complex: one independent clause and one dependent clause).* Have students identify the dependent clauses in the examples and the one word in each that prevents the clause from standing on its own. *(In every case it is the adverbial word that makes it a dependent clause.)*
- Ask students: "What do you notice about the placement of adverbial clauses in the charts?" *(They can come before or after the main clause.)* Ask: "Does a change in position result in a change in meaning?" *(No.)*

Grammar Notes

Note 1

- Review the definition of *clause* with the class *(a group of words that contains a subject and a verb).* Then have students work in groups to come up with a definition of *independent clause (a clause that is a complete sentence on its own)* and *dependent clause (a clause that is not a sentence on its own. It needs another clause to make a complete sentence.)*
- Have groups talk about what they remember about these types of sentences: simple sentence *(a sentence that consists of one independent clause)*; compound sentence *(a sentence with two independent clauses joined by a coordinating conjunction such as and, but, or or)*; a complex sentence *(a sentence with one independent clause and one dependent clause)*. Elicit definitions of these sentences from various groups, filling in gaps in the definitions when necessary.
- Ask: "What is another name for *independent clause*?" *(main clause)* "What is another name for dependent clause?" *(subordinate clause)* "In a complex sentence, in which clause is the main idea usually found?" *(the independent or main clause)*
- Ask: "Why do some of the example sentences have commas while others don't?" *(In the ones with commas, the dependent clause comes first.)*

Note 2

- Have students look at each of the example sentences. Have them identify the subordinating conjunction in each.
- Ask: "What happens to the clause when the subordinating conjunction is removed?" *(It becomes an independent clause.)*

Note 3

- Some of the example sentences deal with future time. Have students look at the verbs in both the main and the subordinate clauses. Ask: "In which clause is the future form used?" *(the main clause)* "What if the order of the clauses is changed?" (Will *is still used only in the main clause.*) "What about *be going to*—can it be used in a dependent clause?" *(No.)*
- Have students work in pairs to take turns saying the example sentences as they are written and then reverse the order of the clauses.
- Ask students: "Are there other subordinating conjunctions that could replace *as soon as* in the first example?" *(when)*

Note 4

- List the subordinating conjunctions in this note on the board and write the following sentences frames:
  I'll sit _____ at the stadium.
  Famous athletes go _____ .
  Put the tickets for the game _____ .
  We can park the car _____ .
- Have students work in groups to complete the sentences with adverb clauses of place. (Examples: *I'll sit where I have the best view at the stadium. We can park the car wherever there is an open space.*)
- Have groups write one or two sentences for each frame. Call on various groups to share their sentences with the class. Ask: "In which sentences is the adverb clause inside the main clause?" *(the sentences created from the first frame)*

Note 5

- Point out that in conversation *because* and *since* are more commonly used than *as* to express reason. In writing, however, *as* is used a great deal.

- Go over the examples with *since* and *as* used to express both time and reason. Have students write a few sentences using *since* and *as* each way. Then have students work in pairs, exchange papers with a partner, and identify which of the partner's sentences have clauses of time and which have clauses of reason. Have students from various pairs share their sentences with the class and have the class identify which type of clause each sentence contains.
- ⏱ In small groups, have students look at Appendix 20 on page A-9 and identify other subordinating conjunctions that express reason. *(because of / due to / on account of the fact that / inasmuch as)* Then have them write sentences using these subordinating conjunctions and share them with the class.

Note 6
- Write the following sentences on the board. Then ask students which conjunction *(even if* or *only if)* goes with each sentence:
  We are taking this trip to the Olympics for sure. _____ we can't get tickets for our favorite events, we are going. *(even if)*
  I'll give you my cell number for emergencies. Use it _____ you need to. *(only if)*
- Have students look at the fourth example. Ask: "How can you use *if* in place of *unless* in this sentence and keep the same meaning?" *(If you don't train a great deal, you won't be a champion.)*
- Ask: "In which of the other example sentences could you use *unless*? What changes would you need to make in each sentence to keep the same meaning?" *(You won't improve unless you practice daily. Bi-Yun won't make the team unless another athlete drops out.)*

Note 7
- Point out that clauses of contrast that show unexpected results can be seen as the opposite of clauses of reason, which have a predictable cause and effect relationship.
- Write some simple sentences that show an unexpected result. For example: *We stayed up all night to watch the competition. I wasn't tired.* Then have students work in pairs to combine these sentences using adverbial clauses. For example: *Though we stayed up all night to watch the competition, I wasn't tired.* Have students from various pairs write their sentences on the board and go over them as a class.

- ⏱ Have students look through Appendix 20 to find additional subordinating conjunctions that can introduce clauses of contrast. *(in spite of / despite the fact that)*

⏱ **Identify the Grammar:** Have students identify the grammar in the opening reading on pages 323–324. For example:
  As I write this editorial, the World Cup is in full swing in South Africa.
  But **while sports may look good on the surface**, problems are lurking underneath.
  Because he penalized a player in the 2008 European Championships, a British referee received death threats.
  When the Olympics began about 2,700 years ago in Greece, the contests were related to war.
  We see it **wherever we look**, and it's certainly not decreasing.

Go to **www.myfocusongrammarlab.com** for grammar charts and notes.

Step 3: Focused Practice (pages 329–333)
See the general suggestions for Focused Practice on page 4.

Exercise 1: Discover the Grammar
- Have students complete the exercise and work in groups of three to compare answers.
- Go over the answers as a group, clarifying any discrepancies among students' answers.

Exercise 2: Word Order
- Have students complete the exercise. Go over the answers as a class.
- ⏱ Have students decide in pairs which Grammar Note applies for each answer.

Exercise 3: Combining Sentences
- Have students complete the exercise, then have pairs work together to compare answers.
- Have students from each pair write their sentences on the board. As you go over these sentences, ask students what other subordinating conjunctions would work in each sentence without changing the meaning.

Exercise 4: Writing Adverb Clauses
- Have students look at the pictures and describe what they see. Ask: "What teams are playing? What sports? What is the score? Who is probably going to win?"
- Have students read the first item. Brainstorm ways to complete the sentence. (Example: *The Sharks will win the game provided that the ball goes in the basket.*)

- Have students complete the exercise. Go over the answers as a class. Then have students work in pairs to read the completed sentences to each other.

Exercise 5: Editing

- Have students work in pairs to complete the exercise.
- Have students from each pair write their corrected sentences on the board and explain their corrections to the class.
- (!) Have students read the corrected text aloud to each other in pairs.

Go to **www.myfocusongrammarlab.com** for additional grammar practice.

Step 4: Communication Practice (pages 334–338)

See the general suggestions for Communication Practice on page 5.

Exercise 6: Listening

A
- Establish a purpose for listening. Read the instructions and the question. Remind students to think about the question as they listen.
- Play the audio. Go over the answer with the class.

B
- Establish a purpose for listening. Have students read the questions. Remind them to think about the questions as they listen.
- Play the audio. Since these questions require complex answers, you may want to play the audio more than once.
- Have students complete the exercise and work in pairs or groups of three to compare their answers. Then have students identify what type of adverb clause was required for each sentence.

Exercise 7: Pronunciation

A
- Have students read and listen to the Pronunciation Note.
- Say the examples aloud and have students repeat.

B
- Have students quickly read the sentences. Play the audio for the first sentence and go over the example answer as a class. Make sure students can hear the pause and understand why the comma has been added.
- Have students complete the exercise and work in pairs to check their answers.

C
- Have students practice saying the sentences. Circulate and help as needed.
- (!) Have students take turns saying the sentences again in pairs, first with the clauses in the order that they appear and then reversing the order of the clauses.

Exercise 8: Personal Inventory

A
- Read the instructions and go over the picture and the example with students. Brainstorm other sentences about the future with *when*.
- You may want to have students review the *Be Careful!* note in Note 3 about the use of *will* and *be going to* in complex sentences with time clauses. Ask: "Do you use *will* or *be going to* in the dependent clause?" *(No. Use simple present instead.)*
- Have students complete the exercise individually.

B
- Have pairs discuss their answers. Then have them exchange books and check each other's sentences for correct punctuation.
- Call on students to tell the class about their partners' answers.

Exercise 9: Picture Discussion

A
- Have students look at the picture and describe what they see. If needed, explain vocabulary such as *brawl, punch,* and *rivalry.*
- Have students discuss the events in the picture and the questions in the instructions. Circulate and help as needed.
- (!) Have students talk in groups about similar sports incidents that they have witnessed or heard about.

B
- Call on students from each group to share their ideas with the class.
- Have the class vote on whether sports have become too violent.

Exercise 10: Writing

A
- Read the instructions and the topics. Point out that in this writing assignment students will be expressing an opinion in the topic sentence of the first paragraph and providing reasons, facts, and evidence to support that opinion in the rest of the essay. Have students identify the topic sentence in the example and articulate what the writer's opinion is.

- Have students identify the sentence in the example in which the author provides the reason for his opinion. (*In particular, I strongly believe that sports provide opportunities to people who don't have many other opportunities.*) Point out that the next sentence is the beginning of an example that the writer uses to support the reason he states.
- Elicit from students that this essay will most likely have two to three more paragraphs that provide additional reasons and examples for their opinions.
- Have students write their essays in class or as homework.

B
- Have students use the Editing Checklist to revise and rewrite as needed. As an alternative, have them work in pairs to correct each other's work.
- (!) Post the essays around the room. Have students circulate and read each essay. Have students choose one essay that has a viewpoint opposite to their own but also has a convincing argument. Then discuss them as a class.

OUT OF THE BOX ACTIVITIES

Reading, Speaking, and Listening
- Bring in (or have students bring in) advertisements for sports equipment or any other kind of item that is suitable for people who practice sports. Have students work in small groups. Hand out several advertisements to each group. Have students study the advertisements and discuss the message behind each one. Encourage students to use adverb clauses of reason, condition, and contrast as they describe the messages. Write the following examples on the board to prompt students:
  You will beat your opponent only if you wear [brand].
  Since our equipment is the best, you won't be able to reach the top without it.
  Although it's expensive, you can't afford not to have it.
  If you drink [brand], you will have more energy.
- Follow up by having students share with the class their views about the advertisements and their messages.

Speaking, Listening, Writing, and Reading
- Write the following sentences on the board:
  It's not whether you win or lose that's important; it's how you play the game.
  The only thing that matters is winning.
- Then write the following sentence on the board:
  The only thing that matters is winning. Given the roots of the Olympic games in war, this ancient Greek ideal might make sense.
- Have students work in small groups to decide which of these ideals provides a better guiding principle for modern sports. Then have them write a three- to four-paragraph opinion essay expressing their view. Remind students to focus on using adverb clauses in their writing.
- Have students work in pairs to correct each other's essays using the Editing Checklist.

Go to **www.myfocusongrammarlab.com** for additional listening, pronunciation, speaking, and writing practice.

Note:
- See the *Focus on Grammar Workbook* for additional in-class or homework grammar practice.

Unit 19 Review (page 339)
Have students complete the Review and check their answers on Student Book page UR-3. Review or assign additional material as needed.

Go to **www.myfocusongrammarlab.com** for the Unit Achievement Test.

Grammar: ADVERB AND ADVERBIAL PHRASES

Unit 20 focuses on the form and uses of adverb and adverbial phrases and the reduction of various types of adverb clauses to phrases.

- A *clause* is a group of words with a subject and a verb that expresses time. A *phrase* does not have a subject and a verb that expresses time. A phrase often has a present or past participle.

- Some adverb clauses can be shortened to adverb phrases in ways similar to the ways adjective clauses can be shortened: by reducing them or changing them. Negative adverb phrases contain the word *not* or *never* before the participle.

- Adverb clauses can be reduced to adverb phrases when the clause has a form of *be*. Omit the subject and *be*. You can reduce the adverb clause to a phrase only if the subject in both clauses of the sentence refers to the same person or thing. Adverb phrases can come first or second in the sentence. If the original sentence has commas, keep the commas in the reduced sentence.

- Some adverb clauses can be changed to adverb phrases when the clause has no form of *be*. Omit the subject and change the verb to its *-ing* form. You can reduce the adverb clause to a phrase only if the subject in both clauses of the sentence refers to the same person or thing. Keep the subordinating conjunction (*after, before, since,* or *while*) and the original punctuation.

- Change a simple past or past perfect verb in an adverb clause to the *-ing* form or to *having* + past participle in an adverb phrase.

- *Upon* or *on* + *-ing* in an adverb phrase usually has the same meaning as *when* in an adverb clause.

- The subordinating conjunction is sometimes omitted in a phrase. A phrase without a subordinating conjunction is called an adverbial phrase. In a time clause, the subordinating conjunction can be omitted when the clause is changed to an adverbial phrase if the meaning remains clear. However, do not omit the subordinating conjunction in a passive construction.

- Adverb clauses of reason can be changed to adverbial phrases, but *because, since,* or *as* at the beginning of a clause must be omitted in the adverbial phrase.

- A clause with a passive verb can be changed to an adverbial phrase with a past participle. If the subordinating conjunction can be omitted without changing the meaning, delete the subject and any auxiliaries in the passive sentence.

Theme: COMPASSION

Unit 20 focuses on language that is used to describe stories and discuss acts of compassion.

Step 1: Grammar in Context (pages 340–342)

See the general suggestions for Grammar in Context on page 1.

Before You Read

- Have students work in small groups to discuss the questions, or discuss them as a class.
- You may also want students to share stories they know about people who have shown compassion in the midst of personal pain and suffering.

Read

- You may want to have students scan the text for the following words and guess at their meanings using context clues. Have them jot down the definitions in their notebooks. Have students share their definitions. Discuss and clarify them as a class:

ruins	the parts of buildings that are left after the rest have been destroyed
shatter	to break suddenly into very small pieces or to make something break this way
outdistance	to run, ride, etc., faster than other people, especially in a race so that you are far ahead
alert	to officially warn someone of a problem or danger, so that he or she can be ready to deal with it
coma	a state in which someone is unconscious for a period of time, usually after a serious accident or illness
transplant	the operation of moving an organ, piece of skin, etc., from one person's body to another
civility	a high level of civilized behavior
irony	a situation that is unusual or amusing because something strange happens or the opposite of what is expected happens or is true

pledge   to make a formal, often public, promise to do or give something to an organization, country, etc.

- Write the following questions on the board:
  1. Why did the Greens try to escape from the criminals? *(They thought their new car could outrun them.)*
  2. Why were the Greens attacked? *(The criminals thought they were carrying precious stones.)*
  3. Why did Nicholas's parents offer to donate his organs to Italians in need of them? *(to return good for evil and so that someone could have the future he lost)*
  4. What happened to the Greens after their return to the United States? *(They began to receive requests to speak about their son and the importance of organ donation.)*
  5. How did they react to these requests? *(They realized that they had found their life's work.)*
- Establish a purpose for reading. Have various students read each of the questions aloud. Remind students to think about these questions as they read and listen to the text.
- Play the audio and have students read the text. Have students discuss the questions in pairs or groups of three. Then have students from each group share answers with the class.

After You Read

A. Vocabulary
- Have students work in pairs. Have them cover the definitions in the right-hand column and guess at the definitions of the boldfaced words. Have them discuss their guesses with their partners.
- Have students complete the exercise individually. Go over the answers as a class. As you talk about each answer, have students share what their initial guesses were.

B. Comprehension
- Have students complete the exercise individually. Then have them compare answers in pairs.
- Call on various students to share their answers with the class. Have them point out the place in the text where they found the answer to the question.

Go to **www.myfocusongrammarlab.com** for an additional reading, and for reading and vocabulary practice.

Step 2: Grammar Presentation (pages 343–346)

See the general suggestions for Grammar Presentation on page 2.

Grammar Charts
- Have students scan the charts for the spaces marked Ø. Ask :"Why are no adverb phrases possible here? *"(because the subjects of the two clauses are not the same)*
- Have students look at each of the charts. Ask: "What are the two types of adverb clauses that are the focus of these charts?" *(adverb clauses of time and reason)* Ask: "What is the main difference between the first chart and the others?" *(The first chart relates to the reduction of active time clauses with* be. *The rest focus on time clauses with verbs other than* be, *reason clauses, and clauses with passives—all of these involve more complicated changes to reduce to phrases.)*
- Write the following questions on the board: In reducing or changing adverb clauses to phrases:
  What words from the clause were omitted in the phrase?
  What word forms were changed?
- Have students work in four groups. Assign each group one chart to examine and answer the questions for each example sentence. If you have a large class, you may have more than one group working on each section.
- Have students form new groups of four, making sure that there is one person from each of the previous groups in the new groups. Have students in the new groups share their answers to the questions about the chart that they examined.

Grammar Notes

Note 1
- Have students read the note. Then ask: "What are the two ways that adverb clauses can be made into phrases?" *(by reducing the original clause [omitting words] or, for some clauses, by changing the words)*

Note 2
- Have students read the note. Then ask: "When can adverb clauses be reduced to phrases?" *(when the clause has a form of* be *and the subjects in both clauses of the sentence refer to the same person or thing)*

Note 3
- Have students look at the examples. Ask: "How are the verbs in these examples different from the ones in the previous examples?" *(They are not forms of* be. *They are other verbs:* visited *and* saw.) "How do we change these clause to adverb phrases?" *(omit the subject and change the verb to its* -ing *form)*

- Write sentences such as the following on the board and have students complete them with information about a real or fictional vacation:
  After _____ , we checked into our hotel.
  While _____ , we made plans for the next day.
  Before _____ , we had lunch in a restaurant.
  After _____ , we went shopping at . . .
  Before _____ , we visited . . .

Note 4

- Have students read the note. Ask: "What are the two ways to reduce a simple past or past perfect verb in an adverb clause?" (*omit the subject and change the verb to the* -ing *form or to* having + *past participle*)
- Say a simple past or past perfect sentence with an adverb time clause with *after* and have students reduce the clause in both ways. (Example: *After I'd woken up, I realized my alarm clock was broken. / After waking up, I realized my alarm clock was broken. / After having woken up, I realized my alarm clock was broken.*)
- ⏱ Have students continue the same activity in groups of three. Each student takes turns saying a sentence, changing the clause to an *-ing* phrase, and changing the clause to a phrase with *having* + past participle.

Note 5

- Have students read the note. Explain that adverb clauses with *when* often do not sound correct when reduced to adverb phrases in the normal way described in Notes 1 through 4. A good rule of thumb is to replace *when* with *upon* or *on*.
- Say an example sentence with *when* and have students reduce the clause to a phrase. Example: When he boarded the plane, he immediately fell asleep. (*Upon / On boarding the plane, he immediately fell asleep.*)
- Have students continue practicing this in pairs.

Note 6

- Have students read the note and the example sentences.
- You may want to point out that this sort of change is most common when the events in the adverb phrase and the main clause are happening at the same time. Subordinating conjunctions such as *after* and *before* cannot usually be omitted because this will change the meaning.

Note 7

- Have students read the note.
- Write some sentences on the board and have students reduce the clauses to phrases. For example:
  Since the Greens were compassionate people, they chose to donate Nicholas's organs. (*Being compassionate people, the Greens chose to donate Nicholas's organs.*)
  As he wasn't willing to stop for the thieves, Mr. Green kept driving. (*Not willing to stop for the thieves, Mr. Green kept driving.*)
  Because they had been affected by this tragedy, the Greens wanted to help other people. (*Having been affected by this tragedy, the Greens wanted to help other people.*)

Note 8

- Have students work in pairs to generate three or four sentences with adverb clauses that have passive verbs. Have them base their sentences on the reading. (Example: *Because he was hit by a bullet, Nicholas was critically injured.*)
- Then have pairs exchange sentences and reduce the adverb clauses to phrases. (Example: *Hit by a bullet, Nicholas was critically injured.*)
- Go over the *Be Careful!* note and write several sentences with adverb clauses on the board for students to transform into phrases. For example:
  Before they were affected by this tragedy, the Greens were a happy family. (*Before being affected by this tragedy, the Greens were a happy family.*)
  Then write the following sentence on the board and ask students if it is a possibility:
  Affected by this tragedy, the Greens were a happy family. (*No. Deleting the subordinating conjunction and* be *changes the meaning, and the resulting sentence doesn't make sense.*)

⏱ **Identify the Grammar:** Have students identify the grammar in the opening reading on pages 340–341. For example:

Having spent a wonderful day exploring the ruins at Paestum in southern Italy, Reg and Maggie Green were driving south in the area of Italy known as the boot, **their children Nicholas and Eleanor sleeping peacefully in the** back seat.

Not knowing what to do, Reg carefully weighed the options.

Shots rang out, **shattering both windows on the driver's side of the car.**

Go to **www.myfocusongrammarlab.com** for grammar charts and notes.

Step 3: Focused Practice (pages 346–352)

See the general suggestions for Focused Practice on page 4.

Exercise 1: Discover the Grammar

A

- Have students complete the exercise individually and work in pairs to compare answers.
- Call on students from various pairs to share their answers with the class.

B

- Read the instructions and go over the example with the students.
- Have students complete the exercise individually.
- Call on various students to share their answers with the class.

Exercise 2: Adverb Clauses to Phrases

- Have students complete the exercise individually.
- Go over the answers as a class. Have various students write their shortened sentences on the board.

Exercise 3: Clauses / Phrases

A

- Establish a purpose for reading. Write the following questions on the board:
  1. What happened to the elephant Damini? Why? *(She apparently died of grief after the death of another elephant she was close to.)*
  2. How did the two elephants come to be in the same zoo? *(Damini was taken from owners who were illegally transporting her and brought to the zoo; Champkali was brought on "a kind of maternity leave.")*
  3. How did Champkali die? *(She died after giving birth to a stillborn calf.)*
  4. Why do people think Damini was experiencing grief? *(She shed tears and lost interest in food. Also, an expert said that elephants are very social animals that form close bonds with others and experience emotions.)*
- Have students read the questions. Then have them read the article and find the answers.
- Go over the answers as a class.

B

- Have students read the instructions for each item. Make sure everyone understands that the instructions are different from item to item. Answer any questions about how to complete the exercise.

- Have students complete the exercise individually and work in pairs to compare answers. Then go over the answers as a class.
- For the *yes / no* items, have various students explain why their answers are correct. For the rewrite items, have various students write their sentences on the board and explain them.

Exercise 4: Adverb Phrases / Main Clauses

- Many students will find this activity quite challenging, so you may want to guide them using the following steps.
- Have students look at the pictures. Point out that the pictures tell a story. Have students work in pairs or groups to work out the plot of the story. Explain that students should just work out the story for now and not worry about grammar. Call on a few groups to tell the story in their own words.
- Write the key events of the story on the board. If your class needs extra help, you may want to write a description of each picture using full adverb clauses. Examples:
  1. When a tourist couple came out of the train station, they saw a boy selling guidebooks.
  2. When the boy saw the couple, he said to the man, "Guidebook, sir?"
  3. Because they didn't have any money, they told the boy they couldn't buy anything.
  4. After they thought about the situation, they decided to buy a guidebook from the boy.
  5. When they found a bank, they went inside and changed money.
  6. When they returned to the train station, the boy was gone.
  7. After they learned from a policeman where the boy was, they went to find him.
  8. After they'd found the boy, they bought a map.
- Go over the example and have students complete the exercise in pairs or small groups. Have strong students write sentences using their own ideas. If students need more help, have them work with the sentences you wrote on the board and reduce or change the adverb clauses.
- Go over the answers as a class. Have students practice telling the story again, this time using adverb phrases wherever possible.

Exercise 5: Editing

- Have students check their answers in pairs. Then call on students to explain each error and correction.

Go to **www.myfocusongrammarlab.com** for additional grammar practice.

Step 4: Communication Practice (pages 353–356)

See the general suggestions for Communication Practice on page 5.

Exercise 6: Listening

A

- Have students read through the list of subjects. Remind them to keep these subjects in mind as they listen to the audio.
- Play the audio and have students complete the exercise.
- Go over the answers as a class. You may need to play the audio again to clarify discrepancies in students' answers.

B

- Have students read the questions. Remind students to think about the questions as they listen. Then play the audio, pausing as needed so students have time to write their answers.
- Have students compare their answers in small groups. Then go over the answers as a class.
- ⏱ Provide copies of the audioscript and have students practice reading it in pairs. Then have one pair read the audioscript to the class.

Exercise 7: Pronunciation

A

- Have students read and listen to the Pronunciation Note. Say the examples aloud and have students repeat.

B

- Play the audio, pausing as needed so students have time to circle their answers.
- Go over the answers as a class.

C

- As students repeat each sentence, circulate and provide feedback as needed.

Exercise 8: Personal Inventory

A

- Circulate as students are writing. Provide help as needed.

B

- Have two pairs work together and discuss their sentences.
- Have each student report at least one sentence about his or her partner to the class.

Exercise 9: Group Discussion

A

- Read the instructions and the questions. If needed, have students reread the article on Student Book pages 340–341.
- Go over the example answer. Remind students to give reasons and extra information when they answer the first question, not simply answer *yes* or *no*.
- Have students discuss the questions in pairs. Circulate and help as needed.

B

- Call on students to share their partners' answers with the class.

Exercise 10: Writing

A

- Point out that this is a narrative essay— students will be telling the story of something that happened or that they witnessed.
- Remind students that effective narrative writing includes sensory details. Have students look at the example and identify the sensory details. (*I suddenly felt the car slow down and heard a grinding noise.*)
- Have students work in pairs or small groups to brainstorm ideas of events to write about. Then have students write their essays, either in class or as homework.

B

- Have students use the Editing Checklist to correct their work. Then have them revise and rewrite as needed. As an alternative, have them work in pairs to edit each other's work.
- Have students work in small groups to share their writing with one another.

OUT OF THE BOX ACTIVITIES

Reading, Speaking, Listening, and Writing

- Bring in stories (or have students bring them in) that deal with love and compassion. They can be fictional stories or fables such as "Androcles and the Lion" or true stories from magazines, newspapers, or organizations that help people in need, such as UNICEF.
- Have students work in groups to read and discuss the stories. Then write the following example on the board:
  Having run away from his master, Androcles made for the woods. On seeing the lion in pain, Androcles grew bold and decided to help.
- Have students look at the grammar charts again. Have them use ideas from the stories to write sentences using adverbial phrases. Have students from various groups share their sentences with the class.

Listening and Speaking

- Have students reread the opening text. Point out that the outpouring of sorrow, the reactions of shame on the part of Italians, and the Greens' receiving Italy's highest honor indicate that organ donation was probably very unusual in Italy at that time.
- Have students discuss the following questions in small groups:
  1. What are the attitudes toward organ donation in your nation or region?
  2. Are you a registered organ donor? Would you be if you were asked? Why or why not?
  3. What are the arguments for and against organ donation in your culture?
  4. How have attitudes toward organ donation changed in your lifetime?

Go to **www.myfocusongrammarlab.com** for additional listening, pronunciation, speaking, and writing practice.

Note:
- See the *Focus on Grammar Workbook* for additional in-class or homework grammar practice.

Unit 20 Review (page 357)

Have students complete the Review and check their answers on Student Book page UR-3. Review or assign additional material as needed.

Go to **www.myfocusongrammarlab.com** for the Unit Achievement Test.

UNIT 21 OVERVIEW

Grammar: CONNECTORS

Unit 21 focuses on the forms, meanings, and uses of three types of discourse connectors.

- There are three main types of connectors: coordinating conjunctions, subordinating conjunctions, and transitions.
- Coordinating conjunctions join two independent clauses. They are usually preceded by a comma. Subordinating conjunctions connect ideas within a sentence. They come at the beginning of subordinate (dependent) clauses. If the subordinate clause comes first in the sentence, it is followed by a comma. Unless it sets up a contrast, a subordinate clause that follows an independent clause is not preceded by a comma.
- Transitions connect ideas between sentences or larger sections of text. Transitions that connect sentences can come at the beginning, end, or within a sentence. At the beginning of a sentence, a transition is preceded by a period or semicolon and followed by a comma. At the end of a sentence, it is preceded by a comma.
- There are five types of transitions that connect sentences. These can show addition, condition, contrast, effect / result, and time.
- Transitions that connect larger blocks of text usually come at the beginning of a sentence and are followed by a comma. They have a variety of uses: to list ideas in order of time or importance, to give examples, to summarize, or to add a conclusion.

Theme: MEMORY

Unit 21 focuses on language that is used to talk about different types of memory and how we can improve our ability to remember.

Step 1: Grammar in Context (pages 358–360)

See the general suggestions for Grammar in Context on page 1.

Before You Read

- Have students work in pairs to discuss the questions.

- Have various students share their answers with the class and list them on the board. Save them for future reference.

Read

- ⏱ Write unfamiliar vocabulary on the board. Have students scan the text for each word and read the entire sentence in which the word appears. Ask what they think each word means and discuss the meanings as a class. For example:

worrisome	something that makes you anxious
deterioration	the state of becoming worse or developing into a bad situation
vivid	memories, dreams, descriptions, etc. that are so clear that they seem real
the real trick	the best way to solve a problem or to get a good result

Point out that using context to guess meanings of unknown words is an important reading comprehension skill that will help students to more easily understand what they read.

- Write the following questions on the board (or prepare them as a handout):
  1. What are the two types of memory that the author distinguishes between? *(long-term and short-term)*
  2. Where do short-term memory operations occur? *(the frontal lobes of the brain)*
  3. As we age, how much mass do the frontal lobes lose per decade? *(as much as 5 to 10 percent)*
  4. According to the author, what is one way to remember names? *(create a mental picture you can relate to the person, place, or thing you want to recall)*
- Establish a purpose for reading. Have students read the questions. Remind students to think about the questions as they read and listen to the text.
- Have students read the text. Discuss the answers to the questions as a class.

After You Read

A. Vocabulary

- Have pairs look at the sentences on the left and identify what the part of speech of each boldfaced word is. For example, *core* in the first sentence is used as a noun. Have them do the same for each of the definitions on the right. For example, *lessen the seriousness of a harmful action* is a verb plus object. Point out that understanding how an unknown word is used in a sentence can often help readers understand the meaning.
- Have pairs complete the exercise, discussing the part of speech for each boldfaced word and its definition as an aid to selecting an answer.
- Have two pairs work together to check their answers. Clarify any discrepancies in students' answers as a class.

B. Comprehension

- Have students complete the exercise individually and then compare answers in pairs or groups of three.

Go to **www.myfocusongrammarlab.com** for an additional reading, and for reading and vocabulary practice.

Step 2: Grammar Presentation (pages 360–364)

See the general suggestions for Grammar Presentation on page 2.

Grammar Charts

- Have students look at the examples in the first chart. Ask: "Is the meaning expressed by the different sentences the same or different?" *(pretty much the same)* "Why would a speaker or writer choose one form over another?" *(Each form has a slightly different emphasis, allowing the speaker or writer to choose the best one to connect with what came before.)*
- ⏱ Photocopy the remaining charts individually, but white out various sections of each chart. Then make enough copies for the class. Have students complete the charts in small groups. Then have them check their answers against the charts in their books.

Grammar Notes

Note 1

- Have students name as many coordinating conjunctions as possible from memory, and write them on the board. Then have students look at the charts and complete the list. Repeat the process for subordinating conjunctions and transitions.

Note 2

- Remind students that an independent clause has a subject and a verb. Have them identify the subjects and the verbs in the first two example sentences. *(I forget / I write / I heard / you did mean)*

- 🕐 Since students studied adverb clauses in the previous unit, they should be familiar with subordinating conjunctions and the comma rules. To establish the connection between these and other connectors, have students transform the first two examples in Note 1. Have them change the structure of the first sentence to a complex sentence using a subordinating conjunction. *(Although I try hard, I can never remember new people's names.)* Then have them change the second sentence to two independent clauses joined by a coordinating conjunction. *(I can't remember her name, but I can remember her face.)*

Note 3

- You may want to point out that some transitions, such as *however,* can be used comfortably in all sentence positions indicated. Others are more restricted. Tell students that, when in doubt, the initial position is always safe.

- 🕐 In small groups, have students look at Appendix 21 on page A-9. Ask them to identify words that could replace the transition words in the example sentences. Go over their choices as a class.

Note 4

- Have students read the note and the examples. Write the following on the board in three columns.

	In addition, . . .	. . . his memory didn't improve.
Tom bought a book about how to improve your memory.	Otherwise, . . .	. . . he bought some audio CDs.
	However, . . .	. . . he had a difficult time remembering names.
	As a result, . . .	. . . his memory improved.
	Before that . . .	. . . his anxiety in new situations may have increased.

- Have students connect the sentence at the left with transitions and clauses to create logical sentences. (Example: *Tom bought a book about how to improve your memory. In addition, he bought some audio CDs.*)

- Brainstorm other transitions that could replace the ones in the chart. (Example: in addition *can be replaced with* additionally, furthermore, plus, *etc.*)

Note 5

- Point out that sentence connectors help us anticipate the kind of information that is coming next when we read or listen. The transitions that connect blocks of text show us the broad outlines of a writer's or speaker's overall plan.

- Have students reread "Try to Remember," underlining the transitions that connect blocks of text. Then go over these as a class.

- 🕐 Have students look at Appendix 22 on page A-10 in pairs. Ask them to choose transitional words or phrases that can replace those in the text. Discuss those as a class.

🕐 **Identify the Grammar:** Have students identify the grammar in the opening reading on pages 358–359. For example:

You're with a friend, **and** suddenly up walks somebody you've known for a long time.

However, just as you say, "Nancy, I'd like you to meet . . . ," your mind goes blank.

I wouldn't be too concerned, **though**, **for** it's also very common.

I was worried about memory loss on my part; **therefore**, I decided to do some research into the problem.

First: There are two types of memory, long-term and short-term.

Go to **www.myfocusongrammarlab.com** for grammar charts and notes.

Step 3: Focused Practice (pages 364–368)

See the general suggestions for Focused Practice on page 4.

Exercise 1: Discover the Grammar

A

- Have students complete the exercise individually. Then have them compare answers in pairs.
- Review the answers as a class.
- ⏱ Have students look at the opening reading in pairs and find more examples of each type of connector. Have them write the sentences in random order on a piece of paper. Have pairs exchange papers and label each connector as indicated in the exercise.

B

- Have students complete the exercise individually. Then have them discuss their answers in groups.
- Circulate as students are working. Identify any items that seem problematic and go over them as a class.

Exercise 2: Combining Sentences with Connectors

- Have students complete the exercise individually and work in groups of three to check their answers.
- Have students from each group write their sentences on the board. Discuss the sentences as a class.

Exercise 3: Completing Sentences with Connectors

- Have students complete the exercise individually and work in pairs to compare answers.
- Go over the answers as a class.
- ⏱ Have students practice reading the completed text to each other in pairs.

Exercise 4: Writing Sentences with Conjunctions / Transitions

- Have students look at the pictures and describe what they see. Answer any questions about vocabulary.

- Point out that the pictures tell a story. Have students work in groups to work out the story in their own words. Call on a few groups to tell the story.
- Have students read the instructions and the prompts in parentheses. Brainstorm sentences to write for the first item. (Example: *Hank woke up late, and he didn't take a shower. In addition, he didn't have breakfast.*)
- Have students complete the exercise individually and compare answers in pairs. Call on students to write their sentences on the board.

Exercise 5: Editing

- Have students complete the exercise individually and compare answers in pairs.
- Call on various students to write their corrected sentences on the board. Have students explain their corrections to the class.
- ⏱ Have students practice reading the corrected text aloud to each other in pairs.

Go to **www.myfocusongrammarlab.com** for additional grammar practice.

Step 4: Communication Practice (pages 369–372)

See the general suggestions for Communication Practice on page 5.

Exercise 6: Listening

A

- Have students read the sentences. Remind students to keep these sentences in mind as they listen.
- Play the audio and have students complete the exercise.
- Go over the answers with the class. Replay the audio if needed.

B

- Have students read the questions. Then play the audio and have students complete the exercise. You may need to play the audio more than once in order for students to write answers for all of the questions.
- Have students work in groups to check their answers.
- Go over the answers as a class. If needed, play the audio again so students can check their answers.

Exercise 7: Pronunciation

A

- Have students read and listen to the Pronunciation Note. Say the examples aloud several times and have students repeat.

B

- Play the audio, pausing after each item, so students have time to write answers.
- Have students compare their answers in pairs.
- Call on students to write their answers on the board, including the commas or semicolons they added. Discuss the sentences as a class.

C

- Circulate as students practice saying the sentences. Give help as needed.

Exercise 8: Game

- Read the instructions and go over the example with the class. To demonstrate how to play the game, read the example sentences aloud. Students take notes with their books closed. Then have students say or write down the example sentences using their notes.
- Divide the class into teams. Set a time limit, and have the teams write statements with connectors. Then have students play the game while you keep score.
- ⏱ Have members of each team exchange statements with each other or the opposite team. Then have students write sentences with the same information and meaning but different connectors. Have students share the original and rewritten sentences with the class.

Exercise 9: Picture Discussion

- Have students look at the picture. Help with vocabulary as needed.
- Read the instructions and have students complete the exercise in pairs. Remind them to focus on using various types of connectors. Have students from various pairs share their observations with the class.

Exercise 10: Writing

A

- Review the structure of an essay. This assignment will most likely include an introductory paragraph, one or two body paragraphs, and a concluding paragraph. Point out that this assignment will be a narrative about a past event, and the topic sentence in the example identifies a specific event.
- Have students brainstorm an event to write about. Then have them choose one event and list details associated with the event. Make sure they eliminate any details that are not related to the event.
- Have students write their essays, either in class or as homework.

B

- Have students use the Editing Checklist to correct their work. Then have them revise and rewrite as needed. As an alternative, have them work in pairs to edit each other's work.
- Have students share their writing in small groups.

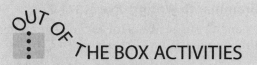

OUT OF THE BOX ACTIVITIES

Reading, Speaking, Listening, and Writing

- Have students conduct an Internet search on tips for improving memory. Have them print out material and bring it to class.
- Have students exchange articles in pairs and underline the connectors. Then have them discuss what they found and identify what type of connector each one is.
- Have students write two paragraphs about one of the methods to improve memory that they discussed. Remind them to use various types of connectors. In the first paragraph, have them explain how the method works. In the second paragraph, have them express their views on the method.

Listening and Speaking

- Have students watch relevant parts of the movie *50 First Dates,* a romantic comedy about a veterinarian named Henry Roth (Adam Sandler), who falls in love with Lucy Whitmore (Drew Barrymore). Lucy never remembers that she is dating Henry because she suffers from short-term memory loss, a disorder which causes her to forget everything every night.
- Have students discuss the following questions in small groups:
  What would you have done if you were Henry?
  How does Henry's father behave?
  How does Lucy's father behave?

Go to **www.myfocusongrammarlab.com** for additional listening, pronunciation, speaking, and writing practice.

Note:

- See the *Focus on Grammar Workbook* for additional in-class or homework grammar practice.

Unit 21 Review (page 373)

Have students complete the Review and check their answers on Student Book page UR-3. Review or assign additional material as needed.

Go to **www.myfocusongrammarlab.com** for the Unit Achievement Test.

From Grammar to Writing (pages 374–376)

See the general suggestions for From Grammar to Writing on page 9.

Go to **www.myfocusongrammarlab.com** for an additional From Grammar to Writing Assignment, Part Review, and Part Post-Test.

PART IX OVERVIEW

CONDITIONALS AND THE SUBJUNCTIVE

UNIT	GRAMMAR FOCUS	THEME
22	Conditionals; Other Ways to Express Unreality	Intuition
23	More Conditions; The Subjunctive	Advice

Go to **www.myfocusongrammarlab.com** for the Part and Unit Tests.

Note: PowerPoint® grammar presentations, test-generating software, and reproducible Part and Unit Tests are on the *Teacher's Resource Disc.*

UNIT 22 OVERVIEW

Grammar: CONDITIONALS; OTHER WAYS TO EXPRESS UNREALITY

Unit 22 focuses on the forms, meanings, and uses of a variety of structures that express real conditions or unreality.

- Conditional sentences describe situations that occur (or do not occur) because of certain conditions. They consist of two clauses: a dependent condition clause and an independent result clause. There are two types of conditionals: real and unreal.

- Real (or factual) conditionals describe situations that occur regularly or are likely or possible in the future. Unreal conditionals describe situations that are untrue, unlikely, or impossible in the past or present. In conditional sentences, the clause can occur in either order without a change in meaning. Either or both clauses can be negative.

- We use present real conditionals to talk about general truths, scientific facts, or habits and repeated events. The simple present is used in both clauses. We can also use the present progressive in the *if* clause. In future time situations, use the simple present or the present progressive in the *if* clause and the future with *will* or *be going to*, *may*, *might*, *can*, or *could* in the result clause.

- Use the present unreal conditionals to talk about unreal, untrue, imagined, or impossible conditions and their results. Use the simple past form of verbs in the *if* clause. If the verb is *be*, use *were* for all persons. In the result clause, use *could*, *might*, or *would* + the base form of the verb.

- Use the past unreal conditional to talk about past unreal, untrue, imagined, or impossible conditions and their unreal results. Use the past perfect in the *if* clause and *could, might, or would have* + past participle in the result clause. We can use past unreal conditionals to express regret about a situation that actually happened in the past.

- Times in the *if* clause and the result clause are sometimes different. Present unreal and past unreal conditionals can be mixed in the same sentence.

- We often use unreal conditionals to express regret or sadness. We can also use *wish* + a noun clause to express sadness or desire for a different situation. *If only* has a meaning similar to that of *wish*. *If only* is followed by a noun clause without *that*.

Theme: INTUITION

Unit 22 focuses on language that is used to talk about intuition and speculation.

Step 1: Grammar in Context (pages 378–380)

See the general suggestions for Grammar in Context on page 1.

Before You Read

- Have students work in groups to discuss the questions or discuss them as a class. If students discuss the questions in groups, have students from each group share their ideas with the class.

Read

- You may want to discuss these words and their meanings:

serial killer someone who has killed several people, one after the other, often in the same way

curb the edge of a street, between where people can walk and cars can drive

- Write these questions on the board:
  1. On what kind of day did the story take place? *(very hot)*
  2. In American culture, which sex is supposed to have intuition? *(females)*
  3. Why was Donna unhappy about stopping to help Mr. Wilkerson? *(At first, she was afraid he might do harm to them. Then she was also concerned that by the time they got to the yard sale, all the good merchandise would be gone.)*
  4. Did Donna think the man's story about traveling around the country was true? *(No.)*
  5. What was the irony in the story? *(Donna and Thain probably assumed that the man was not very well off. In fact, he must have been quite wealthy if he sent them $100,000.)*
- Establish a purpose for reading. Have several different students read each of the questions aloud. Remind students to think about these questions as they read and listen to the text.
- Have students read the text, or play the audio and have students follow along in their books. Have students discuss the questions in pairs or groups of three. Call on students from each group or pair to share answers with the class.

After You Read

A. Vocabulary

- Have students complete the exercise individually and compare answers in pairs.
- Go over the answers as a class.

- **Note:** You may want to point out that, in this type of exercise, all of the answer choices are the same part of speech as the target word. In this case, looking at the context (the words and sentences around the target word) can help to determine meaning. One way for students to do this is to replace the target word in the sentence with the word choice that they think is correct. If the sentence makes sense and is logical in terms of other sentences, it is likely that the choice is correct.

B. Comprehension

- Have students complete the exercise individually.
- Have students work in pairs to check their answers.

Go to **www.myfocusongrammarlab.com** for an additional reading, and for reading and vocabulary practice.

Step 2: Grammar Presentation (pages 381–384)

See the general suggestions for Grammar Presentation on page 2.

Grammar Charts

- Have students compare the examples in the first two charts (Present and Future Real Conditional; Present Unreal Conditionals). Both talk about present situations. Ask: "Do both use present verb forms?" *(No, the verb forms in the unreal conditionals are past.)*
- Ask: "What about subject-verb agreement in Charts 1 and 2? "*(Subject-verb agreement is normal with the real conditionals. For the present unreal conditional, instead of* it was / wasn't, *we see* it were / weren't, *which is actually subjunctive. Students will learn more about the subjunctive in the next unit.)*
- Have students look at the third chart (Past Unreal Conditionals). Ask: "In Chart 3, what verb forms are used?" *(In the* if *clause, the past perfect is used. In the result clause,* would have + *past participle is used.)*
- Have students look at the last chart (Other Ways to Express Unreality). Ask: "In this chart, what verb forms are used for the present and future?" *(would, could)* "Which form is used for the past?" *(past perfect)* Ask: "In each sentence, what actually happens?" *(She will miss the sale. They can't buy the bureau. They arrived late.)*

Grammar Notes

Note 1

- Have students work in pairs to generate three or four more examples of situations or events that occur regularly or that are likely or possible in the future. (Examples: *It is hot in the summer. My train is late.*) Then brainstorm events that are untrue, unlikely, or impossible. (Examples: *I win the lottery. I am president of the United States.*)
- Have students from each pair share their ideas with the class.

Note 2

- Have students look at the present real conditional examples in Note 2 and point out that either the simple present or the present progressive can be used in the *if* clause.
- Have two students come to the board and change the verbs in *if* clauses of the first two sentences to the present progressive. Have a third student change the verb in the third example to the simple present. Ask: "Do these changes affect the meaning of the sentences?" *(No.)*
- Have students look at the examples that express future time situations. Have various students replace the modals in the result clauses with the other modals listed. Ask: "Do these substitutions change the meaning of the sentences?" *(In some case they do, but only because the modals have different meanings.)*

Note 3

- On the board write this sentence frame:
  If I _____ , I _____ .
  Have students tell you what can go into the blanks, and write these words under the blanks on the board:
  If I _____ , I _____ .
   were   *could*
   simple past   *might* + base form
          would
- Have students think about three things they wish were true, with at least one related to being something and one involving having something. Have them write these as sentences and share them in small groups. For example:
  If I were president of the country, I'd / I wouldn't . . .
  If I had 10,000 extra dollars, I'd . . .
  If I could talk to one famous person in history, I'd talk to . . .

Note 4

- Have students read the note and the examples. Draw students' attention to the *Be Careful!* note. You may want to point out that, in informal speech, many native speakers use *would have* in the *if* clause of past unreal conditionals, but it is still considered incorrect, especially in writing and in formal speech.
- Write the following sentence frame on the board again and have students supply the verb forms. Write them below the blanks:
  If I _____ , I _____ .
   had + past participle   *could have*
            might have + past participle
            would have
- Have students think about things they wish would have been true or things they regret. Have them write about them in sentences using the frame on the board and share their sentences in groups. For example:
  If I had studied English when I was young, I might have gotten my degree by now.
  If I had lived 100 years ago, I would have never left my home village.
  If I had worked more last summer, I could have bought a new motorcycle.

Note 5

- Write the following statements on the board. Have students read the sentences aloud and say whether each clause is about a past or future condition or result.
  If I hadn't read that book, I wouldn't know the answer. *(past condition; present result)*
  If I were rich, I would be in the Bahamas enjoying the sun. *(present condition; present result)*
  If I hadn't been there, I wouldn't have gotten hurt. *(past condition; past result)*
  If my car weren't at the garage, I would have lent it to you. *(present condition; past result)*
- Have students match the conditional sentences with the types of conditions and results they express. Then have students replace the underlined segments with their own ideas.

Note 6

- Point out that the central meaning of *wish* is a desire that a situation be different from what it is. A wish involves a contrary-to-fact situation.

- Have students write down three general situations (not actions) that they want to be different. Then have them make a *wish* statement about each and share these with a partner. (Example: *I don't get to see my wife much because she works a lot. I wish she had a different job.*)
- Next, have them write a sentence with *wish + would / could + base* form expressing a single future action that would change each situation wished about. (Example: *I wish my wife would look for a better job with fewer hours.*)

Note 7

- Have students read the note and the examples.
- Have students write down three things: something they want now, something they regret about the past, and something they'd like to change in the future. Have students express their wishes with sentences starting with *if only*. (Examples: *If only I had a car . . . If only I had passed my history test . . . If only Maria would stop smoking . . .*)

⏱ **Identify the Grammar:** Have students identify the grammar in the opening reading on pages 378–379. For example:

  I **wish** I **had** an iced tea right now.
  I**'d** sure **get** out of this heat **if** I **were** him . . .
  He**'s going to faint if** he **doesn't get** out of the sun.
  He**'ll** probably **kill** us and **steal** the car **if** we **pick** him **up**.
  "**If only** that bureau **would** still **be** there!"

Go to **www.myfocusongrammarlab.com** for grammar charts and notes.

Step 3: Focused Practice (pages 385–390)

See the general suggestions for Focused Practice on page 4.

Exercise 1: Discover the Grammar

A
- Have students complete the exercise individually and compare answers in small groups.
- Call on students from various groups to share their answers with the class. Discuss and clarify any discrepancies in answers among groups.

B
- Read the instructions and go over the example answer with students.
- Have students complete the exercise individually. Call on various students to share and explain their answers to the class.

Exercise 2: Present Real Conditionals

- Go over the example answer with students. Point out that the word *farmers* is capitalized, so the sentence begins with that word.
- Have students complete the exercise individually. Call on various students to write their sentences on the board and go over them as a class.
- ⏱ Have students rewrite the sentences so that the condition and result clauses switch places. (Example: *Item 1: If the springtime temperature drops below zero, farmers sometimes lose their crops.*)

Exercise 3: Present / Future Conditionals

- Have students complete the exercise individually. Then have them check their answers in pairs.
- Go over the answers as a class.
- ⏱ Have students practice the conversation in pairs twice, changing roles after the first practice.

Exercise 4: *Wish / If Only* Sentences

A
- Have students look at the pictures and describe what they see. Ask: "What situation do you think the people want to change?" Brainstorm some ideas. Then read the instructions and go over the example answer as a class.
- Have students complete the exercise individually. Then have students work in pairs to compare answers. Call on students to write their sentences on the board. Discuss the sentences as a class.

B
- Read the instructions and go over the example answer.
- Have students complete the exercise individually. Go over the answers as a class.
- ⏱ Have students take turns reading both sets of sentences (*wish* and *if only*) to each other.

Exercise 5: Mixed / Past Unreal Conditionals

- Have students quickly read the story for unfamiliar vocabulary items. Answer any questions.
- Have students complete the exercise individually and work in pairs to check their answers. Circulate as students are working together, noting any particular items that are problematic for students. Go over the problematic items as a class.
- ⏱ Have students practice reading the text aloud to each other.

Exercise 6: Editing

- Have students complete the exercise individually and work in pairs to check their answers.
- Have various students write their sentences on the board and explain each error and correction.

Go to **www.myfocusongrammarlab.com** for additional grammar practice.

Step 4: Communication Practice (pages 390–394)

See the general suggestions for Communication Practice on page 5.

Exercise 7: Listening

A

- Have students read the list of subjects. Remind them to listen and check the subjects that are *not* mentioned.
- Play the audio and have students complete the exercise.
- Go over the answers as a class.

B

- Have students read the questions. Remind them to keep these questions in mind as they listen.
- Play the audio and have students complete the exercise. You may have to play the audio more than once so students have enough time to write complete sentences.
- Have students work in pairs to check their answers. Go over the answers as a class.
- Give each pair a copy of the audioscript. Have them identify the target structures and whether each is real or unreal.

Exercise 8: Pronunciation

A

- Have students read and listen to the Pronunciation Note. Have students listen as you say the two example sentences, pronouncing the verb in the contracted form.
- Have students listen again and raise their hands if they think the action has already happened. Repeat the sentences randomly several times. After each one, tell students whether they were correct.

B

- Play the audio, pausing as needed so students can circle their answers.
- Go over the answers as a class. You may want to play the audio again to clarify any discrepancies in students' answers.

C

- Circulate as pairs practice saying the sentences. Provide help as needed.

Exercise 9: Conditional Game

- Read the instructions and go over the example with students.
- Divide the class into teams and have them work together to write the questions. Then have students find the answers to the questions. You may want to assign this portion as homework. Or you can provide each team with the following answers:

Team A
1. Where would you be if you were in the capital of Honduras? *(Tegucigalpa)*
2. How old would you have to be if you were the president of the United States? *(at least 35)*
3. Where would you be traveling if the monetary unit was the won? *(South Korea or North Korea)*
4. Where would you be if you were visiting Angkor Wat? *(Cambodia)*
5. Who would you have been if you had been the emperor of France in 1804? *(Napoleon)*
6. Who would you have been if you had been the first prime minister of India? *(Jawaharlal Nehru)*
7. What country would you have been from if you had been Marco Polo? *(Italy)*
8. What mountain would you have climbed if you had been with Edmund Hillary and Tenzing Norgay? *(Mt. Everest)*

Team B
1. How old would you be if you were an octogenarian? *(in your 80s)*
2. Where would you be traveling if you were in Machu Picchu? *(Peru)*
3. What would you be if you were the largest mammal? *(the blue whale)*
4. What country would you be in if you were standing and looking at Angel Falls? *(Venezuela)*
5. Who would you have been if you had been the inventor of the telephone? *(Alexander Graham Bell)*
6. What kind of creature would you have been if you were a stegosaurus? *(a dinosaur)*
7. What would have been your occupation if you were Genghis Khan? *(a powerful ruler and conqueror)*
8. Who would you have been if you had been Siddartha Gautama? *(the Buddha)*

- Have students play the trivia game. Keep score on the board. If your class is large, you might want to have students work in groups of four or six. Then divide each of those groups into two teams.

Exercise 10: Personal Inventory

A
- Have students read the instructions and the prompts. Brainstorm ways to complete the sentences.
- Have students complete the exercise individually. Encourage students to write statements about other people as well as themselves.

B
- Have students compare answers in pairs. Then have students report about each other to the class. Be sure that each person shares at least two sentences about his or her partner.
- **Note:** As a variation and for large classes, have each pair report their answers to another pair instead of the whole class.

Exercise 11: Group Discussion

A
- Give students time to read the opening reading again.
- Have students read the questions and discuss them in small groups.
- Circulate and provide help as needed.

B
- Have students make sure that each person in the group shares something with the class (or, for large classes, with another group) about what the group decided.
- ⏱ Have students discuss these questions: Have you ever received a gift that you thought was too generous? How did it make you feel? Why?

Exercise 12: Writing

A
- Establish some guidelines about this writing task. You may want to specify a certain number of paragraphs for students to write. Remind students that this assignment is essentially a narrative—telling a story about something that has occurred.
- ⏱ Have students use a graphic organizer to brainstorm a list of possible situations and a few details about each one. Then have them choose one situation to write about.

B
- Have students correct their work using the Editing Checklist or have them use the checklist to correct each other's work in pairs.
- Have students revise their writing.

OUT OF THE BOX ACTIVITIES

Writing, Speaking, and Listening
- In small groups, have students outline a biography of Quentin Wilkerson, the generous old man who left the young couple $100,000 in the opening reading. Have them use what little information is given about his life in the story and invent more about him. You may want to write these questions on the board as a guide:
  1. How old is he?
  2. Why is he traveling around the country?
  3. Why is he traveling alone?
  4. Why does he travel by bus?
  5. How did he make his money?
  6. Why doesn't he have any children?
  7. Why won't he be traveling around any more?
- Have each group share their biography outline with the class.

Reading, Speaking, and Listening
- Bring in a magazine or newspaper story about a situation that ended well because someone made the right decision at the right time.
- Have students read the story and discuss: (a) what would have happened if the person had reacted differently; (b) what they think the person wished at that moment; and (c) what they would have done themselves if they had been in that situation.
- You can also choose to have students discuss fictional stories. Two of these are "The Truth About Pyecraft" by H. G. Wells, in which Pyecraft, a fat man obsessed with losing weight, makes a decision which he then regrets, and "The Honest Man and The Devil," by Hilaire Belloc, in which a man decides to have nothing to do with the devil and is then surprised by the consequences of his decision. Have students discuss questions similar to the ones suggested above.

Go to **www.myfocusongrammarlab.com** for additional listening, pronunciation, speaking, and writing practice.

Note:
- See the *Focus on Grammar Workbook* for additional in-class or homework grammar practice.

Unit 22 Review (page 395)

Have students complete the Review and check their answers on Student Book page UR-3. Review or assign additional material as needed.

Go to **www.myfocusongrammarlab.com** for the Unit Achievement Test.

Grammar: MORE CONDITIONS; THE SUBJUNCTIVE

Unit 23 focuses on the forms, meanings, and uses of the subjunctive in implied and inverted conditionals and noun clauses.

- Conditions are sometimes implied rather than directly stated in an *if* clause. In a sentence with an implied condition, there is no change in the result clause, but the clause that expresses the condition may be implied through the use of certain words. The condition clause may precede or follow the result clause.

- Unreal conditions with *had, should,* and *were* are sometimes expressed by inverting the subject and verb and deleting *if*. There is no change in the result clause. The inverted condition clause can precede or follow the result clause. Inverted conditionals with *should* imply that an action or event is not likely to happen. This is much different from the usual meaning of *should.* Negative inversion is formed by adding *not* after the inverted subject and verb. Do not contract *not* and the verb. Sentences with inverted conditional clauses are more formal than conditionals with *if.*

- Although the use of the subjunctive is somewhat uncommon in English, it is commonly used in present unreal conditions with the use of *were. Were* is not used for past situations in conditionals.

- In another form of the subjunctive, we use a noun clause with the base form of the verb. Form the negative by placing *not* before the base form. To form a passive subjunctive, use *be* + the past participle. In passive subjunctives, we can usually omit *that.*

- The subjunctive is used in noun clauses following verbs of advice, necessity, and urgency. Do not use infinitives in subjunctive noun clauses with these types of verbs. However, some of these verbs can be followed by a gerund phrase.

- The subjunctive is also used after adjectives of advice, necessity, and urgency. Subjunctive verbs after these types of adjectives occur in the pattern *it* + *be* + adjective + *that* clause. In this type of clause we do not usually omit *that.*

Theme: ADVICE

Unit 23 focuses on language that is used to ask for and give advice.

Step 1: Grammar in Context (pages 396–398)

See the general suggestions for Grammar in Context on page 1.

Before You Read
- Have students work in pairs or groups to discuss the questions.
- Have various students from each group share answers with the class. Brainstorm advice and solutions for the problems students mention.

Read
- Write these questions on the board (or prepare them as a handout):
  1. What is the problem that Jason writes to Rosa about? *(He's upset because he thinks his college roommate is a slob, and the lack of neatness bothers him.)*
  2. What are Rosa's suggestions? *(Ask Hank if he really likes living this way; show him how to clean up; remind him that Jason has a right to an orderly and clean living space.)*
  3. What does Rosa say is an important thing? *(She says that Hank shouldn't feel criticized.)*
  4. What does Carla feel like at times? *(She feels like she's married to his family members).*
  5. What are two examples that Carla gives to explain her complaint? *(She says that his family members drop in without letting her know they're coming, his sister constantly asks her to do favors for her, and his cousin asks to borrow money but doesn't pay it back.)*
  6. What does Rosa think will help make Carla and Jim's marriage stronger? *(a little bit of communication)*

- Establish a purpose for reading. Have various students read the questions to the class. Remind students to think about the questions as they read and listen to the text.
- Have students read the text. Then have them work in pairs to discuss their answers.

After You Read
A. Vocabulary
- Have students complete the exercise. Go over the answers as a class.
- (⏱) Have students choose four or five of the vocabulary words from the exercise and write original sentences for each one. Then have them compare and discuss their sentences in pairs.

B. Comprehension
- Have students complete the exercise individually and compare answers in pairs or groups of three.
- Have various students share their answers with the class. Clarify any discrepancies in students' answers. Have students refer to the text to defend their answers if needed.

Go to **www.myfocusongrammarlab.com** for an additional reading, and for reading and vocabulary practice.

Step 2: Grammar Presentation (pages 399–402)
See the general suggestions for Grammar Presentation on page 2.

Grammar Charts
- Have students look at the first chart. Ask: "In general, which are easier to construct, implied or nonstandard conditions?" *(nonstandard conditions)*
- Point out that most of the nonstandard condition structures are very commonly used in conversation except for one. Ask: "Which nonstandard condition structure is *not* commonly used in conversation?" (but for, *which is, in fact, quite formal and very rarely used*)
- Have students look at the second chart and describe the difference in form between the inverted conditions and the standard conditions. (*word order, deletion of* if)
- Have students look at the third and fourth charts. Ask: "What do you notice about the form of the verbs in the subjunctive clauses?" *(They're base forms—they don't show agreement with the subject.)*

Grammar Notes
Note 1
- Have students read the note.
- Have students work in pairs to use the example sentences in the first grammar chart to practice forming nonstandard conditions. Have one partner cover the leftmost column and, looking at the implied condition column, re-create the equivalent sentences using *with, without, but for, if so, if not,* and *otherwise.* The other partner provides helpful feedback as needed. Then have partners switch roles.
- Elicit other examples from the class. Start with a prompt. (Example: *I'd better balance my checkbook.*) Have students suggest some nonstandard conditions *(if not, otherwise)* and complete the thought. (Example: *If not / Otherwise, I'm likely to bounce some checks.*)

Note 2
- Have students read the note.
- Have students work in pairs. Have one partner cover the leftmost column in the second grammar chart, look at the standard condition column, and re-create the equivalent sentence as an inverted condition. The other partner provides helpful feedback as needed. Then have partners switch roles.

Note 3
- Students will most likely be familiar with the structures in Note 3 because they studied them in the last unit as present and past unreal conditionals. Point out that *if I were you* is a particularly useful structure in English. If you feel they need more practice with it, have them work in pairs posing problems and offering advice. For example:
S1: My rent is too high.
S2: If I were you, I'd look for a new apartment.

Note 4
- Write these sentences on the board (without underlining the words):
  1. They <u>insist</u> we be available when they drop in.
  2. When I <u>suggest</u> she call first, she becomes angry.
  3. I would <u>recommend</u> she talk with her husband.
  4. I'd <u>rather</u> Jim not tell his parents how I feel.
  5. It's <u>important</u> that Elena not criticize his parents.
  6. I'd <u>propose</u> she communicate directly with him.
  7. It's not <u>advisable</u> for her to be upset.

8. I'd <u>recommend</u> Jason look into ways to help Hank understand.
9. It's <u>essential</u> that we understand each other's points of view.
10. It's <u>imperative</u> for her to communicate with her husband.

- Have students identify the noun clauses and the verbs they contain. **(All but Sentences 7 and 10 have noun clauses.)** Ask: "What do you notice about the verb form in the noun clauses in each of the sentences?" *(It's the base form.)*
- Leave the sentences on the board for Notes 5 and 6.

Note 5

- Have various students underline the verbs in each of the sentences on the board that trigger the use of the subjunctive. Ask: "What do you notice about the use of *that* in these sentences?" (That *is used in some of the sentences and omitted in others*.) "Can *that* be used after the underlined verbs?" *(Yes, but it's not required.)* "Which sentences contain a negative subjunctive?" *(4 and 7)* "How is it formed?" (Not *is added before the base form of the verb*.)
- This note presents some useful alternatives to the subjunctive. Have students look at the sentences again and consider in which cases the subjunctive might be replaced by a gerund phrase. *(2, 6, and 8)*

Note 6

- Have students look at the sentences again. Ask:
  — Which sentences have a structure that is different from the other sentences? *(5, 7, 9, and 10)*
  — What is the different structure? *(In these four sentences the main clause has the pattern* it + be + *adjective.)*
  — How are Sentences 7 and 10 different from Sentences 5 and 9? *(Sentences 5 and 10 have the alternate pattern* it + be + *adjective* + for + *noun or object pronoun* + *infinitive, which is more informal.)*
  — Why does *that* appear in some of these sentences and not others? *(In 5 and 9 it can be omitted, but usually isn't. In 7 and 10* for *replaces* that *and cannot be omitted. In the rest of the sentences* that *is optional.)*

- ⏱ **Identify the Grammar:** Have students identify the grammar in the opening reading on pages 396–397. For example:
  Hank and I were best friends in high school, so when he **suggested we room** together in college I thought it was a great idea.

Had I known what a slob Hank really is, I never would have agreed.
What would you **recommend I do**?
If so, ask him if he really likes having dirty dishes and bugs all over the place.

Go to **www.myfocusongrammarlab.com** for grammar charts and notes.

Step 3: Focused Practice (pages 402–408)

See the general suggestions for Focused Practice on page 4.

Exercise 1: Discover the Grammar

A
- Have students work in groups to compare their answers.
- Have various groups share and explain their answers to the class.

B
- Have students complete the exercise individually. Go over the answers as a class.
- For each incorrect rewrite, have various students write a correct rewrite on the board and discuss them as a class.

Exercise 2: Implied Conditionals
- First, have students work individually to underline the conditional sentences. Go over the answers as a class.
- Next, have students rewrite the sentences they underlined. Have them work in pairs to compare answers. Then go over the answers as a class.
- ⏱ Have students practice the conversation twice in pairs, changing roles after each practice. Then have them practice the conversation again, substituting the sentences with nonstandard conditions they wrote in the exercise.

Exercise 3: Inverted / Implied Conditionals

A
- Have students work individually to complete the exercise and compare answers in groups.
- Call on various groups to share their answers with the class.

B
- Have various students write their sentences on the board and discuss them as a class.
- Have students work in pairs to practice reading the completed text aloud to each other.

Exercise 4: Verbs of Urgency and Subjunctives

- Have students look at the pictures and describe what they see. Read the instructions and go over the example with the class.
- Have students complete the exercise individually and work in groups to share their sentences.

Exercise 5: Adjectives of Urgency and Subjunctives

A
- Have students read the instructions and the words in the box. Go over the example answer so students understand how to use the prompts in parentheses and the words in the box to complete the sentences.
- Have students complete the exercise individually. Go over the answers with the class.

B
- Read the instructions. If needed, show students how to rewrite the first sentence. *(It is desirable for young people to have good self-esteem.)* You may want to point out that students should use *young people* or *them* as nouns or object pronouns.
- Have students complete the exercise. Call on various students to write their sentences on the board. Discuss the sentences as a class.
- ⏱ Have students take turns reading the sentences in Parts A and B in pairs.

Exercise 6: Editing

- Have students complete the exercise individually and work in pairs to check answers.
- Have various students write their corrected sentences on the board and explain each error and correction.

Go to **www.myfocusongrammarlab.com** for additional grammar practice.

Step 4: Communication Practice (pages 409–412)

See the general suggestions for Communication Practice on page 5.

Exercise 7: Listening

A
- Have students read the question. Remind them to think about the question as they listen.
- Play the audio and allow students time to answer the question. Go over the answer as a class.
- ⏱ Have students write down in their notebooks any information that they recall from the listening.

B
- Have students read the questions. Remind them to think about them as they listen.
- Play the audio and have students complete the exercise. You may want to play the audio more than once to allow students enough time to write answers in complete sentences.
- Go over the answers as a class.
- ⏱ Have students look at the information they noted after the first listening. It is likely that they did not remember too much. If so, ask students why they think this is true. *(In Part A, they are listening for a very specific piece of information. For this reason, they may have missed hearing much of the other information).*

Exercise 8: Pronunciation

A
- Have students read and listen to the Pronunciation Note.
- Say the examples aloud several times and have students repeat.

B
- Read the instructions and go over the example answers.
- Play the audio, pausing as needed so students can write their answers.
- Go over the answers as a class.

C
- Circulate as pairs practice. Provide feedback as needed.

Exercise 9: Personal Inventory

A
- Read the instructions and have students look at the prompts. Remind students to pay close attention to the structures in each item.
- Have students complete the exercise. Circulate and help as needed. Have them refer to the grammar charts and notes as needed to complete the sentences.

B
- Have students report about each other to the class.

Exercise 10: Group Discussion

A
- Have students read the statements. Answer any questions about vocabulary.
- Have students complete the exercise. Encourage them to take notes on why they agree, disagree, or are not sure about each item.

B

- Go over the instructions and the example. Point out that the speaker gives reasons for his or her opinion and the other person asks follow-up questions.
- Have students discuss their answers. Circulate, helping as needed.
- Call on groups to report their answers to the class. Be sure that, as students report their group's opinions to the class, each member of the group contributes to the reporting.

Exercise 11: Picture Discussion

- Have students look at the pictures and share what they know about the place. Ask them about what tourists can do there, what the weather is like, what the local customs are, and if there is anything people should or shouldn't do while there.
- Read the instructions and go over the example. Brainstorm other pieces of advice for travel to the United Kingdom. (Examples: *I recommend that she ride a double-decker bus. It's essential that she remembers to drive on the left, not on the right.*) Encourage students to use a variety of verbs and adjectives. If needed, refer students to Appendix 24 on page A-10.
- Have students choose a place they'd like to discuss and form groups with students who chose the same place. Have them complete the exercise. Circulate and help as needed.

Exercise 12: Writing

A

- Have students read the instructions and the example. Brainstorm other examples of good or bad advice that students have taken.
- Explain that students will write a narrative essay. Review the key parts of the essay. (*A statement of whether the advice was good or bad, identification of the situation and a clear description of it, the sequence of events, and the ultimate resolution or outcome.*)
- ⏱ Have students use the prewriting process to plan and organize their essays.
- Have students write their essays, either in class or as homework.

B

- Have students use the Editing Checklist to revise and rewrite as needed or have students work in pairs to correct each other's work.

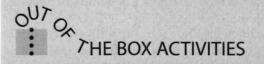

OUT OF THE BOX ACTIVITIES

Writing, Reading, Listening, and Speaking

- Have each student write two letters to an advice columnist seeking advice about two different situations. They can use the opening text as a model.
- Have students give each of their letters to a different classmate. Have students respond to the letters and give their responses to the appropriate student.
- Have students work with a new partner to discuss one of the situations and the advice they received. Make sure students use their own words to describe the situation orally and do not simply exchange papers to read.
- ⏱ Have students change partners and repeat the process for the second letter.

Reading, Listening, and Speaking

- Bring in (or have students bring in) a variety of articles that make suggestions, express opinions, or give advice.
- Have students work in small groups to read one of the articles and discuss it. Have students take notes about their discussion and deliver a group report to the class. Encourage students to use the language they learned in this unit. You may also want to write the following sentence frames on the board:
  The article suggests (that) _____.
  The experts recommend (that) _____.
  You might _____; if so, _____.
  Should you _____, _____.
  Without perseverance, you won't be able to _____.
  With a bit of patience, you'll soon be able to _____.
  It's important (that) _____.
  It's essential (that) _____.
  It's advisable (that) _____.

Go to **www.myfocusongrammarlab.com** for additional listening, pronunciation, speaking, and writing practice.

Note:
- See the *Focus on Grammar Workbook* for additional in-class or homework grammar practice.

Unit 23 Review (page 413)

Have students complete the Review and check their answers on Student Book page UR-3. Review or assign additional material as needed.

Go to **www.myfocusongrammarlab.com** for the Unit Achievement Test.

From Grammar to Writing (pages 414–417)

See the general suggestions for From Grammar to Writing on page 9.

Go to **www.myfocusongrammarlab.com** for an additional From Grammar to Writing Assignment, Part Review, and Part Post-Test.

STUDENT BOOK AUDIOSCRIPT

EXERCISE 6 (page 10)

JIM: Hi, Mary. How are things going? You look like you lost your best friend.

MARY: Not well. I'm having some pretty serious money problems.

JIM: Why? What's wrong?

MARY: Well, someone got hold of my credit card number.

JIM: You mean somebody stole your credit card?

MARY: No, somebody got the number. You've heard of identity theft? Well, this is a good example of it.

JIM: Oh, no! Really? I know that sort of thing happens, but I've never known anyone it happened to.

MARY: Yeah. The whole thing is really upsetting. Whoever got the number has been charging a lot on my card—$8,000.

JIM: How do you think it happened?

MARY: Well, I'm almost positive it was on the Internet. About two months ago I bought some CDs from a website and used my card. They said it was a secure site, but apparently it wasn't.

JIM: So what happens now? You won't have to pay the $8,000, will you?

MARY: Probably not, but I might have to pay something. You're supposed to report thefts like this immediately.

JIM: Didn't you?

MARY: No, not right away. I got a credit card bill with a big purchase on it that I couldn't remember making, but I thought it was probably my mistake, and I didn't do anything for a few days. By the time I reported it, there were a lot of other purchases.

JIM: I'm really sorry. This is terrible.

MARY: Thanks. You know, the Internet makes things easy. Maybe too easy.

JIM: Yeah. It's easy for us to get information, but it's also easy for criminals to get it. That's the downside of the Internet.

UNIT 2

EXERCISE 7 (page 24)

In other news, the first-ever wedding of a couple jumping from a plane in parachutes took place yesterday in the skies over Saskatoon, Saskatchewan, Canada. Samantha Yang and Darrell Hammer hired a minister, Reverend Robert Martinez, to jump with them out of a twin-engine Cessna and marry them in the air before they landed. Yang and Hammer met four years ago at a meeting of the Saskatoon Sky-Divers, of which they have been members for many years. To date, each of them has made over thirty jumps. Interviewed as to why they wanted to get married in such an unusual way, Yang said, "We're just adventurous souls, I guess. We like new and different things. We didn't want a conventional wedding." Hammer agreed, adding, "We were going to get married on a bungee jump, but when we got to thinking about it, we decided that would be just a little too dangerous. Plus, we couldn't find a minister who would bungee-jump with us."

Reverend Martinez had never made a parachute jump before yesterday. Asked if he had ever performed such an unusual wedding ceremony before, Martinez responded, "No, I think this one is the oddest. I used to be a pastor in Arizona. I would get some fairly unusual requests. I mean, for example, once I married two people on horseback. But nothing quite like this."

Would he do another parachute-jump-wedding— or even another parachute jump? "I don't think so," Martinez said. "No, I think this is one for the scrapbook. At this point, I can just say, 'Been there, done that.'"

That's the news on the half hour. Stay tuned for our next broadcast on the hour.

UNIT 3

EXERCISE 6 (page 41)

MOM: Tim? Come on! We're going to be late if you don't get up right now.

TIM: Why? Where are we going?

MOM: To the historical museum. Remember?

TIM: Do we have to? Amy and I want to go to the West Edmonton Mall.

AMY: That's right, Mom. Museums are boring.

DAD: But this is a really interesting museum. There'll be all kinds of thing to learn.

TIM: Why do we have to learn things when we're on vacation?

AMY: Dad, can't you and Mom drop us off at the mall? Then you can go to the museum.

Mom: It's all arranged, kids. We're meeting the tour bus at 9:30. In fact, if we don't get down to the lobby, we're going to miss it.

Tim: Oh, no! Not a tour!

Dad: Yes. Sometimes a tour is the best way to see things.

Amy: I hate tours. If we have to go to the historical museum, can't we at least go by ourselves?

Mom: Come on, kids. We're going to be late.

Amy: Can we go to the mall later?

Dad: Sure. Tell you what: The tour will be over by 12:30. As soon as we get back from the tour, we'll go to the mall.

Tim: Can we go ice-skating at the mall?

Mom: Yes. As a matter of fact, we've got reservations for all of us to skate.

Amy: Right on, Mom!

EXERCISE 7 (page 41)

1. I won't be able to go with you tonight, but I will be able to go tomorrow night.
2. I'm not going to attend college this fall, but I am going to attend in the spring.
3. I will be able to help you tomorrow; unfortunately, I won't be able to help you today.
4. We won't be traveling in Asia in July, but we will be there in August.
5. They won't be moving to a new house in September, but they will be moving in November.
6. We're not leaving this weekend, but we are leaving next weekend.
7. We won't have visited every South American country by the end of our trip, but we will have seen most of them.

UNIT 4

EXERCISE 6 (page 62)

Bev: Hello?

Dad: Hi, Bev. This is Dad.

Bev: Dad! Where are you? Mom's surprise party is supposed to start in 15 minutes. Everybody's already shown up. We're just waiting for you and Ray and Mom.

Dad: Great. You don't think your mother has figured out what's going on, do you?

Bev: No, I'm sure she hasn't. She thinks we're all going to a concert this afternoon. She says she's really looking forward to it.

Dad: Good. Anyway, here's the problem, Bev. Ray and I are at the department store trying to find a gift for your mom, and we can't come up with anything.

Do you think we could get away with not giving her a present today? If we took a little more time, we could find something really nice.

Bev: Dad! Of course not! Everybody who's here has brought something. You and Ray will be the only ones. And Dad, remember what you told me when I was a girl? Don't put things off to the last minute?

Dad: Yes, dear; I know. We should've gone shopping last week. But honey, what do you suggest?

Bev: What about a camera?

Dad: She's got three cameras. In fact, she just got rid of one of her old cameras last week.

Bev: How about some article of clothing?

Dad: Great idea. A dress, maybe?

Bev: Dad! You can't just buy her a dress. She'd never buy a dress without trying on several first.

Dad: Well, Bev, we're running out of time here. Can't you think of something?

Bev: Well, you might get her a blouse. She loves blouses.

Dad: No way, Bev. I tried that once, and your mother hated what I got her.

Bev: Well . . . let's see. How about a couple of nice scarves?

Dad: Good! What material? What color?

Bev: Why don't you look for a couple of silk scarves in some conservative color?

Dad: Good idea. Will do. We'll get there as soon as we can.

Bev: OK, Dad, but hurry up! Mom could be home any minute.

UNIT 5

EXERCISE 6 (page 80)

A

Professor: OK, folks. Today we're going to talk about a question related to hearing. I want to begin by telling you about an experience I had the first time I heard my voice on a recording. It was at a speech class when I was in college. The professor recorded our voices and then played them back. When I heard mine, I said, "That couldn't have been me. There's got to be some mistake. I don't sound like that." Now, I'd venture to say all of you must have had this experience at one time or another. Am I right? Let me see a show of hands . . . Uh-huh, just as I thought. Now, the question is why. Why do we hear our voices differently than others do? Based on what we've been studying, you should be able to figure this out. Allison, what do you think?

ALLISON: I think it must be because we're hearing the sound in a different way.

PROFESSOR: Very good. You've got the right idea. Now, anybody want to expand on that? Bart?

BART: It could be because the sound is traveling through different substances.

PROFESSOR: Right. Go on. Can you explain?

BART: Well, let's see. When somebody speaks, the sound of that person's voice comes to us through the air. We hear our own voice through our head.

PROFESSOR: Good, good . . . Kathy, can you add something?

KATHY: I agree with Bart when he says we hear our own voice through our own head. But don't we also hear it through the air? It might be a combination of the two things.

PROFESSOR: Yes, you're both right. You see, when we hear our own voice, we hear partly through our ears—externally. But we also hear through the bone in our head and through the fluid in our inner ear—internally. Most of the sound we hear internally comes through liquid . . . Now, here's one more question. Which sound is the "real" sound? The way other people hear our voices, or the way we hear them? . . . Darren?

DARREN: I think the sound others hear has to be the real sound.

PROFESSOR: Uh huh, anybody else?

KATHY: I'd say the opposite. The sound we hear must be the real sound.

PROFESSOR: Actually, Kathy is right. Internal hearing is of higher fidelity than external hearing.

B

1. That couldn't have been me.
2. There's got to be some mistake.
3. All of you must have had this experience at one time or another.
4. You should be able to figure this out.
5. It must be because we're hearing the sound in a different way.
6. It could be because the sound is traveling through different substances.
7. It might be a combination of the two things.
8. The sound others hear has to be the real sound.
9. The sound we hear must be the real sound.
10. Internal hearing is of higher fidelity than external hearing.

EXERCISE 6 (page 100)

DR. JINDAL: Hello, Mr. Smith. Have a seat and make yourself comfortable. I'm Larry Jindal.

JOE SMITH: It's good to meet you, Dr. Jindal. I guess you know why I'm here.

DR. JINDAL: Yes. I understand your wife was on one of those TV medical shows and asked the speaker a question about your health. The speaker said you needed to lose some weight?

JOE SMITH: Yeah, that's basically it. My wife insisted I see a doctor, so here I am.

DR. JINDAL: Well, I'm looking at your records here—I see that you're 5 feet eleven, and your weight is 257 pounds. Your cholesterol level is 322. So I'd say the speaker was right. Tell me about your daily routine. How many meals do you eat a day, where do you eat them, how much do you exercise—that sort of thing.

JOE SMITH: Well, I just eat two meals a day—lunch and dinner. I don't really get any exercise, since I work 12-hour days and don't really have time.

DR. JINDAL: What about lunch? Do you take a lunch with you? Eat out?

JOE SMITH: I eat out at various fast-food places near where I work.

DR. JINDAL: And you don't eat breakfast?

JOE SMITH: No. It seems like I never have time. Plus, I never feel like eating anything until about 11 A.M. Then I have a snack at work—usually doughnuts or some other pastry.

DR. JINDAL: Well, I'd say you're at high risk for a heart attack. Your cholesterol is what I'd call dangerously high. Your BMI would be about 35. Anything over 25 is considered overweight.

JOE SMITH: So are you going to put me on a diet?

DR. JINDAL: No. For the most part diets don't work. I'm going to suggest a radical change in your eating habits. That includes eating breakfast—whether you feel like eating it or not. You can still eat a lot of the foods you like, but in much smaller portions. And I want you to start an exercise program. You can begin slowly—say three times a week, with non-strenuous exercise at first. Are you willing? It won't be easy. But you can do it if you work at it.

JOE SMITH: Well, I guess so. There's nothing to lose, I guess.

DR. JINDAL: And a lot to gain.

UNIT 7

EXERCISE 6 (page 115)

WIFE: Anything interesting in the paper?

HUSBAND: Not a whole lot. There's a story about reintroducing wolves into national parks.

WIFE: Oh yeah? What does it say?

HUSBAND: Oh, the usual nonsense. It's on the side of the environmentalists.

WIFE: Why do you think it's nonsense?

HUSBAND: Because it's too pro-environmentalist. It doesn't really look at the viewpoint of ranchers and hunters.

WIFE: Well, you're a hunter, so I'm not surprised. But do you support the ranchers too?

HUSBAND: Yes, I do, basically.

WIFE: Why? Do you think it's a bad thing to put wolves back into the wilderness?

HUSBAND: Well, yes, in a lot of ways I do. Wolves are dangerous creatures. They kill farm animals. They've even been known to kill people.

WIFE: Bill, where are you getting your information? That's an old stereotype.

HUSBAND: All those old stories must mean something.

WIFE: Well, I support the plan to put wolves back into national parks.

HUSBAND: Why?

WIFE: I've done some reading about it. They put a few wolves into Yellowstone National Park back in 1995. They've multiplied quite a bit and have done a lot to restore the balance of nature. There were too many elk there, but the wolves have killed off some of the old and sick ones. Wolves are really intelligent and helpful.

HUSBAND: Hmm. I guess you've got a point. But I still think we have to consider the ranchers' point of view.

UNIT 8

EXERCISE 6 (page 130)

MARY: Mmm. That sure was a great meal. Thanks for suggesting this restaurant, Mike.

MIKE: Glad you liked it. There aren't as many menu choices as at that restaurant we went to last month, but what they serve is really delicious.

STEVE: Yeah. And the prices are lower here, too.

SALLY: Well, guys, Mary and I are going to the ladies' room. Back soon.

STEVE: OK.

MIKE: All right, let me just get the check here . . . Everything looks right . . . Uh-oh!

STEVE: What's wrong?

MIKE: I don't have my wallet! I must have left it somewhere, but I can't think where. Have you got any money, Steve?

STEVE: I don't think so, but let me check. I didn't bring my wallet because you said you were paying . . . Let me just look . . . oh yea, I found a few dollars. How much is the bill?

MIKE: Seventy-five.

STEVE: Oh, too bad. I've got less than $20.

MIKE: Have you got a credit card with you?

STEVE: No, I don't. Actually, Sally and I don't have any credit cards at all. We don't use them.

MIKE: Hmm. Maybe Mary has her card or some money with her. I sure hope so. Otherwise we'll be washing dishes.

MARY: Hi, guys. We're back. Is the bill all taken care of?

MIKE: No, it's not. We've got a problem. I don't have my wallet. Do you have any money, Mary?

MARY: Gee, Mike, I don't know. Let me look . . . Looks like I've got about $25.

MIKE: Well, Steve has about $15. It's still not enough to pay the bill. Do you have your credit card, Mary?

MARY: No, I don't think so . . . Oh, wait a minute, but here's my bank card. We can use it at an ATM. I don't think they take debit cards here.

MIKE: But there aren't any ATM machines here, are there?

MARY: Yes, there are. There's one in the hotel lobby.

MIKE: Whew! Saved. I just wonder what I could have done with my wallet . . .

UNIT 9

EXERCISE 6 (page 144)

A

DR. TANAKA: OK, Josh, let's get started. Our first meeting is only going to be a thirty-minute session. We don't want to make this a brain-breaker. Now, first I want you to tell me exactly how you feel when your teacher asks you to read.

JOSH: I feel like a total, complete idiot. And I feel like I have an ugly, high-pitched, squeaky voice.

DR. TANAKA: Your voice sounds fine, Josh. You're just going through a rapid adolescent growth period, so your voice is changing. It happens to a lot of twelve-year-old boys. All right. Now, the key to getting you over this fear-of-oral-reading problem is to distract you from thinking about how well you're doing. Let's think of a short, easy-to-remember phrase that you can keep in the back of your mind. When you're reading and you start to feel nervous or frustrated, you say it and distract yourself.

JOSH: How about "Roses are red, violets are blue"?

DR. TANAKA: That'll do fine. All right, let's put it to the test. I want you to read this passage. If you start feeling anxious, just start saying the phrase.

JOSH: "It was an icy, dark, stormy evening. It promised to be one of those famous three-dog nights." . . . What's a three-dog night?

DR. TANAKA: It's a night that's so cold you need three large, warm, furry dogs to sleep with to keep you warm. Anyway, you read that beautifully. Did you feel nervous?

JOSH: Just for a second, and I started saying the line from the poem. After that it was fine. I think I'm going to like this.

B

1. Our first meeting is only going to be a 30-minute session.
2. I feel like a total, complete idiot.
3. And I feel like I have an ugly, high-pitched, squeaky voice.
4. You're just going through a rapid adolescent growth period.
5. Now, the key to getting you over this fear-of-oral-reading problem is to distract you from thinking about how well you're doing.
6. Let's think of a short, easy-to-remember phrase that you can keep in the back of your mind.
7. It was an icy, dark, stormy evening.
8. It promised to be one of those famous three-dog-nights.
9. It's a night that's so cold you need three large, warm, furry dogs to sleep with to keep you warm.

UNIT 10

EXERCISE 6 (page 168)

JEAN: Hi, Greg.

GREG: Hi, yourself. How's it going?

JEAN: Great. Hey, do you want to hear a joke?

GREG: A joke? Why do you think I'd want to hear a joke?

JEAN: Don't you like jokes?

GREG: Not usually.

JEAN: Why not?

GREG: Well . . . what bothers me about most jokes is that they're too . . . programmed.

JEAN: I don't know what you mean.

GREG: Somebody tells a joke, and you're expected to laugh, whether you think it's funny or not. Basically, the problem is that you're usually forced to be dishonest.

JEAN: You're too sensitive. Don't laugh if you don't think it's funny.

GREG: But everybody thinks you're a drag if you don't laugh.

JEAN: What? Explain.

GREG: Well, a lot of times I don't get what the point of the joke is. I feel like I'm stupid when that happens.

JEAN: I know what: I'll tell you a funny story—not exactly a joke—and let's see if you understand.

GREG: All right. Go ahead.

JEAN: OK. Here we go. There was a school in Oregon that was faced with a unique problem. A lot of the girls used lipstick, and they would put it on in the girls' bathroom. There was nothing wrong with that, but after they'd put it on, they'd press their lips against the mirror just to make sure the lipstick was on right, and that would leave dozens of lip prints all over the mirror. So finally the principal of the school decided something had to be done about the problem.

GREG: So what did he do?

JEAN: It wasn't a he; it was a she. Anyway, here's what she did: She told some of the girls to report to the bathroom, and she'd meet them there with the school custodian. She explained to the girls that the lip prints were causing a major problem for the custodian because he had to clean the mirrors every day. To show the girls how difficult this was, she asked the custodian to clean one of them. He took a mop with a long handle, dipped it into a toilet, and then cleaned the mirror with it. Ever since then there haven't been any lip prints on the mirror.

GREG: Gross. Pretty funny, though.

JEAN: Are you sure you're not just saying that just so you don't feel stupid?

GREG: Nope. It wasn't exactly a joke, but it was funny.

UNIT 11

EXERCISE 6 (page 186)

ANNOUNCER: We're back, everyone. Once again, my guest today is communication expert Ellen Sands, who is telling us about ways to minimize verbal conflict. Ellen, you've talked about active listening and about stating things positively instead of negatively. What's another way to improve communication?

Ellen Sands: A third way involves speaking about yourself instead of about the other person, especially in a conflict situation. That means focusing on how the other person's statements are affecting you. It does *not* involve returning anger for anger.

Announcer: How about an example?

Ellen Sands: Sure. Here's a situation from my own private practice. A few months back, two sisters, whom I'll call Rosa and Alicia, came to me for help with a family dispute. Their mother had died, and they were arguing about dividing up the family estate. Their mother hadn't left a will, so the situation was pretty complicated. It wasn't long before Rosa and Alicia were at each other's throats. Rosa said, "Alicia, you always got everything because you were Mother's favorite." Alicia was clearly hurt by the criticism and angrily responded, "The problem is that you're a very selfish person." After that it just got worse.

Announcer: What would have been a better way to handle this?

Ellen Sands: Well, Rosa was the aggressive one, but it takes two people to make an argument. Alicia should have spoken about how Rosa made her feel instead of attacking Rosa back. She could have said something like, "You know, Rosa, you really hurt my feelings when you said that." Then she could have said, "I felt disrespected." You'd be surprised how much statements like these can defuse anger and help in a conflict situation.

Announcer: Very interesting! All right, we're going to take another break and then hear more from Ellen Sands.

UNIT 12

EXERCISE 6 (page 206)

Al: Hi, Mom. Hi, Dad. I just thought I'd call and tell you about my week.

Mom: Hi, Al. How are things going now?

Al: Pretty well. I like the dormitory. The supervisor, who lives right down the hall from me, is really helpful. And he doesn't inspect our rooms.

Dad: How about your roommates, son?

Al: I really like the one who's from Minnesota. He's great to hang around with. I'm not so sure about the other one.

Dad: What's the problem with him?

Al: He's always asking to borrow money.

Mom: Well, I hope that stops happening. What about your courses? Are they hard?

Al: Well, my English course, which is really tough, is going to require a lot of writing. So is the history

class that's in the morning. The history class that I have in the afternoon looks like it's going to be the easiest. My math class is going to be a piece of cake.

Mom: One thing I'm curious about—is this an all-male dorm, or are there girls living there too?

Al: Well, there are two parts to the building. The girls live on one side and the guys on the other. And there are three cafeterias. The girls who live on the second floor eat with us at the cafeteria on our floor.

Dad: What about your advisors? Advisors helped me a lot when I was in college.

Al: Well, my advisor, who is from Minneapolis, is wonderful. She's told me just what subjects I have to take.

Mom: OK, now I have another question . . .

EXERCISE 7 (page 208)

1. The man, who lives down the street from me, is a friend of my father.
2. The man who lives down the street from me is a friend of my father.
3. The tie, which has a stain on it, needs to be dry-cleaned.
4. The tie which has a stain on it needs to be dry-cleaned.
5. The teacher who handed out the awards is really a well-known scientist.
6. The teacher, who handed out the awards, is really a well-known scientist.
7. The student who lives close to the campus has low gasoline bills.
8. The student, who lives close to the campus, has low gasoline bills.
9. The garden, which Mary planted, is the most beautiful one of all.
10. The garden which Mary planted is the most beautiful one of all.

UNIT 13

EXERCISE 7 (page 222)

A

Good evening, all you movie buffs. I'm Penelope Truman with this week's *Movie Mania*. Run, don't walk, to the film festival being held this holiday weekend on the university campus. A series of all-time classics, some recent and some of which haven't been shown on the big screen in over a decade, will be shown in the film school auditorium. For the $25 admission price, you can see eight movies. Here are my special picks:

First: *A Beautiful Mind*, the creation of director Ron Howard, is a fascinating biography starring Russell Crowe and based on the life of M.I.T. professor and mathematical genius John Nash, who suffered from schizophrenia and had some very interesting delusions. You have to pay close attention to this one: which characters are real, and which aren't? Ultimately, it's a touching film for which Jennifer Connelly won an Oscar for her performance as Nash's wife.

Second: *Rashomon* is probably the most famous picture of Japanese director Akira Kurosawa and the winner of the Oscar for best foreign film. It's an unusual movie about a rape and murder recounted by four different witnesses of the episode. Set in the Japan of several centuries ago, it deals with the notion that truth is often in the eye of the witness.

Third: We don't see as many musicals as we used to, which is too bad, but they may be making a comeback. Even if you're not a fan of musicals, this one deserves your attention. *Chicago*, starring Renée Zellweger, Richard Gere, and Catherine Zeta-Jones, is a story of the almost lawless times in the city of Chicago after World War I. Zellweger plays a woman on trial for murdering her husband, and Gere plays the lawyer who defends her. Whoever would have thought Gere could sing and dance? Zeta-Jones won an Oscar for her role as Zellweger's fellow prisoner.

Fourth: *Back to the Future*, the movie that was responsible for launching the movie career of Michael J. Fox, is about a teenager who has to travel back in time to arrange for his own parents to meet so that he won't cease to exist! *Back to the Future* is especially fun because it gives us a semi-objective comparison of our own era and an earlier one.

Finally: For all of you old-timers out there a kiss may be just a kiss, but *Casablanca*, showcasing the talents of Humphrey Bogart and Ingrid Bergman, is more than just a movie. This picture, my personal all-time favorite, is a must-see for all regarding themselves as serious movie buffs. This movie, filmed in black and white, may not be a pretty picture, but it's certainly a profound one.

So, there they are. My spies tell me that tickets are likely to sell like hotcakes, in which case you'd better call right away or order your tickets online if you want to attend. I'm Penelope Truman for *Movie Mania*, and I'll see you at the movies.

B

1. Run, don't walk, to the film festival being held this holiday weekend on the university campus.
2. A series of all-time classics, some recent and some of which haven't been seen on the big screen in more than a decade, will be shown in the film school auditorium.
3. *A Beautiful Mind*, the creation of director Ron Howard, is a fascinating biography starring Russell Crowe and based on the life of M.I.T. professor and mathematical genius John Nash.

4. Ultimately, it's a touching film for which Jennifer Connelly won an Oscar for her performance as Nash's wife.
5. *Rashomon* is probably the most famous picture of Japanese director Akira Kurosawa and the winner of the Oscar for best foreign film.
6. Set in the Japan of several centuries ago, it deals with the notion that truth is often in the eye of the witness.
7. *Chicago*, starring Renée Zellweger, Richard Gere, and Catherine Zeta-Jones, is a story of the almost lawless times in the city of Chicago after World War I.
8. *Back to the Future*, the movie that was responsible for launching the movie career of Michael J. Fox, is about a teenager who has to travel back in time to arrange for his own parents to meet so that he won't cease to exist!
9. *Casablanca*, showcasing the talents of Humphrey Bogart and Ingrid Bergman, is more than just a movie. This picture, my personal all-time favorite, is a must-see for all regarding themselves as serious movie buffs.
10. This movie, filmed in black and white, may not be a pretty picture, but it's certainly a profound one.

UNIT 14

EXERCISE 7 (page 245)

Here is breaking news from KKBO News Channel 6. A hit-and-run accident occurred this evening at 8:45 P.M. at the intersection of 4th Avenue and Madison Street downtown. An eight-year-old boy was crossing the intersection alone when he was struck by a blue late-model Toyota Camry. The Toyota disappeared from the intersection immediately, and no information has been received as to the car's license number or the driver's identity. The boy sustained massive injuries and was taken to Downtown Medical Center, where he is being cared for in the Intensive Care Unit. The boy's condition is described as critical. Anyone with information is asked to call 444-6968. A reward is being offered for information leading to the arrest of the driver of the Toyota.

EXERCISE 8 (page 246)

1. The prisoner's being interrogated.
2. The issue's been discussed.
3. Bob's been promoted to police chief.
4. The investigation's being completed.
5. The plane's being hijacked.
6. The boy's being treated for injuries.
7. The report's been written.
8. The mystery's been solved.

UNIT 15

EXERCISE 6 (page 261)

We interrupt our regularly scheduled program to bring you this news bulletin. A massive series of earthquakes has struck the nation, causing extreme damage to most major cities. The earthquakes are said to have registered a 9 on the Richter scale, although this information is considered preliminary. The minister of science has stated that the epicenter of the quakes was located in the Atlantic Ocean some 40 miles west of Gibraltar. According to unconfirmed reports, vast sections of the coastline are reported to be under water as a consequence of a gigantic tsunami that hit the coastal areas after the earthquakes. The exact number of casualties of the tsunami is not known, although it is estimated that more than 200,000 people have drowned. Serious flooding is believed to have occurred in cities farther inland. The president, who was vacationing at his mountain retreat, has returned to the capital. Looting is alleged to be taking place in most major cities, and it is assumed that the president will be speaking to the nation shortly, in an effort to reestablish law and order. As he was boarding his plane for the flight to the capital, the president said, "A grave tragedy has struck our nation. It is to be hoped that the citizens of Atlantis will conduct themselves in a calm, gentle, and law-abiding manner in our time of need." In the meantime, Atlanteans are advised to gather provisions and to head for the highest ground that they can find. Stay tuned for further bulletins.

UNIT 16

EXERCISE 6 (page 281)

JANE: Hello?

BRIAN: Hello. May I speak with Jane Travanti?

JANE: This is Jane.

BRIAN: Jane, my name is Brian Hansen. Dr. Ralph Stevens gave me your number. I understand that you belong to an orienteering club. I'm interested in joining a group like that and getting to know some people, and . . . he suggested calling you to find out some details. Would you mind giving me some information about your club and about becoming a member?

JANE: Sure, I'd be glad to. Are you new in town?

BRIAN: Um, yeah, I've been here about five months and haven't really met anyone. Dr. Stevens thinks I need to stop working so hard and try to enjoy myself more. He's probably right.

JANE: Have you ever done any orienteering before?

BRIAN: No, I haven't. Do you need to be experienced?

JANE: Not necessarily. You can learn. We've got several different levels of participants. You do need to be in good physical condition.

BRIAN: Well, I haven't been doing much exercising lately, but Dr. Stevens says I'm basically in good physical shape. So can you give me some details? How often do you go orienteering, and where do you go, and stuff like that?

JANE: Sure! We try to go at least twice a month, normally on Saturdays. Usually we go to the Sherwood Forest area. Sometimes we only manage to go once a month, but most months it's at least twice. In the summer we get around by fast hiking, but right now we navigate by cross-country skiing. Do you know how to ski?

BRIAN: I tried cross-country skiing a couple of years ago, but I haven't done it since then. I did pretty well at it, though. I still have my skis.

JANE: Great. Let's see . . . what else? Uhmm, the group is pretty diverse. There are some married people and their kids, some singles, all ages. But we're an actual club. We have dues of $40 a year; that's to pay for organizing the activities. Sounds like you'd like the club. It's a good way to make friends. The members really enjoy being together.

BRIAN: Sounds great to me. When's your next activity?

JANE: We're meeting on Saturday morning, the 15th, at 6 A.M. in front of Darcy's Coffee Shop in Stapleton. We'll get to the forest by carpooling. Do you know where Darcy's is?

BRIAN: I think so. But I have a GPS, just in case.

JANE: OK, good. Don't forget to bring your skis. And remember to bring a lunch—hopefully with a lot of high-protein stuff in it.

BRIAN: Super. I'll see you on the 15th at 6 A.M. Thanks a lot.

JANE: Sure. I'll look forward to meeting you in person. Bye.

UNIT 17

EXERCISE 7 (page 296)

Good afternoon. Here is a bulletin from the Mason County Sheriff's Office. Convicted bank robber Charles Gallagher and two other inmates are reported to have escaped from the maximum security prison in Grandview. Listeners may recall that two years ago Gallagher was sentenced to serve a minimum of 20 years without parole. The three prisoners are thought to have escaped in a prison laundry truck. Authorities are not saying how the break-out could have taken place, but according to usually reliable sources, the three men are believed to have been helped in their escape, allegedly by a prison employee. A new state-of-the-art security system was supposed to have been installed two months ago, but because of unexpected delays and postponements, it is not yet in place. Listeners should be aware that the three prisoners are thought to have weapons and are believed to be heading through a rugged mountainous area in the direction of Union City. Listeners are warned not to approach the prisoners but are asked to contact the Sheriff's Office or call the toll-free number, 1-800-555-9999, if they have any information.

UNIT 18

EXERCISE 7 (page 318)

McGaffey: Our next caller is from Singapore. Here's Lu Adijojo. Lu, what's your view?

Lu Adijojo: Hello, Mike. Before I give my viewpoint, I just want to say how much I enjoy your show. I get a chance to listen only once a week or so, but I really like it.

McGaffey: Thanks. That's nice to hear. So how do you feel about what these two callers said? Do you agree with either of them?

Lu Adijojo: Well, I'm sort of in between. Basically, I guess I'm closer to the lady from Canada. I don't totally disagree with Jerry, but I do disagree with what he said about service needing to be voluntary. Like the second caller, I also think it should be required. But I do agree with Jerry about women in combat.

McGaffey: OK. Give me some specifics. Why shouldn't women be in combat?

Lu Adijojo: Well, one reason is that many women of military service age are mothers. I just don't think it's right for women to go off and fight when their children are at home. The motherly role is just too important.

McGaffey: All right. What about his idea that fighting is not feminine?

Lu Adijojo: I agree with the lady on this part. Fighting in combat doesn't mean that a woman in unfeminine. I just think it's not advisable for mothers. We don't allow women in Singapore to fight in combat, and not even pro-military people want to change that.

McGaffey: What do you think about Sarah's idea about national service in every country?

Lu Adijojo: I think it's basically a good idea. But I'm afraid this probably won't happen in most countries because there might not be enough money to carry it out.

McGaffey: All right, Lu. Thanks for your comments. Call me back sometime . . We'll be back after this commercial message.

UNIT 19

EXERCISE 6 (page 334)

Mary: Thanks for tuning in to *Sports Talk*, all you listeners out there. I'm Mary Mobley, and today we're talking with Lillian Swanson, champion swimmer, whose Team Jamaica just won the world championship. Lillian will be participating in the upcoming Olympics as part of the Jamaican national team. Lillian, thanks so much for being here with us.

Lillian: Thanks for having me, Mary.

Mary: There are a million questions I could ask, Lillian, but I'll start with this one: From all appearances, you've had a charmed athletic career. To what do you attribute your success?

Lillian: Well, Mary, whenever I've been asked that question, I've always answered it in the same way: It was because my parents loved and supported me.

Mary: OK. Tell us more. How did it all happen?

Lillian: It started when I was a girl in Jamaica. I learned to swim when I was four. I swam in the Caribbean, and swimming wasn't a big deal. It's the most natural thing in the world in Jamaica. I think I became a good swimmer because I had to swim in the Caribbean, which is a lot more difficult to swim in than a pool.

Mary: Who taught you to swim?

Lillian: My parents. My family and I spent a lot of time at the beach since we didn't have many toys or video games or things like that.

Mary: What did you mean when you said that your parents supported you?

Lillian: Well, when I was 12, I decided I wanted to become a champion swimmer and go to the Olympics someday. My parents said they'd pay for lessons and training if I would stick to my plan and practice regularly. So I did. They helped me become a disciplined person.

Mary: Twelve is pretty young to make a decision like that. Didn't you ever get tired of practicing all the time? And did you ever get discouraged?

Lillian: Sure I got tired of practicing, lots of times. And yes, I got discouraged whenever I had a hard time learning a new stroke.

Mary: Any regrets?

Lillian: None at all. Because swimming is a total passion for me, I can't imagine myself doing anything else. But I owe it all to my parents. Once I started my lessons, they wouldn't let me quit.

MARY: Well, Lillian, thanks very much for talking with us. And good luck in the Olympics.

LILLIAN: Thanks. My pleasure.

UNIT 20

EXERCISE 6 (page 353)

Good afternoon. This is the latest news from the World Broadcasting Network. The cease-fire has been broken in Franconia. Asked whether he would attend next week's peace conference in Geneva, rebel leader Amalde declined to commit himself, saying that the success of the conference depends on the good-faith actions of Mr. Tintor, the country's president. Mr. Amalde went on to say that Mr. Tintor could demonstrate good faith by agreeing to free elections. Interviewed about Mr. Amalde's comments, an aide to President Tintor, speaking off the record, said he did not expect the conference to take place as scheduled. One of the key issues to be discussed is amnesty for the rebels.

Meanwhile, researchers from the Global Health Foundation announced plans to test a new vaccine for AIDS. Acknowledging that the current vaccine is ineffective, the researchers claim that their new vaccine is a marked improvement of the existing one and believe that it holds great promise.

A new nation comes into existence at midnight tonight. To be known as the Central Asian Republic, the new nation has been carved out of the eastern portion of Spartania. According to its president, the new country will need billions of dollars of foreign aid in order to become a viable state.

Finally, here is today's human interest story: In St. Louis, Missouri, 16-year-old Sam Michaels was saved from drowning in a swimming pool by 12-year-old Carrie Hutchinson. Being unable to swim, Michaels had almost given up hope of being rescued. Having heard his cries for help, Hutchinson located him, jumped into the water, and pulled him to safety by using the lifesaving techniques she had learned in swimming classes. Michaels, grateful for the rescue, said he planned to start swimming lessons immediately.

That's the news from the World Broadcasting Network. Stay tuned for further developments.

UNIT 21

EXERCISE 6 (page 369)

LEADER: All right, folks, we're ready to start Part 2 of the workshop. Let's just review the points we made before. First, it's important to get people's names in your short-term memory. When you're meeting clients, it's crucial to be able to remember and use their names. Clients like to be called by their names, so it's good for business. Therefore, it's absolutely essential that you say the people's names when you meet them. Second, you need to notice one particular thing about each person and link that thing with the person's name. For example, suppose the person has strong, prominent eyebrows. And suppose the person's name is Ed. You can link the "e" in eyebrows with the "e" in *Ed*, and then you have an easier . . . Yes, May I help you?

VISITOR: Yes. My name is Keoki Kendall.

LEADER: Excuse me, Mr. Kendall, but we're in the middle of a workshop here. I'd. . .

VISITOR: I won't keep you long. I'm from the university police. I want everyone to stand up. Quick! Everyone! Some money has been stolen from the Registrar's Office, and I need to inspect your belongings. Please empty your purses and backpacks and your pockets onto your desks . . . Thank you. You have all been very cooperative. You may put your things away now. Thank you. Aloha.

BOB: What in the world was that about?

MIKE: Come on, you guys. He wasn't for real.

SARAH: What? Are you kidding?

MIKE: Didn't you notice? He wasn't in uniform. Besides that, Marsha, you didn't really act like this was an interruption. So this must have all been planned.

LEADER: Yes, Mike you're right. It was all planned. But I'll bet he had you going for a minute. Right, Bob?

BOB: I'll have to admit it.

LEADER: All right. The question is what you got out of the experience. Let's see what you remember. How was he dressed?

SARAH: He had on a suit, a tuxedo actually, but he wasn't wearing a white shirt.

LEADER: OK, good. What color was his shirt? . . . No one remembers? All right. What about his shoes? What color were they?

MIKE: Brown?

LEADER: Sorry. As a matter of fact, they were black. What was his name?

SARAH: Uh . . . I . . . I think his first name was . . . Keoki?

LEADER: That's right. Very good. Now why do you think you were able to remember that name?

SARAH: Well, it's an unusual first name—except in Hawaii.

LEADER: Good. Now what was his last name?

Mike: I think it was Kendall. I don't think I would have remembered it, except for the fact that you repeated it when you said, "Excuse me, Mr. Kendall."

Leader: Right. Excellent. Now what was the last word he said?

Bob: *Aloha*.

Leader: Very good. Why were you able to remember it?

Bob: Well, it's not the usual way we say good-bye. Everyone knows the word, of course. But people don't say it much.

Leader: Right. OK. Now let's just sum up the point here. You were able to remember some of the particulars about our visitor but not all of them. It's true that you were distracted. That was deliberate. But . . . most importantly, if you're going to improve your memory and use it well, you're going to have to learn to focus your attention consistently. You were able to remember the flashy things, and that's a good start. But it's the ordinary things you have to work on. You have to pay attention to those things, too.

UNIT 22

EXERCISE 7 (page 390)

Sally: Hi, April. What's wrong? You look upset about something.

April: I am. I wish Bob and I weren't going together.

Sally: Why?

April: He asked me if he could borrow my workbook for French class—to copy it. We have to turn our workbooks in on Friday. I've finished mine, but Bob's done almost nothing.

Sally: I hope you're going to tell me you said no.

April: I said yes.

Sally: April! I wish you hadn't done that.

April: Well, I knew it wasn't a good idea to lend it to him, but I thought he'd break up with me if I refused.

Sally: This is trouble, girl.

April: What would you have done?

Sally: I would have told him no, plain and simple.

April: Easier said than done. He's very persuasive, and he is my boyfriend.

Sally: It's the wrong thing to do.

April: Yeah, I know. If the teacher finds out, she'll fail both of us.

Sally: Probably. But the main problem is that it's just wrong. You worked for your grade. He's done nothing. It's not fair to you, and it's not fair to anyone who's done the work.

April: Well, it's too late now, isn't it?

Sally: Have you given it to him?

April: No, not yet.

Sally: Then it's not too late. If I were you, I'd call him up and tell him I'd changed my mind.

April: How can I do that? What can I say?

Sally: Just tell him you won't be able to do it because your conscience is bothering you.

April: What should I do if he gets mad and says he wants to break up?

Sally: Say good-bye. He's not worth having as a boyfriend if that's his reaction.

April: I guess you're right. Have you got any courage pills?

EXERCISE 8 (page 392)

1. I wish you'd stop riding motorcycles.
2. I wish you'd stopped riding motorcycles.
3. Mary wishes I'd accepted the job.
4. Mary wishes I'd accept the job.
5. I sure wish she'd call me.
6. I sure wish she'd called me.
7. My dad wishes I'd visited more often.
8. My dad wishes I'd visit more often.
9. I wish it'd rained more.
10. I wish it'd rain more.

UNIT 23

EXERCISE 7 (page 409)

Marge: Hello?

Nancy: Hi, Marge. It's Nancy. Got a moment? I need some advice.

Marge: Sure. What's the problem?

Nancy: My daughter Amanda called an hour or so ago and asked me to babysit. When I said no, she almost demanded I do it. I gave in and said yes, but I wish I hadn't. Had I known she was calling, I wouldn't have answered the phone. What would you suggest?

Marge: Has this been happening a lot?

Nancy: Yes, it has. It's the fifth time in three weeks. The last time it happened, it was 10 o'clock at night, and I was feeling sick. I had to call and insist she come and get the kids.

Marge: Did she?

Nancy: Yes, but she was mad. I love her and my grandchildren, but enough is enough.

Marge: What's her problem, anyway? Why is she asking you to baby-sit all the time?

NANCY: Well, both she and Stan have strange work schedules. She's been working overtime.

MARGE: They seem pretty well off to me. Why is Amanda working so much?

NANCY: She and Stan want to buy another house. Personally I think she's been neglecting the children. It's important that she pay more attention to those kids.

MARGE: Well, this isn't a matter of survival. They have a nice enough home already. I suggest you call her back and tell her you've changed your mind. You're not her slave.

NANCY: Thanks, Marge. That was my thought, too. I just wanted some support.

MARGE: Absolutely! You raised one family; you shouldn't have to raise another.

STUDENT BOOK ANSWER KEY

In this answer key, where the contracted form is given, the full form is also correct. Where the full form is given, the contracted form is also correct.

UNIT 1 (pages 2–14)

AFTER YOU READ

A. 1. g   **3.** b   **5.** h   **7.** a
2. f   **4.** e   **6.** d   **8.** c

B. 1. T
2. T
3. F. MySpace and Facebook are social networking sites.
4. F. Facebook became available after MySpace.
5. F. The author says most teachers have outlawed mobile phones in class.
6. T
7. T
8. F. The author thinks staying in near-constant communication with others is often stressful.

EXERCISE 1

A. 2. AP   **7.** AP
3. HA   **8.** AP
4. AP   **9.** HA
5. AP   **10.** HA
6. AP

B. 2. S   **7.** S
3. S   **8.** S
4. A   **9.** A
5. S   **10.** S
6. A

EXERCISE 2

2. walk   **9.** is considering
3. turn on   **10.** think
4. start   **11.** make
5. is giving   **12.** have
6. 'm trying   **13.** 'm doing
7. 's working   **14.** love
8. 'm writing

EXERCISE 3

2. have been   **8.** has been
3. have been living   **9.** has taught
4. has been   **10.** has been teaching
5. has been working   **11.** have had
6. has been writing   **12.** have owned
7. has also written   **13.** have been communicating

EXERCISE 4

2. are looking, frantically   **7.** is thinking, clearly
3. badly, are having   **8.** think, essential
4. rapidly, have   **9.** is, normally
5. feels, bad   **10.** is being, obnoxious
6. am feeling, terrible

EXERCISE 5

It seems
~~It's seeming~~ that I constantly hear the same thing:
We need
"Cell phones are dangerous. ~~We're needing~~ to restrict them. People are dying because of cell phones."
I think
Well, ~~I'm thinking~~ cell phones themselves aren't the problem. I'm completely opposed to restrictions on them, and here's why:

First, people say cell phones are dangerous to health, so they should be limited. Supporters of this idea say there are studies showing that cell phones produce harmful radiation and can even cause cancer. I think this is nonsense. There hasn't been
It sounds
any real proof. ~~It's sounding~~ like just another study
doesn't mean
that ultimately ~~isn't meaning~~ anything.

Second, teachers say we shouldn't allow cell phones in classes because they're a distraction.
angry
I feel pretty ~~angrily~~ about this. Here's an example: Two weeks ago in my history class, a student had her cell phone on because her mother was really sick and might need a ride to the hospital. The student's mother couldn't contact anyone else. Actually, the mother did call, and the student called someone to help her mother. What if the phone hadn't been on?
bad
The teacher would feel pretty ~~badly~~.

Third, people argue that using a cell phone while driving is dangerous. I disagree. It's no more dangerous than turning on the car radio or eating a sandwich. People do those things when they drive. The law says you have to have one hand on the steering wheel at all times. It's possible to use a cell
correctly
phone ~~correct~~ with one hand. I use my cell phone

carefully

~~careful~~; I always keep one hand on the wheel. Maybe there should be training in ways to use a cell phone

well

~~good~~, but we shouldn't prohibit using handheld phones in cars.

This has always been a free country. I hope it stays that way.

EXERCISE 6

A. Not mentioned: cell phones

B. 2. She is having a serious money problem.
3. Someone got hold of her credit card number.
4. This is a good example of identity theft.
5. The person who got the number has been charging a lot on her card.
6. $8,000 is involved.
7. She probably has to pay some back.
8. People are supposed to report problems like this immediately.
9. The Internet makes things easy, maybe too easy.
10. The downside is that it's easy for criminals to get information.

EXERCISE 7

2. A lot of new thi**ng**s are happeni**ng** in the digital world.
3. James has been writi**ng** for a magazine and bloggi**ng** on the Internet for years.
4. The lo**ng**er he spoke, the a**ng**rier we got.
5. Bill is stro**ng**, but Bob is stro**ng**er.
6. My fi**ng**ers are sore because I've been worki**ng** in the yard.
7. He's been si**ng**le for years, but now he's goi**ng** to get married.

UNIT 2 (pages 15–31)

AFTER YOU READ

A. 1. c   5. f
2. e   6. d
3. a   7. b
4. g

B. 1. T   5. T
2. F. Weinlick had not met his bride before the planning of his wedding.
6. F. Arranged marriages have traditionally not been common in America.
3. T
4. F. He advertised for a bride on the Internet.

EXERCISE 1

A. 2. He just didn't know / who he would be marrying
3. Friends would repeatedly ask Weinlick / when he was going to tie the knot
4. Runze hadn't met Weinlick / when she picked up her candidate survey
5. Weinlick had prepared everything / by the time the wedding day arrived

B. 2. F   3. H   4. H   5. F   6. F

EXERCISE 2

2. didn't happen   9. wanted
3. got   10. made
4. came   11. led
5. thought   12. 've never known
6. I've ever met   13. 's always loved
7. called up   14. 've never been able
8. asked

EXERCISE 3

2. 'd sleep   6. used to live
3. would go   7. used to be
4. 'd go   8. 'd spend
5. used to be   9. used to think

EXERCISE 4

2. By the time they both returned to their hometown about a year ago, Jim had completed four years of military service, and Jennifer had graduated from college.
3. By the time they saw each other again, Jennifer had started teaching, and Jim had taken a job as a computer programmer.
4. When they ran into each other in a drugstore one morning, neither had gone out on any dates.
5. Because he had woken up with a splitting headache, Jim drove to Olson's Drugstore.
6. Because Jennifer's younger sister had fallen and hurt herself and needed medicine, Jennifer also went to Olson's.
7. When a week had passed, Jim asked Jennifer out on a date.
8. When Jim and Jennifer had dated for three months, they got married.

EXERCISE 5

Suggested answers:
2. Their marriage was still going strong.
3. They have had four children.
4. They have never regretted getting married without knowing each other well.
5. They have always stressed that commitment is the thing that makes a marriage work.

6. Friends have noted that the Weinlicks are very much in love.

7. There was no guarantee the Weinlicks' marriage would succeed.

EXERCISE 6

May 20

I just had to write today. It's our six-month
                            have been
anniversary. Jim and I ~~are~~ married six months as of today. So maybe this is the time for me to take stock of my situation. The obvious question is whether I'm happy I got married. The answer is "Absolutely."
                            was
When I remember what my life ~~has been~~ like before
                                            I was
we were married, I realize now how lonely ~~I've been~~ before. Jim is a wonderful guy. Since we both work,
        take
we ~~took~~ turns doing the housework. He's really good
                        were
about that. When we ~~have been~~ dating, I wasn't sure
            I'd
whether or not ~~I'll~~ have to do all the housework. But
    didn't have
I ~~wasn't having~~ any reason to worry. Today we split everything 50 / 50. The only complaint I have is that
        snores
Jim ~~snored~~ at night. When I tell him he does that, he only says, "Well, sweetie, you snore too." I don't believe it. But if this is our only problem, I guess we're pretty lucky.
                I've
Well, ~~I'd~~ had a long and tiring day, but it's almost over. It's time to go to sleep.

EXERCISE 7

A. The wedding took place in Canada.

B. 2. Samantha and Darrell have each made over 30 jumps.

3. They've been members of the group for many years.

4. They were originally going to get married on a bungee jump.

5. They thought it would be too dangerous.

6. They couldn't find a minister who would bungee jump with them.

7. No, Reverend Martinez had never done this type of wedding before.

8. Reverend Martinez used to be a pastor in Arizona.

EXERCISE 8

B. 1. 's   **5.** 'd
2. 've   **6.** 'd
3. 'd   **7.** 'd
4. 'd   **8.** 's

C. 1. has   **5.** would
2. have   **6.** had
3. would   **7.** would
4. had   **8.** has

EXERCISE 9

Jack Strait's life is quite different now from the way it used to be. He used to work for a company that sold carpets and flooring. His job required him to do a lot of traveling. He would stay on the road for two or three weeks at a time. It was always the same: As soon as he pulled into a town, he would look for a cheap motel to stay in.

The next morning he'd leave his business card at a lot of different establishments, hoping that someone would agree to see him. If he'd been lucky enough to arrange an appointment in advance, he'd show them his samples. Occasionally they would order a carpet or some linoleum; most often they wouldn't.

Jack's marriage began to suffer. He missed his wife a lot, but there wasn't much he could do about the situation. And when he was on the road, he hardly ever saw his children. He would try to call them in the evenings if he had a spare moment. Usually, however, it was so late that they had already gone to bed. They were growing up without him.

Finally, his wife laid down the law, saying, "Why should we even be married if we're never going to see each other?" Jack decided she was right. He took a risk. He quit his job and started his own business. Things were difficult at first, but at least the family was together.

That was five years ago. Things have changed a lot since then. Jack and his family used to live in a small apartment. Now they own a house. Life is good.

UNIT 3 (pages 32–44)

AFTER YOU READ

A. 1. b   **5.** c
2. d   **6.** a
3. a   **7.** c
4. b   **8.** d

B. 1. lack   **5.** thieves
2. evening   **6.** phrasebook
3. tours   **7.** yourself
4. numbers

EXERCISE 1

A. 2. leave; simple present
    3. 'll be relaxing; future progressive
    4. 'm going to give; future with *be going to*
    5. will help; future with *will*
    6. 'll have been flying; future perfect progressive
    7. land, will be; two actions in the future
    8. 'll have acquired; future perfect

B. 2. P   5. P   8. F
    3. F   6. P   9. P
    4. F   7. F   10. P

EXERCISE 2

2. 'm going
3. 'm taking
4. 'm moving
5. 'll mind, 'm going to mind
6. won't be able to use, 's not
   going to be able to use
7. 'm seeing
8. 'm leaving
9. 'm arriving
10. 'll write

EXERCISE 3

2. 'll meet OR 's going to meet, arrives
3. will visit OR are going to visit, leave
4. finish, will take OR are going to take
5. 'll visit OR 're going to visit, tour
6. fly, 'll buy OR 're going to buy

EXERCISE 4

Answers will vary.

EXERCISE 5

I am writing these words in English because I need the practice. At this moment I am on an airplane over the Pacific Ocean, on my way to a year of study at Columbia University in the United States. The plane left an hour ago. It's a ten-hour flight, so I hope I will have written a lot by the time we ~~will~~ land. I am looking forward to being there, but I am also a little afraid. What ~~do~~ *will* I find when I ~~will~~ get to America? Will the Americans be arrogant and unfriendly? Will I make any friends? ~~Am I~~ *Will I be* happy? My best friend in Korea said, "You ~~don't~~ *won't* make any real friends when ~~you'll be~~ *you're* there." I am not so sure. I guess ~~I~~ *I'll* find out.

These were the words I wrote in my diary on the airplane last month. But I have been here for a month now, and I have found that things are a lot different from what I expected. The majority of people here are friendly. They go out of their way to help you if you need it, and my American friends

invite me to go places. Soon ~~I go~~ *I'm going (OR I'm going to go)* hiking with a group from my dormitory.

Two of the ideas I had about the United States, however, seem to be true. One is that Americans don't pay much attention to rules. One of my best American friends says, in fact, "Rules are made to be broken." The other idea is about the American family. In Asia the family is very important, but some Asian people think the family means nothing in the United States. I don't know if this is true or not. But I think it might be true, since my American friends almost never mention their parents or their brothers and sisters. Anyway, I am going to have a chance to see a real American family. ~~I go~~ *I'm going (OR I'm going to go)* with my roommate Susan to spend Thanksgiving break with her family in Pennsylvania. When I ~~will~~ see her family, maybe ~~I'm going to~~ *I'll* understand more.

EXERCISE 6

A. Edmonton
B. 2. F   7. T
    3. F   8. F
    4. T   9. T
    5. F 10. F
    6. F 11. T

EXERCISE 7

B. 2. I'm, I am
    3. will, won't
    4. won't, we will
    5. won't, they will
    6. We're not, we are
    7. won't have, will have

PART I From Grammar to Writing
(pages 45–48)

1

In late December. <u>Sherry, Akiko, and Lisa took a one-day trip to Barcelona.</u> Not knowing anyone there. <u>They stayed in a youth hostel for a very reasonable price.</u> On their one day in the city. <u>They visited the Sagrada Familia, Gaudí's famous church.</u> <u>All three girls were impressed by the church's beauty.</u> And decided to climb to the top instead of taking the elevator. <u>Nearing the top, Akiko began to feel dizzy and had to start down again.</u> <u>Sherry and Lisa continued climbing.</u> However, even Sherry, who had done a great deal of mountain climbing in Canada. Felt nervous and unprotected at the summit. <u>Both she and Lisa agreed that the view was magnificent.</u> And the climb well worth it. <u>The three decided to return to Barcelona.</u> As soon as they could.

2

Suggested sentence combining:

   In late December. Sherry, Akiko, and Lisa took a one-day trip to Barcelona. Not knowing anyone there, they stayed in a youth hostel for a very reasonable price. On their one day in the city, they visited the Sagrada Familia, Gaudí's famous church. All three girls were impressed by the church's beauty and decided to climb to the top instead of taking the elevator. Nearing the top, Akiko began to feel dizzy and had to start down again. Sherry and Lisa continued climbing. However, even Sherry, who had done a great deal of mountain climbing in Canada, felt nervous and unprotected at the summit. Both she and Lisa agreed that the view was magnificent and the climb well worth it. The three decided to return to Barcelona as soon as they could.

3

Suggested corrections:

   Last summer when my wife and I were traveling in Morocco, we had one of the most interesting bargaining experiences ever. We were in an open-air market in Rabat, and I really wanted to buy a Moroccan *jellaba*, a long, heavy, ankle-length garment. There were several different shops where jellabas were sold, but Heather and I were drawn to one shop in particular. I tried one jellaba on; it fit perfectly, and I knew it was the one I wanted, so I asked the merchant how much it was. He said it was $100. Now I've always been uncomfortable about bargaining, so I was ready to pay his price. Heather took me aside, however, and said that was too much and that he expected me to bargain. When I said I couldn't bargain, she told me that bargaining was part of the game and that I should offer him less. I sighed, tried to swallow the lump in my throat, and suggested $25. He smiled and asked for $75, whereupon I offered $35. He looked offended and shook his head. Heather grabbed my hand and we started walking away. I thought that was going to be the end of the experience, but then the merchant came running after me, saying he'd accept $50. I ended up buying the jellaba for that amount, and I still have it. Since then I've developed courage and gained self-confidence, so as they say, travel is indeed broadening.

UNIT 4 (pages 50–68)

AFTER YOU READ

A. 1. gracious   **5.** praise
    2. pointer   **6.** decline
    3. chuckle   **7.** have someone over
    4. perplexed   **8.** rectify

B. 1. b   **4.** b
    2. b   **5.** a
    3. a   **6.** a

EXERCISE 1

2. b   **4.** a   **6.** a   **8.** b   **10.** b
3. b   **5.** a   **7.** b   **9.** b

EXERCISE 2

2. had to worry   **7.** should you tip
3. supposed to do   **8.** you're supposed to do
4. were supposed to   **9.** Should you leave
     leave   **10.** ought to have given
5. Should we have left   **11.** could have left
6. don't have to leave

EXERCISE 3

Possible answers:
2. should   **5.** are not supposed to
3. should   **6.** must
4. shouldn't have

EXERCISE 4

Possible answers:
2. They should have arranged their shoes so that they were pointing toward the door.
3. They shouldn't have said anything about the gift when they presented it.
4. They shouldn't have taken a rock and roll CD as a gift.
5. Helen shouldn't have taken the sushi.
6. They should have refused the first offer of a drink.
7. They could (OR might) have taken a box of chocolates.
8. They could (OR might) have taken flowers.
9. They could (OR might) have declined the sushi.
10. They could (OR might) have left earlier.

EXERCISE 5

Dear Masako,

   Sorry it's taken me so long to write. I ~~shouldn't~~ *should* have gotten to this weeks ago, but I've been so busy. I'm really looking forward to the holidays and seeing all you guys again.

   School is going well. It's tough but really interesting, and I'm sure I should be studying even more than I have been. Part of the problem is that

I'm taking too many classes. You're only ~~suppose~~ *supposed* to take five a term, but I'm taking six.

Anyway, I've gotten to know a lot of new people, including several Australians. I have this one really good friend, a girl named Jane. She invited me to her house last week for a party. Actually, it was my birthday, but I didn't know she knew that. I thought it was a party like any other. I figured ~~I better~~ *I'd better* take some kind of gift, but I couldn't decide what it should be. Finally I came up with the idea of a bouquet of flowers. As soon as I got to the party, I gave it to Jane, and she was really happy to get it. But then the funniest thing happened. I guess I ought to ~~expect~~ *have expected* something was up from the mysterious way Jane was acting, but I didn't. This was a surprise party—for me! As soon as I took off my coat and sat down, a lot of people jumped up from behind sofas and other places where they'd been hiding and shouted "Surprise! Happy birthday!" I was embarrassed, but I ~~must not have been~~ *shouldn't have been*, because everyone was really friendly, and pretty soon I forgot about my embarrassment. Then they gave me presents. I was about to put them away, but Jane said, "Aren't you going to open them?" I was perplexed and didn't know what to do. In China you ~~shouldn't have opened~~ *shouldn't open* gifts right when you get them, but apparently you are supposed to in Australia. So I opened them. The nicest gift was a new blouse from Jane. She told me I must ~~have gone~~ *go* and try it on immediately, so I did. It's beautiful. Anyway, what a party! I thought I knew all about Australian culture, but I guess I'm not as familiar with it as I thought. The custom of opening up presents in front of the gift giver is a strange one to me.

The weather is kind of chilly. How is it back in Singapore? Nice and warm? ~~I shall~~ *Shall I* bring you something special from Australia when I come?

Well, Masako, I'm running out of space, so ~~I~~ *I've* got to sign off. Write soon.

EXERCISE 6

A. They're at a department store, looking for a birthday present for Mom.

B. *Suggested answers:*

2. Bev says they shouldn't delay getting the gift because everyone else has brought something.
3. He says they should have gone shopping last week.
4. He says they shouldn't get Mom a camera.
5. She thinks they shouldn't get Mom a dress.
6. He thinks it's a bad idea.
7. She thinks they ought to get Mom of couple of silk scarves in a conservative color.
8. She says they'd better hurry up because Mom could be there any minute.

EXERCISE 8

A married couple was traveling in Europe and had just entered a new country. They had been having a wonderful time, but now everything was going wrong. The first problem was finding accommodations. They were supposed to stay at the Grand State Hotel, but when they got to the hotel there was no record of their reservation. The wife said they should have gotten a confirmation number. They hadn't, unfortunately, so they had to spend the night at the train station. The next day they finally found a room at a hotel far from the center of town. There were two rooms available: a large one and a tiny one. Since they were on a tight budget, they decided they had better take the tiny one.

The second problem was communication. They were starving after spending hours looking for accommodations, so they went into a restaurant. A waiter brought them a menu, but they couldn't understand it. The husband said they should have brought along a phrasebook. They hadn't done that, though, so they didn't know what to order.

Time passed. Other people were being served, but they weren't. Frustrated, they decided they had to do something. But what? They noticed that a boy about 11 years old seemed to be listening to their conversation. Soon the boy came over to their table. "Excuse me," he said. "You have to pay for your meal first. Then they'll take your order." The husband and wife were both astonished but grateful. The wife said, "You speak our language very well. Did you study it somewhere?" The boy said, "I lived in Australia for three years. I learned English there." He asked, "Shall I help you order? I can translate the menu."

When the couple got back home, their friends asked them what they had liked best about the trip. The wife said, "Well, the best part was visiting that country where everything went wrong until that boy rectified the problem. At some point, everybody should experience difficulty. You don't have to be miserable, but you need a challenge. That's when you learn things. Maybe that's what people mean when they say travel is broadening."

AFTER YOU READ

A. **1.** d   **3.** e   **5.** f   **7.** c
   2. h   **4.** g   **6.** a   **8.** b

B. **1.** T   **6.** T
   2. T   **7.** F. The ice crystals
   3. F. . . . the island is   may have been
      too far north for   icebergs.
      grapes to grow   **8.** T
   4. F. Pottery fragments
      from Ecuador date
      from about 3000 BCE.
   5. F. The story of
      St. Brendan may
      have caused
      Columbus to believe
      that there was a New
      World.

EXERCISE 1

   2. a   **3.** b   **4.** b   **5.** a   **6.** a   **7.** a   **8.** b

EXERCISE 2

   2. may have had to   **6.** might be meeting
   3. might be   **7.** should be
   4. could be working   **8.** must have been visiting
   5. must have

EXERCISE 3

   2. could have caused
   3. must be
   4. might have brought
   5. could . . . have disappeared
   6. could . . . have existed
   7. had to have existed
   8. must have become
   9. Could there really have been
   10. might be
   11. may have influenced
   12. might still be walking / might still walk

EXERCISE 4

Answers will vary.

EXERCISE 5

One ~~must~~ *might* think that with all the scientific progress made in the last century, researchers would be able by now to answer this very simple question: Why do we itch? Unfortunately, scientists can't answer this question with any certainty. They simply don't know.

There are some clear cases involving itching. If a patient goes to her doctor and complains of terrible itching and the doctor finds hives or some other kind of rash, the doctor will probably say that she ~~must eat~~ *must have eaten* something she was allergic to—or that she ~~must not have been stung~~ *must have been stung* or bitten by some insect. Scientists can easily explain this kind of case. Most itching, however, does not have an obvious cause.

Here's what scientists do know: Right under the surface of the skin there are sensory receptors that register physical stimuli and carry messages to the brain. These receptors detect pain and let the brain know about it. If there is a high level of physical stimulation to the body, the sensory receptors ~~might carried~~ *might carry* a message of pain to the brain. If the level of physical stimulation is low, the sensors ~~might be report~~ *might report* it as itchiness.

There has been a lot of speculation about the function of itching. Some researchers think the function of itching ~~may~~ *may be* (OR *might be* OR *could be*) to warn the body it is about to have a painful experience. Others theorize that early humans ~~might developed~~ *might have developed* itching as a way of knowing they needed to take insects out of their hair. Still others believe that itching could be a symptom of serious diseases such as diabetes and Hodgkin's disease.

One of the most interesting aspects of itching is that it ~~may have be~~ *may be* less tolerable than pain. Research has shown, in fact, that most of us tolerate pain better than itching. Many people will allow their skin to be painfully broken just so they can get rid of an itch.

EXERCISE 6

A. a speech class

B. **2.** a   **4.** b   **6.** a   **8.** a   **10.** a
   3. b   **5.** a   **7.** b   **9.** b

EXERCISE 7

B. **2. A:** have   **4. B:** have   **6. B:** have
   3. A: to   **5. A:** to

EXERCISE 8

Possible answers:
   1. The man must have tried to cash the check. (OR The woman might have given police a description of the thief. OR Someone could have seen the thief break into the woman's house.)
   2. The girl must not have tied the other end of the rope to something. (OR The dog might have broken the rope. OR Someone else could have untied the rope.)

3. The monks must have correctly pointed the signpost in the direction they had come from. (OR Someone else might have come along and told the monks which way to go. (OR The monks could have remembered going there before.

4. The man must have been struck by lightning. (OR The man's car could have caught fire.)

PART II From Grammar to Writing (pages 85–87)

1

Possible answers:

1. Rio de Janeiro is a city where exciting and mysterious things happen.

2. There are several reasons why college isn't for everybody.

3. Wild animals don't make good pets.

4. Regular exercise has many benefits.

2

Possible answers:

1. Public transportation is a better option for me than driving my car.

2. There are several reasons why I prefer seeing movies in a theater to watching them on TV.

3. There are three main reasons why I like planning my own vacation more than going on tours.

4. I can think of three reasons why a cat is a better pet for me than a dog.

UNIT 6 (pages 90–104)

AFTER YOU READ

A. 1. side with   **6.** drag
2. telling   **7.** in moderation
3. obese   **8.** brimmed
4. BMI   **9.** devote
5. champ   **10.** Sunblock

B. 1. b   **2.** d   **3.** d   **4.** c   **5.** c   **6.** b

EXERCISE 1

2. It's OK in moderation, but I wouldn't make a habit of it.

3. Most fast food is full of salt, sugar, cholesterol, and calories.

4. We love its warmth, but it has its dangers.

5. I've treated patients with skin cancer.

6. You should wear sunblock if you're going out in the sun for more than a few minutes.

7. He used to be in good shape when he was a tennis champ, but now he doesn't get any exercise.

8. Your husband would have a BMI of about 35, which puts him in the obese category.

9. Is there a cure for baldness?

10. I've been losing my hair for several years.

EXERCISE 2

2. a work   **9.** Work
3. a history   **10.** fish
4. a talk   **11.** Soda
5. space   **12.** milk
6. a time   **13.** history
7. criteria   **14.** a film
8. time

EXERCISE 3

2. a. some
b. a flash of
3. a. any
b. a game of
4. a. some
b. a piece of
5. a. any
b. a drop of
6. a. any
b. a grain of
7. a. some
b. a piece of
8. a. some
b. a piece of

EXERCISE 4

Answers will vary.

1. The two best films I've seen in the last year are . . .

2. The two funniest people I've ever met are . . .

3. The best advice I've ever had is / was . . .

4. The most enjoyable work I've ever done is / was . . .

5. The most beautiful work of art I've ever seen is . . .

6. The best news I've heard this month is / was . . .

7. The worst traffic I've ever seen is / was . . .

8. The most interesting experience I've had in the last year is / was . . .

EXERCISE 5

Dear kids,

Your mom and I are having *a* wonderful time in

Brazil. We landed in Rio de Janeiro on Tuesday as scheduled and made it to our hotel without any problems. On Wednesday we walked and sunbathed on Copacabana and Ipanema beaches. The only problem was that I didn't put on any sunblock and *a*

got ^bad sunburn. There's ~~a good news~~ ^good news^, though; it's

better today. Actually, there's one other problem:

furniture

We don't have enough ~~furnitures~~ in our hotel room. There's no place to put anything. But everything else has been great. We went to a samba show, and even though it was intended for tourists, it was a lot of fun.

are

The Brazilian people ~~is~~ very friendly and helpful. On Friday we had a flight to São Paulo scheduled for 9:00 A.M., and we missed the bus and couldn't get a taxi. But we were saved by one of the hotel employees, who gave us a ride to the airport. We got there just in time. Now we're in São Paulo. It's an exciting place, but I can't get over the traffic. It took two hours to get from our hotel to the downtown area. Yesterday we had lunch at a famous restaurant where they serve *feijoada*, a typical Brazilian food.

much

It had so ~~many~~ spice in it that our mouths were on fire, but it was delicious. Tonight we're going to have dinner at a very famous restaurant where they serve

meat

every kind of ~~meats~~ you can think of.

The other thing about Brazil that's really

coffee

interesting is the amount of ~~coffees~~ the Brazilians drink. They have little cups of coffee several times a day—called *caffezinho*. We tried it; it's very strong and sweet.

time

That's all for now. Your mom hasn't had ~~a time~~ to go shopping yet, which is good. You know how much I hate shopping.

Love,
Dad

EXERCISE 6

A. His wife was on a TV medical show and asked the speaker about his health.

B. 2. His cholesterol level is 322.
3. Joe skips breakfast daily.
4. He doesn't have time to eat breakfast.
5. He doesn't get any exercise.
6. He eats his midday meal at various fast-food restaurants.
7. Joe is at high risk for a heart attack.
8. The doctor isn't going to put Joe on a diet because for the most part diets don't work.
9. Joe will still be able to eat a lot of the foods he likes.
10. Joe will need to exercise three times a week at the beginning.

EXERCISE 7

3. There were a lot (of) new people in class today.
4. We bought a new piece (of) furniture for the living room.
5. We lost a piece of equipment when we changed offices.
6. Can you pour me a glass of orange juice?
7. I had a delicious piece (of) meat for supper.
8. There was a large group of engineers at the convention.
9. I bought my fiancée a bouquet (of) flowers.
10. There was a basket of eggs on the kitchen table.

UNIT 7 (pages 105–119)

AFTER YOU READ

A. 1. e 4. h 7. b
2. d 5. c 8. f
3. g 6. a

B. 1. F. Easter Island was settled about the year 900 by Polynesians.
2. T
3. T
4. F. The Easter Islanders used canoe rails to move their statues.
5. T
6. T
7. F. Deforestation led to the island becoming dryer.

EXERCISE 1

A. 2. D 5. G 8. N
3. N 6. G 9. D
4. D 7. G 10. D

B. 2. a 3. b 4. a 5. b

EXERCISE 2

Excerpt 1
2. the   8. no article
3. the   9. the
4. the   10. the
5. no article   11. the
6. a   12. the
7. the

Excerpt 2
13. the   19. a
14. the   20. the
15. a   21. the
16. the   22. no article
17. The   23. the
18. the

EXERCISE 3

Excerpt 1

2. the	**6.** the
3. A	**7.** a
4. the	**8.** the
5. the	**9.** no article

Excerpt 2

10. The	**17.** the
11. a	**18.** no article
12. no article	**19.** the
13. an	**20.** the
14. the	**21.** no article
15. the	**22.** the
16. The	**23.** the

EXERCISE 4

1. A TV set is an electronic device that receives electromagnetic waves, converts the waves into images, and displays them on a screen. / The TV set was invented in the 1920s by Farnsworth and Zorinsky.
2. A wheel is a circular device that turns around a central point. / The wheel was invented 5000 to 6000 years ago.
3. A clarinet is a woodwind instrument that uses a reed. / The clarinet was invented around 1700.
4. Guitars are stringed instruments that typically have six strings. / The guitar was invented in the 1400s in Spain.
5. Automobiles are self-powered traveling vehicles. / The automobile was invented in 1874 by Siegfried Marcus in Vienna.
6. Telephones are communication devices that convert sound signals into waves and reconvert them into sounds. / The telephone was invented in 1878 by Alexander Graham Bell.

EXERCISE 5

Many people today are against the nuclear power. I disagree with them for several reasons. First, we need the additional power sources. We are running out of the petroleum. Many environmentalists say we need to develop the use of geothermal and wind energy. I am certainly not against these sources, and we should work on developing them. But they can't do everything. Then there's the suggestion of hydroelectric power. Many say that even though there are the problems with it, it is better than going

a
nuclear. I am big supporter of hydroelectric power,

but it can't provide all the power we need either.

Second, many are against nuclear plants because they believe they are unsafe. They always mention the accidents at Chernobyl and Three-Mile Island as examples. Yes, these were serious problems, but

we have learned from them. There haven't been the major problems with nuclear reactors for many years now. We can make nuclear power safe if we develop the strict controls and inspections. France produces about 77% of its power from nuclear energy. The French have had the issue of getting rid of nuclear waste, but they are working on it. If the French can do it, other countries can too.

Third, once a device is invented or a process is developed, it can't really be abandoned. Willy Brandt, a former German chancellor, said, "We cannot return to the age of nuclear innocence." We don't

a
live in perfect world. There are potential dangers of

using nuclear energy, but there are potential dangers in everything. As far as I am concerned, nuclear

a
power will be necessity in the future.

EXERCISE 6

A. national parks

B.

2. a	**7.** b
3. a	**8.** a
4. a	**9.** a
5. a	**10.** b
6. a	

EXERCISE 7

2. The inhabitants of Easter Island built the statues themselves.
3. The climate of the area was changed.
4. The forests that used to cover the island are gone.
5. The unfortunate truth is that the Earth's resources are limited.
6. Fortunately, that's not the end of the story.
7. The eleven ruling chiefs were responsible for the problem.
8. Are we overfishing the ocean in the mistaken belief that the supply of seafood is unlimited?

UNIT 8 (pages 120–133)

AFTER YOU READ

A.

1. e	**6.** f
2. g	**7.** a
3. d	**8.** b
4. c	**9.** h
5. i	

B.

1. abstract	**5.** purchases
2. government	**6.** germs
3. cash	**7.** electronically
4. service	**8.** strangers

EXERCISE 1

2. Y	**6.** N	**10.** N
3. N	**7.** Y	**11.** N
4. N	**8.** N	**12.** N
5. N	**9.** Y	

EXERCISE 2

2. any	**7.** many
3. less	**8.** few
4. some	**9.** little
5. number of	**10.** a little
6. a lot of	

EXERCISE 3

2. less	**9.** fewer
3. enough	**10.** much
4. more OR some	**11.** few
5. a few OR a couple of	**12.** most of
6. one of	**13.** a couple of OR a few
7. both of	**14.** some OR more
8. $50	**15.** every

EXERCISE 4

2. fewer	**6.** a great deal of
3. more	**7.** the number of
4. less	**8.** The amount of
5. fewer	

EXERCISE 5

My fellow citizens: We are at a time in our history when we need to make some real sacrifices. Recent presidents have made ~~a great deal of~~ *a great many* promises they didn't keep. Tonight you deserve to hear the truth.

On the economy, we've made *a* little progress, but we still have ~~a great many~~ *a great deal of* work to do, so I'm proposing several measures. First, I want to raise taxes on the very wealthy because ~~a few~~ *few* of them really pay their share. Second, many members of the middle class are carrying an unfair tax burden, so I'm asking for a tax cut for them. If I'm successful, most of you in the middle class will pay 10 percent less in taxes next year, though a few of you in the higher-income group may see your taxes rise ~~little~~ *a little*. Third, there are ~~much~~ *many* loopholes in the current law which allow some people to avoid paying any taxes at all; and I want to close these loopholes.

Further problems are that we have very ~~few~~ *little* money available for health care reform, and we've made ~~a little~~ *little* progress in reducing pollution and meeting clean air standards. Therefore, as my final measure, I am asking for a 50-cent-a-gallon tax on gasoline, which will result in many more people using public transportation and should create additional revenue. Thus, we will have enough money to finance our new health care program and will be helping the environment at the same time.

EXERCISE 6

A. Mike chose the restaurant.

B.	**2.** a	**6.** b
	3. b	**7.** b
	4. b	**8.** a
	5. a	

EXERCISE 7

B **2.** I have fewer problems than I used to. (2)
3. She doesn't watch much television. (3)
4. Presidents are under a great deal of stress. (4)
5. We are facing a great many challenges today. (4)
6. The amount of money I earn is minimal. (4)
7. The number of students in colleges is growing. (6)
8. I took each item back to the store. (3)

UNIT 9 (pages 134–149)

AFTER YOU READ

A.	**1.** f	**6.** i
	2. h	**7.** d
	3. j	**8.** g
	4. e	**9.** c
	5. b	**10.** a

B. **1.** F. Constantina Dita takes the lead at about the halfway point.
2. F. Dita is not the favorite.
3. F. Few if any spectators expect Dita to win the gold medal.
4. T
5. F. Dita did not win a medal in the 2004 Athens Olympics. She managed only a 20th-place finish.
6. T
7. T
8. T
9. T
10. F. Expectations take over when we focus too much on goals.

EXERCISE 1

2. The Women's Marathon is about at the halfway point when a Romanian runner surges to the head of the pack.
3. Dita finishes the race with a 22-second lead over the silver medalist.
4. The 38-year-old Dita managed only a 20th-place finish in the 2004 Athens Olympics.

5. Your <u>film-buff</u> [friends] have seen the <u>Academy-Award</u>–<u>winning</u> [*Avatar*].

6. They love its <u>strange-looking</u> [creatures] and <u>awesome</u> <u>special</u> [effects].

7. They admire its <u>serious</u> but <u>heartwarming</u> [treatment] of the <u>age-old</u> [conflict] between exploiters and those they exploit.

8. Children sometimes do not meet their <u>parents'</u> <u>career</u> [expectations] of them.

9. "[Focal] [dystonia]" is an <u>abnormal</u> <u>muscle</u> [function] caused by <u>extreme</u> [concentration].

10. I stand at the top of a <u>steep</u>, <u>icy</u> [slope], plotting my <u>every</u> [move] down the course.

EXERCISE 2

2. new silk
3. ugly purple denim
4. suitable dress-up
5. interesting, important OR important, interesting
6. memorable, good OR good, memorable
7. unstylish, sloppy OR sloppy, unstylish
8. round blue sapphire
9. oval green emerald
10. excellent tomato-and-cheese
11. fancy dress-up
12. beautiful purple denim

EXERCISE 3

2. a one-paragraph
3. a 300-page
4. a six-year
5. a stress-related
6. an eyesight-related
7. a 10-gallon
8. performance-induced
9. a two-month

EXERCISE 4

Possible answers:

2. A long-haired cat came to our house and never left.
3. My dad loves his comfortable old jacket.
4. A surprise birthday party is an amusing and interesting experience.
5. An eleven-year-old child won the national spelling contest.
6. *Slumdog Millionaire* is an award-winning movie.
7. My great-aunt built a three-legged table.
8. I'm fascinated by unusual-looking people.
9. She was wearing a short blue cotton skirt.
10. The Chinese jade bowl we bought is worth a lot of money.
11. My grandmother works in a 60-story building.
12. My daughter can easily lift a 90-pound bag.

EXERCISE 5

FRIDAY: It's midnight, the end of a long day. My

medical school
first week of ~~school medical~~ is over, and I'm exhausted but happy! I'm so glad I decided to go to the university. It was definitely a good decision. I'm not completely sure yet, but I think I want to go

child psychiatry
into ~~psychiatry child~~ because I love working with

ten-year-old
children—especially nine- and ~~ten-years-old~~ kids. Yesterday our psychiatry class visited a large new

troubled middle-class
hospital where many ~~middle-class troubled~~ children go for treatment. I expected to see a lot of boys and girls behaving badly, but most of them were pretty quiet and relaxed. They just looked like they needed some warm, personal attention.

Today in our surgery class we had a bright,

young Brazilian
hardworking teacher, a ~~Brazilian young~~ doctor who was substituting for our usual professor. We got a helpful foreign viewpoint on things.

The only thing I don't like about medical school

disgusting cafeteria
is the ~~cafeteria disgusting~~ food. I'm going to have to

tasty hot Chinese
start getting some ~~hot tasty Chinese~~ food from my local favorite place. Well, it's time for me to get some

new computer
sleep. I hope this ~~computer new~~ program works correctly.

EXERCISE 6

A.
2. F   6. T
3. T   7. F
4. F   8. T
5. T

B.
2. a total, complete idiot
3. an ugly, high-pitched, squeaky voice
4. a rapid adolescent growth spurt
5. fear-of-oral-reading problem
6. a short, easy-to-remember phrase
7. an icy, dark, stormy evening
8. famous three-dog nights
9. three large, warm, furry dogs

EXERCISE 7

1. The film is a serious, profound, heartwarming treatment of an important issue.
2. We have some delicious cheese-and-pepperoni sandwiches.
3. That ugly, grotesque, decrepit building should be torn down.
4. The trip we took was an expensive, silly, miserable waste of time.
5. She's going to wear her new red silk dress.
6. We bought a beautiful new hybrid car.
7. My intelligent, gracious, twenty-five-year-old daughter just got married.
8. Our little old fox terrier is a delight to have in the family.

EXERCISE 8

B. 2. b **3.** b **4.** a **5.** b

1

1. list, was
2. one, has
3. mathematics, is
4. bipolar disorder and schizophrenia, are
5. The director and star, was
6. their, students
7. his or her, Each
8. his, Frank
9. them, students
10. he or she, Everybody

2

1. are
2. was
3. encourage
4. are
5. their
6. his or her
7. have
8. are
9. their
10. is
11. are
12. are
13. has

AFTER YOU READ

A. 1. b **4.** c **7.** b
2. a **5.** a **8.** c
3. b **6.** d **9.** b

B. 1. F. A spirit of one-upmanship characterized the brothers' relationship.
2. T
3. F. The boys' mother did not encourage the spirit of competition between them.
4. F. The boys' mother told them she didn't need anything.
5. T
6. F. The mother didn't need the things her sons gave her.
7. T
8. F. The mother was not aware of what the parrot could do.

EXERCISE 1

A. 1. Moe was sure that the mansion would be her favorite gift.   C
2. What wasn't so admirable was their rivalry.   S
3. All I know is that the chicken you gave me was delicious.   C
4. Their mother said there was nothing she needed.   O

B. 2. Curly was wondering what he could do to top his brothers.
   What can I do to top my brothers?

3. At first he wondered if he could afford it.
   Can I afford it?
4. I don't know if you believed me.
   Did you believe me?
5. I don't know what you mean.
   What do you mean?

EXERCISE 2

2. what the name of the nearest town was
3. if I could borrow his cell phone
4. if there were any towing companies nearby
5. if he knew
6. how long he had lived around there
7. what his name was
8. if he knew anything at all

EXERCISE 3

A. *Possible answers:*
1. I don't know what a pun is.
2. I have no idea what *hyperbole* means.
3. I'm not sure what the humor of the unexpected happening is.
4. I'm not entirely sure how repetition works in humor.
5. I don't have a clue what the humor of the incongruous situation is.
6. I don't know how sarcasm differs from other humor.
7. I have no clue what endorphins are.

B. *Possible answers:*
1. What is a pun?
   A pun is a kind of humor that depends on similarities in sound or meaning between two words.
2. What does hyperbole mean?
   Hyperbole means exaggeration.
3. What is the humor of the unexpected happening?
   An example of the unexpected happening is a woman opening her purse and a bird flying out of it.
4. How does repetition work in humor?
   Repetition works by repeating an element in a humorous story.
5. What is the humor of the incongruous situation?
   The humor of the incongruous situation depends on normal things happening in unusual places.
6. How does sarcasm differ from other humor?
   Sarcasm is often more biting and hurtful than other humor.
7. What are endorphins?
   Endorphins are hormones that are created in the brain when we laugh or exercise that help lessen pain and give us a sense of well-being.

EXERCISE 4

Possible answers:

1. *Honk if you're illiterate.* What's funny about this is that anyone who is illiterate couldn't read the bumper sticker.
2. *If you don't like the way I drive, stay off the sidewalk.* What's funny about this is that it implies that the driver is driving on the sidewalk.
3. *Missing: Husband and Dog. Attention: $200 reward for dog.* What's funny about this is the fact that some wives like to joke about their animals being more valuable than their husbands.
4. *Change is inevitable—except for vending machines.* What the humor depends on here is the fact that "change" is used as a pun.
5. *I'm in no hurry. I'm on my way to work.* What's funny about this is that the driver is driving slowly to delay arriving at work.
6. *Everyone is entitled to my opinion.* What the humor depends on is the similar saying "Everyone is entitled to his or her opinion."
7. *Forget about world peace. Visualize using your turn signal.* What the humor depends on here is a commonly seen bumper sticker that says "Visualize World Peace." This bumper sticker asks people to think of less grand things than world peace (while driving) and to concentrate on driving properly.
8. *Eschew obfuscation.* What the humor depends on is knowing the meanings of *eschew* and *obfuscation. Eschew* is a fancy word for "avoid." *Obfuscation* is a fancy way to say "making things confusing."

EXERCISE 5

1. Make sure ~~is~~ the joke you're telling *is* funny.

2. The best jokes are broad enough so that everyone can enjoy them. Be certain that no one will be embarrassed by ~~that~~ *what* you tell.

3. Ask yourself ~~is~~ *if* the joke you want to tell *is* vulgar. If it is, don't tell it.

4. Before you begin, be certain you remember what ~~are the key details~~ *the key details are*. Run through them in your mind before you start speaking.

5. Make sure ~~what~~ *that* you have everybody's attention when you're ready to start.

6. Be certain ~~whether~~ *(that)* you remember what the punch line of the joke is. Nothing is worse than listening to a joke when the teller can't remember the punch line.
7. The fact ~~can you~~ *(that) you can* remember a joke doesn't guarantee success. You have to make the experience a performance. Be animated and dramatic.
8. ~~If~~ *Whether* to laugh at your own jokes is always a question. Many comedians are criticized because they laugh at their own jokes. Don't laugh at what you're saying. Let others do the laughing.

EXERCISE 6

A. The incident in Jean's story took place in a school in Oregon.

B.
2. The expectation is (that) you will laugh whether or not you think the joke is funny.
3. Everyone thinks (that) you're a drag if you don't laugh.
4. He thinks (that) most jokes are too programmed.
5. He feels (that) he's stupid when he doesn't get the point of a joke.
6. The problem was (that) some girls were putting lipstick prints on the mirrors in the girls' bathroom.
7. The principal decided (that) something had to be done about the problem.
8. The principal wanted to show the girls (that) it was difficult to clean the mirrors.

EXERCISE 7

B.
2. ⌐ 6. ⌐
3. ⌐ 7. ⌐
4. ⌐ 8. ⌐
5. ⌐

UNIT 11 (pages 173–190)

AFTER YOU READ

A.
1. e   6. i
2. c   7. a
3. h   8. b
4. j   9. g
5. f   10. d

B.
1. communication   6. slow
2. more   7. service
3. less   8. positive
4. active   9. schoolchildren
5. Japan

EXERCISE 1

A. **2.** e   **6.** b
   3. f   **7.** g
   4. a   **8.** d
   5. c

B. **2.** C   **6.** I
   3. C   **7.** C
   4. I   **8.** I
   5. I

EXERCISE 2

2. The headline said (that) scientist Linda Buck had unlocked the secret of the sense of smell.

3. The headline said (that) the Mt. St. Andrea volcano might erupt again.

4. The headline said (that) a new tax cut would be passed soon.

5. The headline said (that) unemployment was increasing.

6. The headline said (that) mercury-contaminated fish was dangerous to eat.

7. The headline said (that) a face transplant procedure had been perfected by Spanish surgeons.

8. The headline said (that) three local schools will close next month.

EXERCISE 3

2. Sammi asked, "Where was the Rosetta Stone found?"

3. Roberto asked, "How long did World War II last?"

4. Mei-Ling asked, "Where was Magellan from?" OR "What country was Magellan from?"

5. William asked, "Can a person born outside the United States become president?"

6. Ewa asked, "In what century did the modern Olympics begin?"

7. Amanda asked, "How many countries have joined the European Union?"

8. Zelda asked, "Is population growth increasing worldwide?"

EXERCISE 4

2. I could
3. what she needed
4. she had to write
5. her
6. what the quotation was
7. it was
8. what she thought it meant
9. it was
10. would like
11. was
12. if she thought it meant
13. could learn
14. she understood

EXERCISE 5

Dear Emily,

   I just wanted to fill you in on Tim's school adventures. About two months ago Melanie said she ~~feels~~ *felt* we should switch Tim to the public school. He'd been in a private school for several months, as you know. I asked her why ~~did she think~~ *she thought* that, and she said, "He's miserable where he is, and the quality of education is poor. He says he doesn't really have any friends." I couldn't help but agree. She said she thought we ~~can~~ *could* move him to the local high school, which has a good academic reputation. I ~~told~~ *said* that I agreed but that we should ask Tim. The next morning we asked Tim if he wanted to stay at the private school. I was surprised at how strong his response was. He ~~said~~ *told* me that he hated the school and didn't want to go there any longer. So we changed him. He's been at the new school for a month now, and he's doing well. Whenever I ask him ~~does he have~~ *if he has* his homework done, he says, "Dad, I've already finished it." He's made several friends. Every now and then he asks us why ~~didn't we~~ *we didn't* let him change sooner. He says people are treating him as an individual now. I'm just glad we moved him when we did.

   Not much else is new. Oh, yes—I do need to ask ~~are you coming~~ *if you're coming* for the holidays. Write soon and let us know. Or call.

                 Love,
                 Charles

EXERCISE 6

A. active listening and stating things positively instead of negatively

B. **2.** No, this method does not involve returning anger for anger.

3. Two sisters came to Sands for help resolving a family dispute.

4. They were arguing about dividing up the family estate.

5. Rosa said Alicia had always gotten everything because she had been their mother's favorite.

6. Alicia said the problem was that Rosa was a very selfish person.

7. The first thing Alicia could have said was that Rosa had really hurt her feelings.

8. The second thing Alicia could have said was that she had felt really disrespected.

EXERCISE 7

B. 2. We're on a very tight schedule. ___u___

3. The quality of education is poor at that school. ___u___

4. The chair used a self-righteous tone. ___e___

5. Unfortunately, she never answered him. ___u___

6. Tim will graduate in 2014. ___u___

7. No one will ask any questions. ___i___

8. The modern Olympics began in the 19th century. ___u___

9. Spanish surgeons recently perfected a face transplant procedure. ___u___

10. He says people are treating him as an individual. ___u___

PART IV From Grammar to Writing
(pages 191–193)

1

1. "Dad, I want to quit school and go to work," Jim murmured.

2. "Jim, how would you evaluate your education?" his father queried.

3. "I absolutely hate going to school!" Jim responded.

4. "Jim," Frank said, "you're crazy if you think it's going to be easy to get a job."

5. Frank said, "Jim, don't be a fool!"

6. Jim's parents asked, "Frank, when are you going to start taking your future seriously?"

2

The other night my friend Linh and I had a fun conversation about our recent mishaps. Linh and I are both rather clumsy guys, which can lead us to some hilarious experiences. Linh told me about the time when he'd been invited to a Thanksgiving dinner he'd just as soon forget.

"So what happened?" I asked.

"Well," Linh said, "we were all seated around an enormous table. I guess there were about 12 people there. Several of them were high-society types."

"What were you doing with a bunch of high-society people?" I asked.

"Good question," Linh answered. "Actually, I was visiting my cousin, and I was her guest."

"So what did you do wrong?" I asked.

"I was telling a joke and gesturing energetically with my hands," Linh said. "I was sitting just in front of the door to the kitchen. Just as the maid was bringing in the turkey on a big platter, I made a big gesture and knocked the turkey off the platter. It fell on the floor."

"Oh, no!" I said. "Then what?"

"Well," Linh said, "the hostess just started laughing. She said she was glad she wasn't the only person who had ever done something like that. Then she told the maid to take the turkey back into the kitchen and wash it off. The maid did and eventually brought it back, as good as new."

"How did you feel about the whole thing?" I asked.

"Mortified at first," Linh answered. "But it all turned out OK because of the hostess. It's great when people make you feel you're not the only person who can make a stupid mistake."

UNIT 12 (pages 196–210)

AFTER YOU READ

A. 1. e   5. b
2. h   6. a
3. f   7. c
4. g   8. d

B. 1. F. Most people do not fit perfectly into a personality category.

2. T

3. T

4. F. There is not a correlation between shyness and introversion.

5. T

6. F. A Type B person is an extrovert.

7. T

8. F. A Type D person likes to be told what to do.

EXERCISE 1

A. 2. Y   6. N
3. N   7. N
4. Y   8. N
5. Y

B. 2. who resembles a daisy; I

3. you know; I

4. who started her own greeting card business several years ago; NI

5. whose energies are activated by being alone; I

6. which is why she has hired Paul and Mandy to manage her business; NI

7. whom most people consider a charismatic person; NI

8. which can translate into trouble communicating with others; NI

9. who like routine and tend not to enjoy adventure; I

EXERCISE 2

2. which   7. who
3. which   8. whose
4. who   9. Ø
5. who   10. who
6. whom

EXERCISE 3

Suggested answers:

2. The company, which is named Excelsior Computer, has existed for 15 years.
3. The building where we do most of our work is located downtown.
4. The office that I work in has been remodeled.
5. Darren Corgatelli, whose wife is my aunt, is the boss.
6. Darren, whom I've known since I was a child, is an excellent boss.
7. Sarah Corgatelli, who is Darren's wife, keeps the company running smoothly.
8. I joined the company in 1995, when I graduated from college.
9. I really admire my colleagues, whose advice has been invaluable.
10. Part of my job is telemarketing, which I like the least.

EXERCISE 4

2. which is why
3. the other prisoners respected
4. he's been working for
5. the psychiatrists considered
6. which is the reason
7. who has been in trouble
8. an opinion that / which makes me
9. whom the other prisoners respected
10. for which he has been working
11. whom the psychiatrists considered
12. evidence which (OR that) makes me

EXERCISE 5

Dear Mom and Dad,

Well, the first week of college has been tough, but it's turned out OK. My advisor, who ~~she~~ is also from Winnipeg, told me about growing up there, so we

had something ~~when~~ *that* we could talk about. Since I haven't decided on a major, she had me take one of

those tests *that* ^ show you what you're most interested in.

She also had me do one of those personality inventories that ~~they~~ tell you what kind of person

you are. According to these tests, I'm a person ~~whom~~ *who (OR that)* is classified as an extrovert. I also found out that I'm

most interested in things ^ *that* involve being on the stage

and performing in some way, ~~that~~ *which* doesn't surprise me a bit. I always liked being in school plays. Remember? I signed up for two drama courses. Classes start on Wednesday, and I'm getting to know

the other people in the dormitory ~~which~~ *where* I live. It's pretty exciting being here.

Not much else right now. I'll call in a week or so.

Love,
Alice

EXERCISE 6

A. Al doesn't like the fact that one of his roommates is always asking to borrow money.

B.
2. a		6. b	
3. b		7. a	
4. a		8. b	
5. b		9. a	

EXERCISE 7

2. more than one man
3. one tie
4. more than one tie
5. more than one teacher
6. one teacher
7. more than one group of students
8. one group of students
9. one garden
10. more than one garden

UNIT 13 (pages 211–228)

AFTER YOU READ

A.
1. g	5. b
2. d	6. e
3. f	7. c
4. a	8. h

B.
1. critic	5. exploiters
2. cooking	6. interconnectedness
3. government	7. India
4. reconcile	8. environment

EXERCISE 1

A. *Students should draw a line between the circled noun and underlined clause.*

2. Mandela reaches out to (François Pienaar) with whom he develops an enduring friendship.
3. The picture stars (Morgan Freeman) and (Matt Damon), both of whom play their roles to near perfection.
4. (Clint Eastwood), whose films I always go to, directed with great skill.
5. Science-fiction (films), a compelling example of which is *Avatar*, continue to be popular.
6. The movie is a (story) in which the Pandorans vanquish some exploiters from Earth.

7. The American couple's Mexican ⬭housekeeper, to whom they've entrusted their children, takes the kids to her son's wedding in Mexico.
8. In the process he finds the lovely ⬭Latika, from whom he's become separated.

B. 2. who is caught in a dead-end job
   3. which stars Meryl Streep and Amy Adams
   4. which is set on a planetary moon called Pandora
   5. which was directed by James Cameron of *Titanic* fame
   6. that are rivaled by those of few other films
   7. that was left in Morocco by a Japanese man
   8. which features Dev Patel and Freida Pinto as hero and heroine

EXERCISE 2

2. both of which were directed by James Cameron
3. all of whom are highly regarded European directors
4. all of which have earned a great deal of money
5. all of whom have played the role of James Bond
6. neither of whom is known as a singer

EXERCISE 3

2. *Spider-Man*, based on the popular comic book, is one of the highest-earning movies of all time.
3. *The Pirates of the Caribbean*, starring Johnny Depp, are all very popular.
4. Clint Eastwood has directed many big movies, including *Million Dollar Baby*, *Gran Torino*, and *Invictus*.
5. The Harry Potter novels, written by J.K. Rowling, have translated well to the screen.

EXERCISE 4

2. Many science fiction films have been financially successful. They include *Spider-Man*, *Jurassic Park*, and *Avatar*.
3. The top-earning animated films are *Finding Nemo* and *Shrek 2*. I've seen both of them.
4. *The Hurt Locker* was the best picture of 2009. It features lesser known actors.
5. *Beverly Hills Chihuahua* stars Drew Barrymore and Andy Garcia. I respect both of them.

EXERCISE 5

Answers will vary.

EXERCISE 6

Dear Brent,
   Sarah and I are having a great time in Los Angeles. We spent the first day at the beach in Venice and saw where <u>The Sting</u> was filmed—you know,
that famous movie ~~starred~~ *starring* Paul Newman and Robert Redford? Yesterday we went to Universal Studios and learned about all the cinematic tricks, most of
~~that~~ *which* I wasn't aware of. Amazing! The funny thing is that even though you know the illusion presented on the screen is just an illusion, you still believe it's real when you see the movie. Then we took the tram tour around the premises and saw several actors working,
some of ~~which~~ *whom* I recognized. I felt like jumping off the tram and shouting, "Would everyone famous please give me your autograph?" In the evening we went to a party at the home of one of Sarah's
friends, many of ~~them~~ *whom* are connected with the movie business. I had a really interesting conversation with a fellow working in the industry who claims that a
lot of movies ~~making~~ *made* these days are modeled conceptually after amusement park rides. Just like the rides, the movies start slowly and easily, then they have a lot of twists and turns ~~are~~ calculated to scare you to death, and they end happily. Maybe <u>Pirates of the Caribbean</u> is an example. Pretty fascinating, huh? What next?
   Sorry to spend so much time talking about movies, but you know what an addict I am. Anyway, I'll let you know my arrival time, which I'm not sure of yet, so that you can pick me up at the airport.

                              Love you lots,
                              Amanda

EXERCISE 7

A. *Casablanca* is her all-time favorite.
B. 2. F   7. F
   3. F   8. F
   4. T   9. T
   5. F   10. F
   6. T

EXERCISE 8

2. a. æ   b. eɪ
3. a. aʊ   b. ʌ
4. a. oʊ   b. ɑ
5. a. ɪ   b. aɪ

EXERCISE 9

A Beautiful Mind
(2002) C-135 m.
Rating: ★★★ Director: Ron Howard
Starring: Russell Crowe, Jennifer Connelly, Ed Harris, Paul Bettany, Christopher Plummer, Adam Goldberg, Judd Hirsch, Josh Lucas, Anthony Rapp, Austin Pendleton

An unusual story inspired by incidents in the life of John Nash, a brilliant West Virginia mathematician who flowers at Princeton in the late 1940s and goes to work at M.I.T. But his marriage and sanity are put to a painful test. The central story twist is amazing—and completely unexpected. Crowe is excellent as usual, and the film offers an overdue showcase for Connelly as the student who becomes his wife. Oscar winner for Best Picture, Director, Supporting Actress (Connelly), and Adapted Screenplay (Akiva Goldsman). PG-13.

PART V From Grammar to Writing
(pages 229–232)

1

1. **a.** College students who live close to campuses spend less money on gas.
   b. College students, who are expected to study hard, have to become responsible for themselves.
2. **a.** People, who are the only animals with a capacity for creative language, have highly developed brains.
   b. People who live in glass houses shouldn't throw stones.
3. **a.** The car, which was invented in the late 19th century, has revolutionized modern life.
   b. The car that I would really like to buy is the one in the far corner of the lot.
4. **a.** Science fiction movies, which have become extremely popular in the last two decades, often earn hundreds of millions of dollars for their studios.
   b. The science fiction movies that have earned the most money collectively are the *Star Wars* films.
5. **a.** The panda that was given to the National Zoo died recently.
   b. The panda, which is native only to China, is on the Endangered Species List.
6. **a.** A film directed by Steven Spielberg is likely to be a blockbuster.
   b. *A Beautiful Mind*, directed by Ron Howard, won the Academy Award for best picture.
7. **a.** Many Canadians, including Donald Sutherland and Michael J. Fox, are major international film stars.
   b. A film directed by Pedro Almodóvar is likely to be a financial success.

2

Dear Mom and Dad,

Thanks again for bringing me down here to the university last weekend. Classes didn't start until Wednesday, so I had a few days to get adjusted. I'm signed up for five courses: zoology, calculus, English, and two history classes. It's a heavy load, but they're all courses that will count for my degree. The zoology class, which meets at 8:00 every morning,

is going to be my hardest subject. The history class that I have in the morning is on Western civilization; the one that I have in the afternoon is on early U.S. history. Calculus, which I have at noon every day,

looks like it's going to be relatively easy. Besides zoology, the other class that's going to be hard is English, which we have to write a composition a

week for.
I like all of my roommates but one. There are four of us in our suite, including two girls from Texas

and a girl from Manitoba. Here's a picture of us. Sally, who is from San Antonio, is great; I feel like

I've known her all my life. She's the one on the left. I also really like Anne, the girl from Manitoba. She's

the one on the right. But Heather, the other girl from

Texas, is kind of a pain. She's the one next to me in

the middle. Heather is one of those people who never tell you what's bothering them and then get hostile. All in all, though, it looks like it's going to be a great year. I'll write again in a week or so.

Love,
Vicky

UNIT 14 (pages 234–249)

AFTER YOU READ

A. 1. b **6.** b
  2. c **7.** c
  3. a **8.** d
  4. d **9.** a
  5. a

B. 1. F. The flight Cooper hijacked originated in Portland.

2. T

3. F. The money Cooper received was in twenty-dollar bills.

4. F. The passengers were not aware of what Cooper was doing.

5. F. A portion of Cooper's money was discovered by an eight-year-old boy.

6. F. It is not known whether or not Cooper was killed by the impact of his fall and the weather conditions.

7. T

8. F. Some people think Cooper got away with the crime.

EXERCISE 1

2. was handed; a
3. was being hijacked; a
4. had . . . been photocopied; c
5. has been discovered; a
6. were found; a
7. had to have been killed; c
8. has not been divulged; b

EXERCISE 2

2. T; are caught
3. I; disappear
4. I; go
5. T; is helped
6. T; are rewarded
7. I; don't realize
8. T; are watched

EXERCISE 3

2. are being questioned
3. was being opened
4. was being helped
5. are being withheld
6. are currently being interviewed

EXERCISE 4

2. haven't been cracked
3. was sighted
4. was found
5. was determined
6. had been abandoned
7. had been set
8. might have been threatened
9. was caused
10. has not been proved OR proven
11. was considered
12. was accompanied
13. were received
14. have been discovered
15. Could she and Noonan have been killed
16. shouldn't be solved

EXERCISE 5

A. 1. b **2.** b **3.** a **4.** a **5.** b **6.** b

B. 2. have them enlarged
3. getting his car tuned up
4. have a taillight replaced
5. got lunch delivered
6. gotten analyzed
7. had completed the work
8. had finished the report
9. had it typed
10. having their kitchen remodeled

EXERCISE 6

In our day we believe in science and have the feeling that every question can be ~~explain~~ *explained* and every problem can be solved. But some of us want the opposite. We don't want everything to be explained. We like puzzles. We feel that mystery is needed in our lives.

The mysterious crop circles that have ~~been~~ appeared around the world in the last 25 years or so are an example of this. These formations have *been*ˆ reported in more than 20 countries, including the United States, Canada, and Australia. But most of them have been found in grain fields in southern England. These circles, which are large and flat, are caused by a force that flattens the grain but does not destroy it. They are still ~~been~~ *being* made.

How have these circles been produced? By whom have they been made? Since the first discovery of the circles, many explanations have been proposed. According to some people, the circles have been made by spirit creatures like fairies. Others say they have been caused by "Star Wars" experiments or are messages that have been ~~leaving~~ *left* by extraterrestrials visiting our planet. Two British painters, David Chorley and Douglas Bower, say they ~~were~~ made the crop circles over a period of years as a joke. If this is true, however, how can we explain the crop circles in Australia and Canada and other places? They couldn't all have ~~being~~ *been* made by Chorley and Bower, could they?

In 2002, director M. Night Shyamalan released his movie *Signs*, which is about the crop circle question. The movie shows clearly that the crop circles *were*ˆ made by invading aliens from beyond our solar system. This is one interesting and enjoyable theory. More explanations like it ~~get~~ *are* needed. What's fun is speculation. The mystery doesn't need to be solved.

EXERCISE 7

A. A hit-and-run accident occurred this evening.

B. 2. The boy was struck by a Toyota Camry.
3. The boy was crossing the intersection alone.
4. The car disappeared immediately.
5. The boy sustained massive injuries.
6. The boy was taken to Downtown Medical Center.
7. The boy is being cared for in the Intensive Care Unit.
8. His condition is described as critical.

9. Anyone with information is asked to call 444-6968.
10. A reward is being offered.

EXERCISE 8

1. 's being; happening now	6. 's being; happening now
2. 's been; already done	7. 's been; already done
3. 's been; already done	8. 's been; already done
4. 's being; happening now	
5. 's being; happening now	

EXERCISE 9

Student A's Clues and Student B's Completions
(1.) I was born, or maybe I should say I was created . . . **(2.)** . . . at 5:00 in the morning on August 6, 1762.
(2.) An all-night card game . . . **(3.)** . . . was being played at a gaming table.
(3.) I was created by . . . **(4.)** . . . an Englishman named John Montagu, the fourth earl of the place I was named after.
(4.) The "hero" type of me gets its name . . . **(1.)** . . . because of the hero-sized appetite that's needed to eat one.

Student B's Clues and Student A's Completions
(5.) The snack ordered by my creator was composed of . . . **(6.)** . . . some slices of meat between two slices of bread.
(6.) It's almost certain . . . **(9.)** . . . that I'm being eaten somewhere in the world this very minute.
(7.) My creator was hungry but too busy to leave the game, . . . **(8.)** . . . so he ordered a snack to be delivered to the gaming table.
(8.) Two slices of bread with a filling between them . . . **(5.)** . . . have been known by my name since then.
(9.) And the "submarine" type of me . . . **(7.)** . . . is shaped like a submarine.

Correct order of the clues: 1, 3, 2, 7, 5, 8, 4, 9, 6
Mystery object: a sandwich

UNIT 15 (pages 250–265)

AFTER YOU READ

A. **1.** c **3.** a **5.** b **7.** d
2. d **4.** d **6.** a **8.** c
B. **1.** Americans **5.** toothbrush
2. bathroom **6.** dentists
3. sink **7.** therapists or psychiatrists
4. shaving **8.** illnesses

EXERCISE 1

A. **2.** S **4.** S **6.** O **8.** O **10.** S
3. O **5.** O **7.** O **9.** O
B. **1.** **a.** no **b.** no
2. **a.** no **b.** no
3. **a.** yes **b.** yes
4. **a.** yes **b.** yes

EXERCISE 2

2. are surrounded by	7. is made up of (OR is divided into OR is composed of)
3. is divided into (OR is composed of OR is made up of)	
4. is located (OR is found)	8. is divided into
5. is composed of (OR is made up of)	9. are found (OR are located)
6. is bordered by	10. are found in (OR are located in)

EXERCISE 3

A. **2.** was thought to be
3. is claimed to have been (OR is claimed to be)
4. are regarded as
5. were believed to be
6. have been considered
7. is said to live
8. was regarded as
9. is assumed to have been (OR is assumed to be)
10. are alleged to be
B. **3.** It is claimed that Lee Harvey Oswald was the assassin of President John Kennedy.
5. In the Middle Ages, it was believed that fairies and other spirit creatures were real.
7. It is said that Bigfoot, supposedly a large, mysterious forest creature, lives in the Pacific Northwest.
9. Today, it is assumed that William Shakespeare was the author of the plays credited to him . . .
10. From time to time, it is alleged that certain people are criminals . . .

EXERCISE 4

Answers will vary.

EXERCISE 5

Every area of the world has its own legends, and Asia is no different. One of the most famous Asian legends is about the Abominable Snowman, also called the yeti, of the Himalayas. Is the yeti just a

believed
legend that is ~~believe~~ because people want things to be real, or does he really exist?

is
The yeti thought to be a huge creature—perhaps

as tall as eight feet. His body is supposed to be

is said
covered with long, brown hair. He ~~says~~ to have
a pointed head and a hairless face that looks
something like a man's. It is claimed that he lives
near Mount Everest, the highest mountain in the

is located
world, which ~~locates~~ on the border of Nepal and
Tibet.

Sightings of the yeti have been reported for
centuries, but the yeti was made known to the rest of
the world only in 1921. In that year, members of an
expedition to climb Mt. Everest saw very large tracks
in the snow that looked like prints of human feet. No
conclusive evidence of the yeti's existence was found
during that expedition, but interest was stimulated.
Other expeditions were undertaken. In 1951, explorer
Eric Shipton led a search in which some gigantic,
human-appearing tracks were found. Once again, the
yeti himself was not seen. In 1969, Sir Edmund

as
Hillary, who is regarded ^ one of the greatest climbers

ever, arranged another expedition, this time with the
intention of not only seeing the yeti but of capturing
him. Once again, tracks were discovered, but that
was all. Hillary eventually decided the footprints

be
might simply ^ considered normal animal tracks

enlarged by the daytime melting of the snow. In
1964, Boris F. Porshev, a Russian scientist, said
that he believed that the yeti actually existed. He
theorized that the yeti is a surviving descendant of

have lived
Neanderthal man, a creature who is believed to ~~live~~
from 200,000 to 25,000 years ago and is thought
by some to be an ancestor of modern humans.
Porshev has never actually been able to spot the yeti,
however.

The mystery continues. Does the yeti really exist,
or do people just want to believe he exists? It seems
to me that there must be more to this mystery than
just melted tracks. Centuries of reports by
Himalayan trail guides must mean something.

been
Besides, other yeti-type creatures have ^ reported—

most notably, Bigfoot in North America. Time will
tell, but maybe we shouldn't be so quick to dismiss
the Abominable Snowman as nothing more than an
entertaining story.

EXERCISE 6

A. The locale is the "lost continent of Atlantis."

B. **2.** F   **4.** T   **6.** F   **8.** T
    3. F   **5.** T   **7.** F   **9.** F

EXERCISE 7

2. The people **spend** a **great** deal of time on the
appearance and **health** of their bodies.
3. The **president says** that a **great** tragedy has
struck the **nation**.
4. It is **alleged** that **they came** from the East.
5. It is **said** that **strange** creatures like the **yeti**
may actually **exist**.
6. **Every day** each **member** of the family **enters**
the room.
7. The countries of **Haiti** and the Dominican
Republic are located on the **same** island.
8. **Betty's letter** arrived on **Wednesday** afternoon.

PART VI   From Grammar to Writing
(pages 266–268)

1

Rolleen Laing poured herself a second cup of
coffee as she ate her breakfast, which consisted of a

an
fried egg, ^ orange, and a piece of dry toast. She was

62 years old and had been successful as a university

a
professor, ^ writer of detective fiction, and an amateur

detective. Just then the telephone rang. It was Harry
Sadler, a local police detective. Ever since Rolleen
had helped Harry crack a murder case several years
previously, she had been called in as an unofficial
consultant on several cases. She had helped Harry
solve cases involving a hit-and-run victim, a

a
murdered TV executive, and, most recently, ^ koala

stolen from the city zoo.

"Hi, Rolleen. This is Harry. You're needed on
another case. It's a robbery this time. Some thieves
broke into the art museum and stole a van Gogh,

a
a Picasso, ^ Gauguin, and a Matisse. Meet me at the

museum at 10:00, OK?"

2

On the evening of August 6, 1930, Judge Joseph
Force Crater, a wealthy, successful, and good-looking
New Yorker, disappeared without a trace. Earlier in
the evening he had been seen with friends at a

observed
Manhattan restaurant and ~~they observed him~~
departing. At 9:10 P.M. he walked out the door of the
restaurant and hailed a taxi. He was soon driven
away. No one ever saw or heard from him again. It
was 10 days before he was even reported missing. On
August 16, his wife called his courthouse,

asked the secretary

~~the secretary was asked~~ of his whereabouts, and learned that he was probably off on political business. This news reassured Mrs. Crater somewhat, but when he still hadn't turned up by August 26, a group of his fellow judges started an investigation. A grand jury was convened, but its members could not come to any conclusion as to what had happened to Judge Crater. They theorized that the judge might have developed amnesia, ~~might have~~ run away voluntarily, or been a crime victim. His wife disagreed with the first two possibilities, holding that he had been murdered by someone in the Tammany Hall organization, the political machine that controlled New York City at the time. The mystery remains unsolved to this day. Crater could have been killed

murdered by a girlfriend

by a Tammany Hall agent, ~~a girlfriend could have murdered him~~, or kidnapped by an organized crime group. He might in fact have suffered from amnesia,

he might have planned his own disappearance

or ~~his own disappearance might have been planned by him~~. Reports of Judge Crater sightings have continued to surface over the last several decades.

UNIT 16 (pages 270–284)

AFTER YOU READ

A. 1. d 3. g 5. a 7. h
2. f 4. e 6. c 8. b

B. 1. Convenience 5. writer
2. kayaking 6. socializing
3. contacting 7. honest
4. age 8. listened

EXERCISE 1

A. 2. O 4. C 6. C 8. C
3. OP 5. OP 7. O

B. 2. Y 4. Y 6. N 8. Y
3. N 5. Y 7. Y

EXERCISE 2

A. 2. vegetating 10. working
3. worrying 11. playing
4. not having 12. collecting
5. not working 13. singing
6. making 14. not singing
7. socializing 15. singing
8. having 16. orienteering
9. meeting

B. 2. Bob's helping 6. my becoming
3. My boss's criticizing 7. their being
4. Her living 8. Our getting
5. Mary's advising

EXERCISE 3

2. seeing 7. studying
3. having enrolled 8. helping
4. assigning 9. passing
5. arguing 10. having told
6. having said

EXERCISE 4

Suggested questions:
1. Do you prefer being asked out on a date or asking someone yourself?
2. Are you more interested in entertaining yourself or in being entertained by others?
3. Do you prefer preparing dinner yourself or being invited to dinner by friends?
4. Do you like being told what to do or giving orders?
5. Do you like figuring things out yourself or being shown how to do things?
6. Do you prefer being given advice by friends or giving your friends advice?

Answers to the questions will vary.

EXERCISE 5

Dear Adam,

I've been here for three days and am having a

wishing

great time, but I can't help ~~wish~~ you were here too.

letting

Tell your boss I'm really angry at him. Not ~~let~~ you take any vacation time qualifies him for the Jerk-of-the-Year Award. (Just kidding. Don't say that!)

Believe it or not, the first night I missed hearing all the city noises, but I haven't really had any

getting

trouble ~~to get~~ used to the peace and quiet since then.

rushing

Everything's all so relaxed here—there's no ~~rush~~

writing

around or ~~write~~ things down in your Daily Planner.

Getting

~~Get~~ out of New York City was definitely what I needed, even if it's only for two weeks. The ranch has

riding   *rafting*

lots of activities—horseback ~~ride~~, river ~~raft~~ on the Rio Grande, hiking in the wilderness—you name it. The ranch employees do everything for you—being taken care of is nice, for a change, and I love being chauffeured around Santa Fe in the ranch limousine. Tonight a group of us are going out to a country western dance place called Rodeo Nites in Santa Fe, so having taken those two-step dance lessons last summer will come in handy. It's just too bad you couldn't come along so we could both have a good time. Tomorrow we're all going to Taos Pueblo to watch some weaving being done and to see some Native American dancing, which is great because

learning
I'm really interested in ~~learn~~ more about Native
seeing
American culture. And I'm looking forward to ~~see~~
Carmen at the Santa Fe Opera on Saturday.

I'll write again in a day or two. Miss you lots.

Love,
Louise

EXERCISE 6

A. 1. You have to be in good physical shape.
   2. He'll use his GPS to find the coffee shop if
     necessary.

B. 2. F   **7.** T
   3. F   **8.** F
   4. T   **9.** T
   5. F   **10.** T
   6. T

EXERCISE 7

B. 2. The suspect I suspect is the one on the far left.
   3 The band is going to record a new record for
     their CD.
   4. A desert is a place that people desert.
   5. The dictator is going to subject the subject to
     difficult questioning.
   6. The students are going to present their teacher
     with a wonderful present.

UNIT 17 (pages 285–302)

AFTER YOU READ

A. 1. e   **3.** b   **5.** h   **7.** d
   2. f   **4.** g   **6.** c   **8.** a

B. 1. T   **5.** T
   2. F. The word *postpone*   **6.** T
     has a neutral sense.   **7.** F. We should not
   3. T   avoid difficult or
   4. F. Dr. Stevens believes   painful things.
     it is never appropriate   **8.** T
     to procrastinate.

EXERCISE 1

A. 2. O   **4.** SC   **6.** O   **8.** S
   3. S   **5.** O   **7.** SC   **9.** O

B. 1. T   **3.** F   **5.** T
   2. F   **4.** T   **6.** F

EXERCISE 2

  2. warned me not to   **7.** expected to pass
     put off   **8.** required us to write
  3. wanted me to make   **9.** refused to accept
  4. was important to   **10.** caused me to fail
     experience   **11.** advised me to retake
  5. forced me to study   **12.** encouraged me to
  6. was fortunate to   start
     graduate

EXERCISE 3

  2. not to have heard   **6.** to have been hit
  3. not to have understood   **7.** to have fed
  4. to have gotten   **8.** not to have done
  5. to have finished

EXERCISE 4

  2. to be helped by a   **5.** to be stopped by a
     passing motorist   police officer
  3. your phone service   **6.** to be questioned by
     to be disconnected   your teacher
  4. to be notified by the
     police

EXERCISE 5

Suggested answers:

  2. Jack types too slowly to finish the report on
     time.
  3. Marcy will have enough money to buy her
     friend's car.
  4. Eve waited too long to start preparing the meal.
  5. Sally didn't eat enough to stay healthy.
  6. Carlos is intelligent enough to pass the course.

EXERCISE 6

          to
    I just had ˄ write tonight. Until now I've never
            to
had the courage ˄ do this, but now I do. I've decided to
confront
~~have confronted~~ Sarah about her irresponsibility.
This is something that has been bothering me for
some time now, but somehow I've always been
        to
reluctant ˄ force the issue. So here's the situation:

Sarah invites people to do things, but she doesn't
follow through. Last week she asked my fiancé, Al,
      to
and me ˄ have dinner, and she also invited our friends
                     to
Mark and Debbie. The four of us made plans ˄ go to
her house on Friday evening. Something told me I
          to ask
should call Sarah ~~asking~~ what we should bring, and
it's a good thing I did. Sarah said, "Dinner? I'm not
having dinner tonight. I know I mentioned it as a
possibility, but I never settled it with you guys. You
misunderstood me." Well, that's just silly. She told
   to plan
us ~~planning~~ on it for Friday evening at 7 P.M. When I
told the others, they were furious. Al said, "I don't
      to be
expect ~~being~~ treated like royalty. I do expect to be

treated with consideration." So tomorrow I'm going to call Sarah up and make my point. I'm not going to allow her ^to^ make my life miserable.

Enough for now. Time for bed.

EXERCISE 7

A. He received a 20-year minimum sentence.
B. 2. The prisoners are believed to have escaped in a prison laundry truck.
   3. They are believed to have been helped by a prison employee.
   4. It was supposed to have been installed two months ago.
   5. The prisoners are thought to have weapons.
   6. They are believed to be heading in the direction of Union City.
   7. Listeners are warned not to approach the prisoners.
   8. They are asked to contact the Sheriff's Office.

EXERCISE 8

2. a	**4.** æ	**6.** ^	**8.** a	**10.** æ	**12.** æ
3. ^	**5.** æ	**7.** a	**9.** ^	**11.** a	

PART VII From Grammar to Writing
(pages 303–306)

1

Suggested corrections:

1. Ramiro loves camping, ~~to collect~~ *collecting* stamps, and surfing the Internet.
2. Lately I've been trying to stop speeding in traffic, ~~to schedule~~ *scheduling* too many activities, and rushing through each day like a crazy person.
3. To have a happier family life, we should all focus on eating meals together, on airing our problems and concerns, and on ~~take~~ *taking* time to talk to one another.
4. I'm advising you not to sell your property, ^*not to*^ take out a loan, and not to buy a new house right now. (OR not to sell your property, take out a loan, and buy a house . . .)
5. Most presidents want to be reelected to a second term, ^*to be*^ taken seriously by other world leaders, and to be remembered fondly after they leave office.

6. To be hired in this firm, you are expected to have earned a bachelor's degree and ~~having~~ *to have* worked in a bank for at least two years.

2

Suggested corrections:

   What are you most afraid of? Are you worried about being cheated, ~~to lose~~ *losing* your job, or contracting a deadly disease? Well, if you're like the vast majority of Americans, you fear standing up, ~~to face~~ *facing* an audience, and ~~to deliver~~ *delivering* a speech more than anything else. Surveys have found that anxiety about public speaking terrifies Americans more than dying does. Somehow, people expect to be laughed at, ridiculed, or ~~to be~~ scorned by an audience. Many college students fear public speaking so much that they put off taking a speech class or even ~~to think~~ *thinking* about it until their last term before graduation. Speech instructors and others familiar with the principles of public speaking stress that the technique of desensitization works best for overcoming speech anxiety. This idea holds that people can get over their fear of speaking in public by enrolling in a course, ~~to attend~~ *attending* the class faithfully, and ~~to force~~ *forcing* themselves to perform the speech activities. Once they have discovered that it is rare for people to die, ~~making~~ *to make* fools of themselves, or to be laughed at while making a speech, they're on their way to success. Consequently, their anxiety becomes a little less each time they get up and talk in public. It may take a while, but eventually they find themselves able to stand up willingly, ~~speaking~~ *speak* comfortably, and ~~expressing~~ *express* themselves clearly.

UNIT 18 (pages 308–322)

AFTER YOU READ

A. 1. a   3. b   5. a   7. b
     2. c   4. b   6. c   8. d
B. 1. voluntary   3. feminine   5. fair
     2. against   4. required   6. unfeminine

EXERCISE 1

2. basically; S	**7.** just; F
3. obviously; S	**8.** only; F
4. even; F	**9.** Not only . . . but also; N
5. clearly; S	**10.** only; F
6. Little; N	

EXERCISE 2

Each sentence can have the sentence adverb in two other positions.

2. Unfortunately, military service can be dangerous.
3. I'm against the death penalty essentially because I consider it cruel and unusual punishment.
4. There's certainly a lot more violence in movies than in the past.
5. Nuclear weapons can be eliminated, hopefully.
6. Perhaps a vaccine against AIDS can be found.
7. The prime minister's position is clearly wrong.
8. Actually, there's increasing opposition to people's owning SUVs.

EXERCISE 3

2. b   **3.** a   **4.** b   **5.** b   **6.** a

EXERCISE 4

2. Rarely do women fight alongside men in combat.
3. In no way is military service useless.
4. Neither will poverty (be completely eliminated).
5. Not only do we need to stop global warming, but we also need to find new energy sources.
6. Never had it occurred to me that SUVs, could harm the environment . . .

EXERCISE 5

2. even . . . has . . .
3. Only . . . have . . .
4. Not only . . . but they also allow . . .
5. Only men are required . . .
6. Only in . . . are women required . . .

EXERCISE 6

Dear Dad,

I'm waiting for the 5:25 train, so ~~just I~~ *I just* thought I'd drop you a note. I've been at the global warming conference. Actually, I almost didn't get to the conference because ~~almost we~~ *we almost* didn't get our taxes done on time. We stayed up late last night, though, and I mailed the forms this morning.

I hate income taxes! Only once in the last ten years ~~we have gotten~~ *have we gotten* a refund, and this time the form was so complicated that ~~Vicky got even~~ *even Vicky got* upset, and you know how calm she is. Maybe we should move to Antarctica or something. No taxes there.

Besides that, we've been having problems with Donna. It's probably nothing more serious than teenage rebellion, but whenever we try to lay down the law, she gets defensive. Rarely if ever ~~she takes~~ *does she take* criticism well. The other night she and her friend stayed out until 1 A.M., and when we asked what they'd been doing she said, "We were just talking and listening to music at the Teen Club. Why can't you leave me alone?" Then she stomped out of the room. Fortunately, Sam and Toby have been behaving like angels—but they're not teenagers!

Meanwhile, Donna's school has started a new open-campus policy. Students can leave the campus whenever they don't have a class. ~~Even they don't~~ *They don't even* have to tell the school office where they're going and when they'll be back. No way do Vicky and I approve of that policy! School time, in our view, is for studying and learning, not for socializing. Little do those school officials realize how much trouble unsupervised teenagers can get into.

Well, Dad, here ~~the train comes~~ *comes the train*. I'll sign off now. Write soon.

Love,
Ken

EXERCISE 7

A. The caller is from Singapore.
B. **2.** a   **4.** a   **6.** d   **8.** b
   3. c   **5.** a   **7.** b

EXERCISE 8

1. Bill can even understand this <u>math</u>.
2. Even <u>Bill</u> can understand this math.
3. I don't just <u>agree</u> with Nancy.
4. I just <u>don't</u> agree with Nancy.
5. We don't even <u>understand</u> you.
6. Even <u>we</u> don't understand you.
7. Only <u>women</u> can visit this club.
8. Women can only <u>visit</u> this club.

UNIT 19 (pages 323–339)

AFTER YOU READ

A. 1. Venues
2. inevitable
3. lurking
4. Stamina
5. prevalence
6. also-ran
7. Partisanship
8. awry

B. 1. war
2. peace
3. excellence
4. fame
5. bargain
6. salaries
7. violence
8. local

EXERCISE 1

2. *contrast*
   <u>While sports may look good on the surface</u>, <u>problems are lurking underneath</u>.

3. *reason*
   <u>Because he penalized a player in the 2008 European Championships</u>, <u>a British referee received death threats</u>.

4. *time*
   <u>When the Olympic games started about 2,700 years ago in Greece</u>, <u>the contests held were basically those related to war</u>.

5. <u>Running paralleled the physical exertion you</u>
   condition
   <u>might have to make</u> <u>if an enemy was chasing you</u>.

6. *contrast*
   <u>Although athletes still try to achieve their personal best</u>, <u>the emphasis has shifted away from the individual pursuit of excellence</u>.

7. <u>I wondered why tickets are so expensive</u> until I
   time
   <u>remembered the key factor: player's salaries</u>.

8. <u>Baseball is cheaper</u>, <u>though it's not really a</u>
   contrast
   <u>bargain at an average ticket cost of $27</u>.

9. *place*
   <u>We see violence</u> <u>wherever we look</u>.

10. *time*
    <u>Once we assume violence is inevitable</u>, <u>it will be almost impossible to stop</u>.

EXERCISE 2

2. If the score is forty-love, one player's score is zero.
3. You can't play this game unless you have ice skates.
4. You go to the free-throw line after you've been fouled.
5. Though you can't use your hands, you may use your head.
6. You've finished the course when you've run 26.2 miles.
7. Your team can't bat until the other team makes three outs.
8. If your team scores a touchdown, it earns six points.

EXERCISE 3

2. Although (OR Though OR Even though OR While) Greek city-states were often at war with one another, Olympic contestants stopped fighting during the games.
3. The ancient Olympic games were outlawed by the Roman emperor Theodosius I after they had been held for over 1,000 years.

4. He outlawed them in 393 because (OR since) Romans thought Greeks wore too few clothes.
5. French educator Pierre de Coubertin revived the Olympics since (OR because) he thought they would promote international peace.
6. Tug-of-war was dropped from the Olympics in 1920 when (OR after OR because OR since) American and British athletes disagreed about how it should be played.
7. New Olympic sports often first appear as demonstration events before they are adopted as medal sports.
8. Any sport can potentially become a medal event if (OR provided that) it can be scored and fulfills certain criteria.

EXERCISE 4

Suggested answers:

1. if the player makes the basket.
2. unless the player misses the basket.
3. Although the Blues are losing,
4. even though very few people are watching.
5. Because the slope was icy,
6. until conditions

EXERCISE 5

A lot of people are criticizing school sports these days. Some say there's too much emphasis on
while
football and basketball, ~~if~~ there's not enough emphasis on education. Others say the idea of the scholar-athlete is a joke. Still others say sports provide a way of encouraging violence. I think they're all wrong. If anything, school sports help prevent violence, not encourage it. Why do I think sports are a positive force?

because (OR *since* OR *as*)
For one thing, sports are positive ~~even though~~ they give students opportunities to be involved in something. Every day on TV we hear that violence is increasing. I think a lot of people get involved in crime when they don't have enough to do to keep
you
themselves busy. After ~~you'll~~ play two or three hours of basketball, baseball, or any other kind of sport, it's hard to commit a violent act even if you want to.

Second, sports teach people a lot of worthwhile things, especially at the high school level. If they play on a team, students learn to get along and work with
When (OR *Whenever*)
others. ~~Wherever~~ their team wins, they learn how
loses
to be good winners; when their team ~~will lose~~, they find out that they have to struggle to improve. They discover that winning a few and losing a few are part

of the normal ups and downs of life. Also, there's no doubt that students improve their physical condition by participating in sports.

Finally, sports are positive ~~although~~ *because* (OR *since* OR *as*) they allow students who do not have enough money to go to college to get sports scholarships and improve their chances for a successful life. ~~Unless~~ *If* a young basketball player from a small village in Nigeria can get a scholarship to play for, say UCLA, he will have a chance to get an education and probably make his life better. If a young woman with little money is accepted on the University of Toronto swim team and gets a scholarship, she'll have the chance to earn a college degree and go on to a high-paying job. *Although* (OR *Though* OR *Even though*) ~~Because~~ school sports programs have some deficiencies that need to be corrected, their benefits outweigh their disadvantages. I should know because I'm one of those students who got a sports scholarship. School sports must stay.

EXERCISE 6

A. Lillian is from Jamaica.

B. *Suggested answers:*

2. She learned to swim when she was four.
3. Lillian thinks she became a good swimmer because she had to swim in the Caribbean.
4. They spent a lot of time at the beach because they didn't have many toys or video games.
5. When she was 12, Lillian decided she wanted to become a champion swimmer and go to the Olympics someday.
6. Lillian's parents agreed to pay for lessons if Lillian would stick to her plan and practice regularly.
7. She got discouraged whenever she had a hard time learning a new stroke.
8. Lillian can't imagine herself doing anything else because swimming is a total passion for her.
9. Once Lillian started her lessons, her parents wouldn't let her quit.

EXERCISE 7

2. Elena swam laps while I did my calisthenics.
3. Even though the team scored ten runs, they still didn't win.
4. In case you haven't heard, the manager was fired.
5. I always manage to go to a gym whenever I'm traveling.
6. He makes a lot of money now that he's a major league player.
7. The coach was not popular with his players, although he took them to the championship.
8. Tickets to the game were very expensive, though I'd have to say the expense was justified.

9. She always warms up by swimming extra laps before she begins a competition.
10. After Daoud scored the winning goal, he was mobbed by his teammates.
11. The team won't make the playoffs unless they win their next eight games.
12. Once he started wearing contact lenses, he became a much more accurate player.

UNIT 20 (pages 340–357)

AFTER YOU READ

A. 1. g   3. f   5. a   7. i   9. d
    2. e   4. j   6. b   8. h   10. c

B. 1. boot   5. transplant
    2. bandits'   6. moved
    3. driver's   7. mistake
    4. coma   8. trial

EXERCISE 1

A. 1. Upon opening the door, he saw blood oozing from Nicholas's head.
2. **Nicholas** lay in a coma for two days after being rushed to a hospital.
3. **Upon** returning to the United States, Nicholas's parents received requests to tell their son's story.
4. **They** were placed on trial after being turned over to the police.

B. 2. Y   3. Y   4. N   5. N   6. Y   7. Y   8. Y

EXERCISE 2

2. Reg carefully considered the options before he sped away.

Reg carefully considered the options before speeding away.

3. Because the criminals were a deadly threat, Reg floored the gas pedal.

cannot be shortened.

4. When Reg saw a police car parked on the shoulder, he pulled over to alert the authorities.

Seeing a police car parked on the shoulder, Reg pulled over to alert the authorities.

5. As ⟨Nicholas⟩ lay on his deathbed, ⟨Reg and Maggie⟩

decided that something good should come out of

the situation.

cannot be shortened.

6. Because the ⟨criminals⟩ thought the Greens had

precious stones, ⟨they⟩ fired shots that killed

Nicholas.

Thinking the Greens had precious stones, the

criminals fired shots that killed Nicholas.

EXERCISE 3

B. 2. no

3. She came to the zoo last year after being taken from owners.

4. no

5. yes

6. On April 11, Champakali died while giving birth to a stillborn calf.

7. Damini stood still in her enclosure. She barely nibbled at the two tons of food in front of her.

EXERCISE 4

2. Noticing their interest in him, the boy offered them a guidebook.

3. They told the boy they couldn't buy anything, not having any money.

4. Impressed by the boy's responsibility, they decided to go back and buy a guidebook.

5. Finding an exchange kiosk, they changed some money.

6. Having gotten some local money, they looked for the boy but couldn't find him.

7. After being told where the boy might be, they located him.

8. Having found the boy, they bought a map from him.

EXERCISE 5

If you're at all like me, you tire of requests to help

others. ~~Barraging~~ *Barraged* by seemingly constant appeals for money to support homeless shelters, the Special Olympics, or the like, I tend to tune out, my brain numbed. I don't think I'm selfish. But ~~subjecting~~ *subjected* to so many requests, I only remember the flashy ones.

By arguing that I don't have enough money to help others, I am able to ignore the requests. Or at least that was the way I saw the situation before *being* ^ sent by my magazine to South America to do a human interest story on homeless children. Having heard many TV requests asking viewers to sponsor a child overseas, I always said to myself, "I'll bet the money is pocketed by some local politician." My opinion changed when I saw the reality of the life of a poor child.

After
~~While~~ landing in Santa Simona, I took a taxi to my hotel in the center of town, where I met Elena, *Sitting* a girl of 10 or 11. ~~Sat~~ on a dirty blanket on the sidewalk in front of the hotel, she caught my eye. Elena was trying to earn a living by selling mangoes. Smiling at me, she asked, *"Mangos, señor?—Mangoes, sir?"* I bought some mangoes and some other fruit, and we talked together. Elena's life had been difficult. Her parents were both dead, and she lived with an elderly aunt. Having *had* polio at the age of five, she now
^
walked with a limp. She and her aunt often went hungry.

Investigating
~~Investigated~~ the question the next day, I talked to several different authorities. Having become convinced that money from sponsors does in fact get to those who need it, I knew my attitude had to change. Learning that I could sponsor Elena for less than a dollar a day, I began to feel ashamed; after all, I spend more than that on my dogs. But what remains most vivid in my mind is my vision of Elena. She didn't beg or feel sorry for herself. Selling her mangoes, she earned a living, and her spirit shone through in the process. So I say to all of you reading this: The next time you hear an ad about sponsoring a child, pay attention.

EXERCISE 6

A. Not mentioned: an oil spill in the Mediterranean; World Cup news

B. 2. Mr. Tintor could demonstrate good faith by agreeing to free elections.

3. The president's aide spoke off the record.

4. They acknowledged that the current vaccine is ineffective.

5. The new nation is to be known as the Central Asian Republic.

6. It will need billions of dollars of foreign aid in order to become a viable state.

7. He had almost given up hope of being rescued because he was unable to swim.

8. Hutchison rescued him by using the lifesaving techniques she had learned in swimming class.

EXERCISE 7

2. Italians
3. confrontation
4. confronted
5. criminals
6. criminality
7. irony
8. ironic
9. realized
10. reality

UNIT 21 (pages 358–373)

AFTER YOU READ

A. 1. d 3. f 5. c 7. e
2. h 4. a 6. b 8. g

B. 1. F. Forgetting things such as another person's name is quite common.
2. T
3. T
4. F. Our long-term memory holds up better than our short-term memory.
5. T
6. T
7. F. There is evidence that staying mentally active can slow memory deterioration.
8. T

EXERCISE 1

A. 2. T 3. T 4. S 5. T 6. C
B. 2. therefore; R
3. First; O
4. Thus; R
5. Meanwhile; T
6. moreover; A
7. Furthermore; A
8. Most importantly; O

EXERCISE 2

Suggested answers:

2. He was having problems remembering his appointments, so he bought a daily planner.
   He was having problems remembering his appointments; therefore, he bought a daily planner.
3. It's important for Nancy to take her medications, but she forgot today.
   Although it's important for Nancy to take her medications, she forgot today.
   It's important for Nancy to take her medications; however, she forgot today.
4. Jack remembers everyone's name, and he never forgets a face.
   Jack remembers everyone's name; besides that, he never forgets a face.

EXERCISE 3

2. first
3. second
4. however
5. therefore
6. In addition
7. Meanwhile
8. otherwise
9. In fact

EXERCISE 4

Possible answers:

1. Hank didn't have time to take a shower, and he didn't have time to eat breakfast.
   Hank didn't have time to take a shower. In addition, he didn't have time to eat breakfast.
2. He ran out of the house, but he left his wallet on the table.
   He ran out of the house. However, he left his wallet on the table.
3. He was driving too fast, so a police offer stopped him.
   He was driving too fast. Consequently, a police officer stopped him.
4. Hank didn't have his driver's license, and he didn't have his car insurance.
   Hank didn't have his driver's license. Besides that, he didn't have his car insurance.
5. While this was happening, Hank's co-workers were waiting for him at work.
   Meanwhile, Hank's co-workers were waiting for him at work.
6. Hank's boss told him he had to improve his memory, or there could be serious consequences.
   Hank's boss told him he had to improve his memory. Otherwise, there could be serious consequences.

EXERCISE 5

Yesterday I drove my car to the downtown campus of the college. I usually have trouble finding a parking place, ~~however~~ *but* this time it was almost impossible. There were simply no parking places anywhere near the campus, so I had to park in the downtown mall, which is about a mile away. When I finished class, I walked back to the mall. ~~Therefore~~ *However*, I couldn't remember where I'd parked my car! Believe it or not, it took me 45 minutes to find it, and I was about ready to panic when I finally did. That was the last straw. I've decided that I'm going to send my car to a new home in the suburbs.

I used to think that a car was the most wonderful thing in the world. I loved the freedom of being able to come and go to my part-time job or to the college whenever I wanted. A year ago I was in a carpool with four other people, ~~nevertheless~~ *but* I hated having to wait around if my carpool members weren't ready to leave, so I started driving alone.

However
~~Although~~, I've changed my mind since then. Now it's clear to me that there are just too many disadvantages to having a car in town. For example, sitting stalled in your car in a traffic jam is stressful; besides, it's a phenomenal waste of time. In addition, it would cost me $200 a month to park my car in the
in addition (OR *besides* OR *moreover*)
city (which is why I don't do that); ~~therefore~~, there's always the chance it will be vandalized.
Consequently (OR *Therefore* OR *Because of this*)
~~Nonetheless~~, I've decided to leave it at my cousin Brent's house in the suburbs. Otherwise, I'll end up going broke paying for parking or memory improvement. My car will have a good home, and I'll use it just for longer trips. When I'm in the city,
or
though, I'll take the bus or the tram, ~~otherwise~~ I'll walk. Who knows? They say you can meet some interesting people on the bus. Maybe I'll find the love of my life. My only problem will be remembering which bus to take.

EXERCISE 6

A. True things: The visitor has a Hawaiian name; the visitor is wearing a tuxedo.

B. *Possible answers:*

2. People like to be called by their names, and it's good for business.
3. You need to notice one particular thing about a person and link that thing with the person's name.
4. The visitor told everyone to stand up.
5. **a.** The visitor wasn't in uniform.
   b. The leader didn't act like this was an interruption.
6. It's not the usual way to say good-bye.
7. They have to learn to focus their attention consistently.

EXERCISE 7

B. 2. Frank has an excellent memory, but he doesn't use it to good advantage.
3. Marta was having trouble remembering things, so she signed up for a memory course.
4. Marta was having trouble remembering things; consequently, she signed up for a memory course.
5. You need to start writing things down; otherwise, you'll miss out on key appointments.
6. You need to start writing things down, or you'll miss out on key appointments.
7. I have trouble remembering people's names, yet I can always remember their faces.

8. I have trouble remembering people's names; on the other hand, I can always remember their faces.
9. You live awfully far away to visit; besides, you never come to see me.
10. You live awfully far away to visit, and you never come to see me.

PART VIII   From Grammar to Writing
(pages 374–376)

1

Recently the life of Stella and Hank Wang has improved in several ways. <u>First</u>, they both secured new jobs that make them better off financially. Stella got a position as a proofreader and editor at a publishing company pioneering new workplace methods, and Hank was hired as a full-time consultant for an engineering firm. <u>Second</u>, their new jobs have made their lives much less stressful. The difference between their new jobs and their old ones can be summed up in one word: flextime. Until they secured these new positions, Stella and Hank had a very difficult time raising their two small children. They were at the mercy of a nine-to-five schedule; <u>consequently</u>, they had to pay a lot for day care. In order to get to work on time, they had to have the children at the day care center by 7:30 every morning. Both of their new companies, <u>however</u>, offer a flextime schedule. As long as Stella and Hank both put in their 40 hours a week, they are free to work when it is convenient for them. <u>Besides that</u>, they can take turns staying home with the children, and day care is just a memory. <u>Most importantly</u>, Stella and Hank feel that they are now doing a good job of parenting. The children are much happier because they are getting the attention they need.

2

Suggested answers:

There are a number of reasons why I prefer going out to movies to watching DVDs on TV. <u>First</u>, I often fall asleep when watching the TV screen, no matter how interesting the DVD is. The other night, for example, I was watching *Gone with the Wind* on my flat screen TV. It was compelling for a while, but pretty soon my eyelids starting getting heavy, and before I knew it I was in dreamland. <u>Second</u>, watching movies is basically a social experience. There's a lot to be said for experiencing the group reaction to a film seen in a theater. When I watch movies on a TV screen, <u>however</u> (OR <u>though</u>), I'm often alone. I love my cat, but she doesn't make many perceptive comments about movies. <u>Most importantly</u> (OR <u>Finally</u>), the TV screen, no matter how large it is, diminishes the impact you get when watching a movie on the big screen. I have a 58-inch flat screen TV, and I love the programs I see on it. It's not the same as going out to a cinema, <u>though</u> (OR <u>however</u>). <u>Consequently</u>, (OR <u>Therefore</u>,) my recommendation is to find a friend who also likes movies and go out to the flicks.

UNIT 22 (pages 378–395)

AFTER YOU READ

A. 1. c **3.** b **5.** a **7.** c **9.** a
   2. a **4.** c **6.** b **8.** d

B. 1. yard **5.** diabetic
   2. faint **6.** insulin
   3. kill **7.** merchandise
   4. married **8.** wealthy OR rich

EXERCISE 1

A. 2. R **4.** R **6.** R **8.** R
   3. R **5.** U **7.** U

B. 2. present **6.** mixed
   3. present **7.** past
   4. future **8.** past
   5. present

EXERCISE 2

2. If diabetics don't take their insulin, they sometimes go into shock.

3. We will run out of energy if we don't develop alternate energy sources.

4. If global warming continues, the polar icecaps could melt.

5. A Venus flytrap dies if it doesn't get enough water.

6. If present population trends continue, the world will reach nine billion by 2060.

EXERCISE 3

2. will you give
3. I will
4. What would you do
5. you found
6. I'd take
7. it weren't
8. I wouldn't be
9. I'd keep
10. How would you feel
11. you were
12. I'd want
13. If I were
14. I'd call
15. I'll do
16. if you really think

EXERCISE 4

A. 2. They wish it weren't raining.
   3. He wishes she would say yes.
   4. He wishes she would change her mind.
   5. She wishes she hadn't broken her leg.
   6. She wishes she were playing.

B. 2. If only it weren't raining.
   3. If only she would say yes.
   4. If only she would change her mind.
   5. If only I hadn't broken my leg.
   6. If only I were playing.

EXERCISE 5

2. were coming
3. wouldn't have done
4. had been
5. would have turned out
6. they hadn't
7. wouldn't have picked
8. I'd been betting
9. you would have won
10. you'd bet
11. You'd be
12. wouldn't be
13. you'd made it

EXERCISE 6

This has been one of those days when I wish I ~~would have~~ *had* stayed in bed. It started at 7:30 this morning when Trudy called me up and asked me for "a little favor." She's always asking me to do things for her and never wants to take any responsibility for herself. She acts as if the world owes her a living. I wish she *didn't* ~~doesn't~~ think like that. Today she wanted me to take her to the mall because she had to get her mother a birthday present. At first I said I couldn't because I had to be downtown at 11 A.M. for a job interview. Trudy said she'd do the same for me if I ~~would ask~~ *asked* her. Then she said it wouldn't take long to drive to the mall, and I'd have plenty of time to get downtown from there. I gave in and agreed to take her, but something told me I shouldn't. If I had listened to my inner voice, I might have had a job right now. When we were on the freeway, there was a major accident, and traffic was tied up for over an hour. By the time we got to the mall, it was 11:30, so I missed the appointment. I think I probably *would have gotten* ~~would get~~ the job if I had managed to make it to the interview, because my qualifications are strong. If only I ~~wouldn't have~~ *hadn't* listened to Trudy! I just wish she *didn't* (OR *wouldn't*) ~~doesn't~~ ask me to do things like this. If she asks me again, I hope I can resist.

EXERCISE 7

A. Not mentioned: math class; turning in a completed term paper; finding a new boyfriend

B. *Possible answers:*
   2. Sally wishes April hadn't told Bob he could copy her workbook.
   3. April thought Bob would break up with her if she refused.
   4. Sally would have told him no.
   5. The teacher will fail both of them if she finds out.

6. Sally would call Bob up and tell him she had changed her mind.
7. April should tell him she won't be able to do it because her conscience is bothering her.
8. If Bob gets mad and says he wants to break up, April should say good-bye.

EXERCISE 8

B. 2. 'd stopped   **7.** 'd visited
  3. 'd accepted   **8.** 'd visit
  4. 'd accept   **9.** 'd rained
  5. 'd call   **10.** 'd rain
  6. 'd called

UNIT 23 (Pages 396–413)

AFTER YOU READ

A. 1. h   **3.** j   **5.** a   **7.** b   **9.** c
  2. f   **4.** g   **6.** i   **8.** d   **10.** e
B. 1. room   **6.** drop
  2. neat   **7.** marrieds
  3. order   **8.** designated
  4. used   **9.** criticize
  5. fairness

EXERCISE 1

A. 2. IV   **4.** IM   **6.** IV   **8.** S
  3. S   **5.** IV   **7.** IM   **9.** IM
B. 2. Y   **3.** N   **4.** N   **5.** Y   **6.** Y

EXERCISE 2

2. If so, that would solve your problem.
3. And if not, what can I do?
4. Without cigarettes, I can't make it through the day.
5. You can do it with a buddy who has the same problem.
6. I'd hate my job without my friends.

EXERCISE 3

A. 2. Had she known   **4.** with   **6.** If not
  3. otherwise   **5.** If so
B. 2. If she had known   **5.** If they were hiring
  3. if she didn't find a   **6.** If they weren't
     job   hiring
  4. If she had a bit of
     luck

EXERCISE 4

Suggested answers:
2. (that) they be given higher wages (OR the company give them higher wages)
3. (that) her husband / Jin see a doctor
4. (that) they / the company acquire the small company

5. (that) the couple / they buy the house
6. (that) the woman / she visit Bangkok

EXERCISE 5

A. 2. necessary that they take   **5.** crucial that they communicate
  3. important that they find   **6.** advisable that they stay
  4. essential that they make
B. 2. It is necessary for them to take responsibility for their own actions.
  3. It is important for them to find satisfying employment.
  4. It is essential for them to make most of their own decisions.
  5. It is crucial for them to communicate with each other.
  6. It is advisable for them to stay in touch with family and close friends.

EXERCISE 6

Dear Hei-Rim,

It's time I wrote and filled you in on what's been happening since I left Russellville. I finally got a job! Remember when you suggested I just ~~went~~ ^{go} walking around, getting a sense of what St. Louis was like? A few weeks ago I was getting rather worried since I had spent most of the money I had saved to get me through the job-hunting period. It's not all that easy for someone fresh out of college to find a job, you know. I had gotten to the point where it was absolutely essential that I ~~found~~ ^{find} something or come back to Russellville. So I decided to follow your advice. ^{Had I known} ~~I had known~~ how easy this would be, I would have tried it the first week I was here. I started walking around in the downtown area, and before I knew it, I saw a beautiful little florist's shop. I walked right in, unafraid, and asked if they needed anyone. Can you believe that they did?

I was really happy in my job until my boss hired a new assistant manager who has been making my life miserable. Among other things, he ^{demands (that) I make} ~~demands me to make~~ coffee for him. He also ^{insists (that) I do} ~~insists that I'm doing~~ other things that aren't in my job description. I took this job to work with plants, not to serve him coffee. I think I need to tell him where I stand. It's important that he ~~stops~~ ^{stop} treating me as his personal assistant.

I have a few days off for the holidays. Do you have some time off? If so, how about coming down here

for a visit? Wouldn't that be fun? I have a spare
bedroom in my apartment. If you can come, I
suggest (that) you drive
~~suggest you to drive~~, as it isn't far. Please write or
email and let me know.

Love,
Doris

EXERCISE 7

A. The daughter is working so much because she
and her husband want to buy a new house.

B. 2. The daughter almost demanded (that) she do
it.

   3. Had she known who was calling, she would
not have answered the phone.

   4. She had to call and insist (that) she come and
get the kids.

   5. It is important (that) the daughter pay more
attention to the kids.

   6. She suggests (that) the mother call her
daughter back and tell her she has changed her
mind.

EXERCISE 8

B. 2. a. Circle the "c" in *muscular*.   **b.** Cross out the "c" in *muscles*.

   3. a. Cross out the "n" in *autumn*.   **b.** Circle the "n" in *autumnal*.

   4. a. Circle the "g" in *designated*.   **b.** Cross out the "g" in *designed*.

   5. a. Cross out the "b" in *bomb*.   **b.** Circle the "b" in *bombarded*.

   6. a. Cross out the "b" in *crumbs*.   **b.** Circle the "b" in *crumbled*.

PART IX From Grammar to Writing
(pages 414–416)

1

Suggested corrections:

   1. Nancy says she wants to do something
worthwhile. If so, she should consider volunteer
work. (*period*)

   2. I need to get a bank loan; otherwise, I'll have to
file for bankruptcy. (*semicolon*)

   3. Donna didn't want to stop for the old man, but
Thain persuaded her it was a necessity. (*comma
and coordinating conjunction*)

   4. While I was learning to be assertive, I learned
many things about myself. (*subordinating
conjunction and comma*)

   5. Feeling dominated by her mother-in-law, Nancy
needed to take assertive action. (*Make the first
clause an adverbial phrase.*)

2

Possible corrections:

   Call it either intuition or good vibrations.
Whatever you want to call it, it works. Last summer I
was on a committee to hire a new head nurse at the
nursing home where I work. We interviewed two
candidates as finalists, a man named Bob and a
woman named Sarah. On paper, Bob was better
qualified; he had a master's degree while Sarah had
only a bachelor's degree. However, Sarah was the one
who really impressed us. She answered all of the
questions straightforwardly and simply, while Bob,
on the other hand, evaded some of our questions
while simultaneously trying to make us think he
knew everything and could do everything. All of us
on the committee just liked Sarah better; in fact, she
got the job because she was the person we all felt we
wanted to work with. Our intuition wasn't wrong;
she's turned out to be a wonderful nurse.

Single-User License Agreement

System Requirements

WINDOWS®	MACINTOSH®	BOTH
• Windows XP/Vista/7	• Mac OS X (10.4 & 10.5)	• 256 MB RAM minimum (512+ MB recommended)
• Intel Pentium processor 1GHz or higher	• PowerPC & Intel processor 1GHz or higher	• Monitor resolution of 1024 x 768 or higher
• Internet Explorer® 7.0 or higher OR Firefox® 2.0 or higher	• Safari® 2.0 or higher OR Firefox® 2.0 or higher	• Sound card and speakers or headphones
		• 500 MB hard disk space
		• 10X CD-ROM drive or higher
		• Adobe Flash 8 plug-in or higher
		• Internet Connection: DSL, Cable/Broadband, T1, or other high-speed connection
		• Microsoft® PowerPoint Viewer

Installation Instructions

WINDOWS®

- Insert the CD-ROM into the CD-ROM drive of your computer. On most computers, the program will begin automatically.

If the program does not begin automatically:

- Open "My Computer."
- Right-click on the CD-ROM icon.
- Click on Open.
- Double-click on the "Start" file. Leave the CD-ROM in the computer while using the program.

MACINTOSH®

- Insert the CD-ROM into the CD-ROM drive of your computer.
- Double-click on the CD-ROM icon on your desktop.
- Double click on the "Start" file. Leave the CD-ROM in the computer while using the program.

Note: The original CD-ROM must be in the CD-ROM drive when you use the program.

TECHNICAL SUPPORT

For Technical Product Support, please visit our support website at www.PearsonLongmanSupport.com. You can search our **Knowledgebase** for frequently asked questions, instantly **Chat** with an available support representative, or **Submit a Ticket/Request** for assistance.